Energy

ENERGY

GERARD M. CRAWLEY
Michigan State University

Macmillan Publishing Co., Inc.
NEW YORK

Collier Macmillan Publishers
LONDON

Copyright © 1975, Gerard M. Crawley

Printed in the United States of America

All rights reserved. No part of this book may be reproduced or transmitted in any form or by any means, electronic or mechanical, including photocopying, recording, or any information storage and retrieval system, without permission in writing from the Publisher.

Macmillan Publishing Co., Inc.
866 Third Avenue, New York, New York 10022

Collier-Macmillan Canada, Ltd.

Library of Congress Cataloging in Publication Data

Crawley, Gerard M
  Energy.

  Including bibliographies.
    1. Power resources. 2. Environmental policy.
3. Energy conservation. I. Title.
TJ153.C7   333.7   74-5716
ISBN 0-02-325580-3

Printing: 2 3 4 5 6 7 8   Year: 6 7 8 9 0

I think it only fair to confess that I stumbled, or perhaps was pushed, into the subject of energy and the environment. In the summer of 1971, the chairman of our teaching assignment committee asked me if I was willing to give a few introductory physics lectures in a course on energy which was being organized for the next year. Only after I agreed did I learn that the person who gave these lectures was also responsible for the whole course. I therefore spent a number of frantic months trying to organize the course and reading some fraction of the mass of material on energy, pollution, and environment that was being published in scientific journals, in newspapers, and by the United States government. This book is based on the course which was first offered, for both science and nonscience students, at Michigan State University in the spring of 1972.

One thing I learned both from reading and from conferences was that there are very few "experts" on the subject. For example, I heard Dr. Ed David, President Nixon's science advisor, accused with some justification of not being aware of the implications of the second law of thermodynamics. There is a bewildering amount of material written, much of it conflicting. I hope in this book to try to present a balanced view neither shrilly antiscientific nor complacently overconfident that technology can solve all problems. I believe there is a reasonable hope that we can meet the challenge, although the solutions will involve not only selected technical advances but also a rather radical reappraisal of our values and political priorities.

What I attempted to do in the course, and will also attempt in this book, was to give first an introduction to the scientific background of the energy problem. I believe that it is necessary to be able to make quantitative estimates so as better to assess both the problems and proposed solutions. Second, a discussion of alternative energy sources

V

is given which focuses on the general question of resources. Third, the problems associated with the growing use of energy, even with ample resources, are considered. The value and potential savings from energy conservation are next discussed. Finally, the implications of these questions, particularly the limitation of energy use, on various other areas, social, economic, and political, are taken up.

Let me add a little about the approach in this book. The prime motivation is to consider the particular problem of energy use in a manner that will be valuable to both science and nonscience students. Energy is not used primarily as a vehicle to teach physics, although I confess that I was surprised after first teaching the course by how much physics had been covered. Rather the aim is to expose students to an important problem that has significant scientific dimensions in which the role of a quantitative, scientific approach, both its uses and its limitations, can be seen fairly clearly. Sufficient physics is introduced to enable nonscience students to grapple with the scientific and quantitative aspects of the problem. I believe that this is required by the nature of the problem and, in addition, serves as a useful exposure of nonscience majors to scientific principles and approaches. Science students should generally find the physics discussions quite elementary although my experience with the course was that most found the physics coverage a useful review.

There is one final point I should like to make. If the ultimate solution to the energy problem requires a change in values, then it is necessary for many people to become aware of the real issues involved. I hope that this book will make some, albeit small, contribution to this educational task. The electrical power industry and the Atomic Energy Commission have in the past been very reluctant to expose their real problems to public view. I believe that this attitude is a mistake and is now costing them dearly. I hope that, by making people aware of the issues, good sense will prevail without disastrous consequences for us and our children.

Finally I should like to acknowledge the encouragement and insights offered by a number of my colleagues at Michigan State University, particularly Sherwood Haynes (Physics), Aaron Galonsky (Physics) Roger Hinrichs (Physics), Bill Kelly (Physics), Sam Austin (Physics), Harvey Edwards (Physics), Jim Butcher (Entomology), Herman Koenig (Engineering), Amritlal Dhanak (Engineering) and Bob Snow (Lyman Briggs College). A number of students, particularly Rick Watts, Martha Shephard, and Joe Finck, also made valuable suggestions. In addition, a number of other people were extremely helpful, including Roy Wells of Consumers Power Company, Bud Cornell, Agnes Sheehan, and particularly Mike McCormack, Chairman of the United States House of Representatives Task Force on Energy.

Most thanks are due to my wife, Margaret, for her critical reading of the manuscript and her continued support.

G. M. C.

CONTENTS

viii
Contents

PART **TWO**

ENERGY USE: PAST, PRESENT, AND FUTURE   59

ix
Contents

PART

ENERGY RESOURCES 91

Chapter 10   The Transient Resource: Fossil Fuels 93

Chapter 11   An Awkward Alternative: Fission 109

Chapter 12   One Hope for the Future: Fusion 135

PART

OTHER PROBLEMS   187

PART FIVE
FURTHER IMPLICATIONS OF ENERGY USE   229

CHAPTER

Energy and Pollution: an Introduction

1-1 The Problems of Power

One Saturday in early fall, as I sat at home with the weather gray and wet outside, the power failed for the second time in two weeks. As the food began spoiling in the refrigerator and my wife began to worry about being able to cook dinner, it struck me very forcibly how much we depend on the electricity piped into our homes and how naked we feel when stripped of its support. This small problem, which fortunately was only one of inconvenience, emphasized for me once again the larger question of our use of energy which has increased so dramatically this century and is still increasing today.

This larger problem, our future energy resources, immediately raises a number of very complex questions embracing many disciplines from physics, engineering, and geology to sociology, political science, and perhaps even theology. The answers to these questions are not easily found. In some cases this is because the technical information is not available or is apparently conflicting. How soon will energy be available from fusion? Will solar power be practical on a large scale? No one knows for certain. Another obvious example is nuclear power. Will this solve the energy crisis, as many of its proponents claim, or will it merely further blight our environment with radioactive isotopes and leave future generations an unwanted legacy of radioactive waste to dispose of?

In other cases, difficulties arise because the answers require value judgements about the quality of life—a subject upon which we are not yet able to agree. For example, if we consider the question of our

1

resources of oil and natural gas, we see some of the conflicts that immediately arise. Most of us want the advantages that an advanced technology can supply, such as central air conditioning, a power boat, or a vacation home. But in providing these even to the affluent in the United States we may deplete the world's oil and gas resources so much that we finish up with no transportation facilities and no plastics or synthetics. Or again, consider our rivers and our air. Do we want smoke stacks pouring oxides of sulfur and nitrogen into the air, corroding our buildings, not to mention our lungs? Are we willing to pay more for higher grade fuels? How long will they last? These are all questions that require answers, and they will be taken up in more detail in later chapters.

There is a great deal of discussion at present in the mass media, in scientific journals, and even in the congressional record about the current "energy crisis" in the United States. Almost daily we are bombarded by articles in newspapers, weekly news magazines and televi-

Figure 1-1
Cover from *Newsweek,* January 22, 1973. This is one of many examples of magazine, newspaper, television, and radio coverage of energy problems in the past few years. [Reproduced by permission of Newsweek, Inc.]

sion informing us about various facets of the crisis (Figure 1-1). Is such an "energy crisis" real or merely a subterfuge by energy companies to raise prices? If by crisis, we mean a time when critical decisions must be made, there is no doubt that the United States is presently in such a situation.

However most discussion has focused on comparatively short term problems such as the lack of gasoline in summer or fuel oil in winter or the increasing electrical shortages in both seasons. These are problems that are not caused by the total drying up of resources either in the United States or abroad. The lack of refineries, diminishing exploration incentives, and growing political sophistication among oil producing countries have all contributed. The slow growth of the nuclear alternative has also been partly responsible and has caught the power companies unprepared. Little emphasis on research and development by the power companies and their suppliers have left the industry in a comparative technological backwater. Thus, poor planning on the part of power companies, which have been called the poorest managed and most inefficient of all big business, has been another contributing factor to the present problems.

Although these current problems may be extremely trying, an even more rapid expansion of generating, refining, and port facilities will, in principle, help to alleviate them for the next decade or two. The longer term solutions are more difficult. Perhaps our current energy problems have a value in that they give us a dramatic glimpse of a longer term problem that will be caused by a real lack of resources and may arise in the not too distant future. The examination of long term energy resources will be one of the main concerns of this book.

1-2 Pollution

Let us suppose that we do find sufficient resources to meet our energy needs. There is another and perhaps even more serious problem that must be faced. We have all become aware of an increasing number of pollution problems. (See, for example, Figure 1-2.) These range from the small annoyance of noisy people with their electric generators, trail bikes, and record players in our national forests to more serious problems that affect us more acutely. The death of Lake Erie should have a great impact, especially on the midwestern states, and hopefully inspire us to make a greater effort to save our other lakes. The growing air pollution in the southwest from the massive Four Corners power plant is already spoiling another priceless resource, clear desert air.

Figure 1-2
Air pollution from Consolidated Edison Plant, East 14th Street, New York City.
[Courtesy of BLACK STAR. Photo by Richard L. Stack.]

Perhaps one of the most frightening waste pollution problems concerns the ocean. I remember the ocean as clear, salty, almost the epitome of freshness; but now I read of mile-wide, smelly, sticky messes outside New York City where garbage boats daily add to the cancer (Figure 1-3). Or again Jacques Costeau, a pioneer in underwater exploration, reports that visibility in the Mediterranean has decreased tremendously in the 30 or so years he has been diving there. And 30

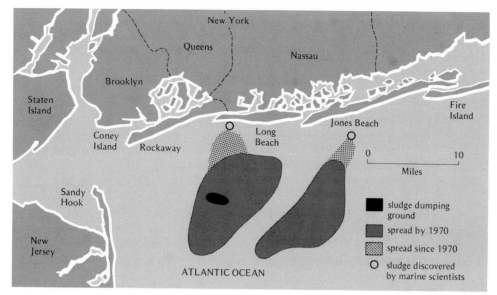

Figure 1-3

Distribution of sludge off Long Island. The sludge, organic and inorganic solid waste left after garbage passes through sewage-treatment plants, has been dumped at the rate of 5 million cubic yards (5×10^6 yd³) a year—enough to cover Central Park. As a result, there is a 25 square mile (25 mi²) area called the "dead sea" 10 miles out in the Atlantic; generally, it ends 6 miles from the Long Island shore and 10 miles from the New Jersey shore to the south. It was believed the sludge would endanger only marine life, but it has now been discovered a $\frac{1}{2}$ mile away from Long Island's South Shore, one of the world's finest recreational seacoasts. [Information from *The New York Times,* December 16, 1973.]

years is but a fleeting instant on any geological scale of time. Imagine what it will be like in another 30 years.

1-3 Thermal Pollution

But bad as these problems are, there is a potentially more deadly and inescapable form of pollution to which little attention has yet been paid, thermal pollution. The earth lives in a delicate heat balance, receiving energy from the sun, reflecting much of it back into space, and using the remainder to produce the wonderful complexity we see around us. But as we continue to tap an increasing amount of the energy stored on the earth over billions of years, we may find ourselves in danger of disturbing this balance with catastrophic consequences. Such effects are already observable in many of our cities. The average temperature of the cities is already significantly higher than that in the surrounding countryside, with attendant alterations in the microclimate nearby. This is another important topic that will be explored later in this book.

1-4   A Quantitative Approach

You might be wondering why a scientist should be responsible for a book on environment—a physicist at that—not even a biologist or a geologist. I would like to argue that, when we examine some of the questions I have pointed out earlier, it is very important to be quantitative in our approach. This is necessary both to decide which are the important questions and also to examine the solutions by "putting in some numbers." William Thompson, later Lord Kelvin, a famous physicist of the nineteenth century wrote:

> I often say that when you can measure what you are speaking about, and express it in numbers, you know something about it; but when you cannot express it in numbers, your knowledge is of a meagre and unsatisfactory kind; it may be the beginning of knowledge, but you have scarcely, in your thoughts, advanced to the stage of science, whatever the matter may be.

By being quantitative I shall first of all help you to become familiar with some of the technical terms used by scientists and engineers so that you are not frightened off by the jargon. Most of the concepts are not really very difficult and need only a little sophistication to master them. A quantitative approach involves making estimates of the size of effects using numerical methods as far as possible. This helps to emphasize the real problems and prevents digression to minor issues. If thousands of people are really dying from air pollution each year, does it make sense to expend one's energies in picking up candy wrappers?

Or again, suppose the claim is made that thermal differences in the ocean will provide sufficient energy for the world's needs. Apart from economic or political questions, it is valuable to be able to estimate from basic physics principles whether such a project is feasible. At what efficiency will it operate? How large would the project have to be? These are questions that can be answered by some simple numerical calculations.

A quantitative understanding is also important because it helps us to realize the limitations of such an approach. There is still a widespread belief, fostered by dramatic successes in medicine and in space, that technology can solve any problem. I think that one should be very careful when one applies this notion to many of the problems we face today. Sociologists and psychologists have adapted the techniques learned in the "hard" sciences to social problems. However, although a physicist can work with an idealized system, the assumptions made by the social scientist to "quantify" the problem may make the solution meaningless. As Professor Marc Ross, a physicist at the University of Michigan writes,

. . . nonspecialists can be and need to be 'critics' of quantitative techniques applied to public questions. It is usually not the computation itself but its basis and its interpretation which requires investigation. Very often, the layman, or specialist in another field, who has mastered certain basic concepts will be able to make a useful assessment of quantitative techniques by means of simple consultation at the source and of rough estimation.

What I plan to do first is to give you some idea of the meaning of the various terms we will be using in this book so that you will be in a better position to make a quantitative response to both the questions raised and the answers proposed. The next chapter will begin with the fundamental structure of the world about us—atoms and nuclei. This understanding will be particularly important for the discussion of fission and fusion in later chapters.

Questions

1. What kinds of pollution do you find personally extremely repulsive? Why?
2. Are some forms of pollution more fundamental than others? Discuss the role of energy as a fundamental pollutant.
3. Critically discuss a recent article on the "energy crisis" from a national magazine or newspaper.
4. What are some of the major causes of the recent "energy crisis?" Is the crisis due, for example, to the United States or the world running out of oil or natural gas? Discuss some steps that might be taken to help alleviate the current problems.
5. Why is it useful to be familiar with basic concepts and with the vocabulary of technical terms in a discussion of energy problems? List examples of problems where a quantitative approach would be valuable.
6. "The 'energy crisis of 1973–74' was manufactured by the large oil companies to drive up prices and increase their profits." Give reasons for or against this point of view.

7. Currently the United States used 18×10^6 barrels of oil per day of which 11×10^6 are domestic and 7×10^6 barrels are imported at a cost of about $10 per barrel. If we increase petroleum use about 5% per year, with the domestic supply constant, by how much will the United States import bill increase per year under these conditions?

Bibliography

Some recent general discussions of the energy problem are given in the following references.

[1] *Scientific American,* September 1971.

[2] *Technology Review,* October/November 1971; December 71; and January 72.

[3] Science and public affairs. *Bulletin of the Atomic Scientists,* September 71; October 71; and November 71.

[4] *New York Times,* July 7, 8, and 9, 1971.

[5] *Intertechnology Corporation Report C645.* National Science Foundation, November 1971.

[6] Briefings before the Task Force on Energy. U.S. House of Representatives 92nd Congress; 1st session Serial M 70-3180, 1971; 2nd Session Serial Q, 73-9020, 1972.

[7] *Energy—The Ultimate Resource.* Study Submitted to the Task Force on Energy, 92nd Congress; 1st Session Serial J 68-1840, 1971.

[8] *The Economy, Energy and the Environment.* A Background Study prepared for the Joint Economic Committee, Congress of the United States 46-3660, Sept. 1970.

[9] K. F. Weaver: The search for tomorrow's power. *National Geographic,* November 1972.

[10] J. Priest: *Problems of Our Physical Environment.* Addison-Wesley, 1973.

[11] A. L. Hammond, W. D. Metz, and T. H. Maugh, II. *Energy and the Future.* American Association for the Advancement of Science, 1973.

PART

SCIENTIFIC BACKGROUND

Atoms, Nuclei, Electrons, and Electricity

2-1 Models

When we stand near the top of a mountain and see the cloud-attended ridges stretching off in the distance or lie on a beach and listen to the surf, the world seems almost infinitely varied and complex. Yet we sense only a tiny fraction of the input of information that is reaching us every instant. Occasionally, if one happens to be on a wide plain or desert on a clear night far from the lights of civilization and looks at the sky, one might sense with awe the vastness of space. It is hard to realize that the light from some of those twinkling stars has been travelling for thousands of years at the incredible speed of 186,000 miles per second, to reach our eyes here on planet earth.

Difficult as it is to grasp the immensity of the distance scale of the heavens, I think that the world of very small sizes, of atoms and nuclei, is even more unreal to most of us. Because there is no way in which our senses can directly experience, particularly "see," objects that are a million times smaller than the thickness of a hair, it is necessary to make "models" of these objects which are similar to things we can see and touch. However, you should remember that, although these descriptions can become very sophisticated and use a good deal of complex mathematics, they are still only models and await further refinement.

This divorce from the world of our senses also means that there are some questions that are perfectly valid in the macroscopic world we inhabit but are meaningless in the microscopic world of the atom. For example, whereas we continually describe objects by their color, it is meaningless to ask the color of a nucleus.

11

2-2 Atoms and Elements

Suppose, like Alice in Wonderland, we start shrinking down and down in size. As we become smaller and smaller we pass through a series of new and complex worlds, the world of bacteria, viruses, and single cells till we come to the level of molecules—the smallest objects that exist stably in our normal world.

If we shrink even further, a simplicity begins to emerge from among the myriads of different molecules. We are in the world of the atom and have shrunk to only a ten thousand millionth of our normal size (Figure 2-1). Each atom consists of a tiny core or **nucleus,** which is very heavy if we try to push on it, but is still far too small to see clearly. We will have to do some more shrinking to examine the nucleus more closely. In addition to the nucleus, there are other particles we can "see" whizzing around. These are the **electrons,** which are at least 2000 times lighter than the nucleus. The simplest atom of all has just one electron. This is the atom of the element **hydrogen.**

A model of the element carbon is shown in Figure 2-2. The six electrons are shown in orbits around the central nucleus, which is scaled up relative to the electron orbit size to make it visible. Thus atoms are mainly empty space filled only by the light, speeding electrons. If we expanded the atom so that the outermost electron shells moved in

Figure 2-1
This is a picture of the tip of a tungsten needle taken with a field ion microscope. The small white dots, for example, the single dot in a dark circle to the left of center in the picture, are individual atoms of tungsten. A group of three atoms can be seen near the center.
[Courtesy Dr. Jack Bass, Michigan State University.]

Figure 2-2

A model of the $^{14}_{6}$C atom. The solid lines represent orbits of the six electrons, indicating that the electrons are not stationary. The central core, the positively charged nucleus, is shown about 1000 times too large on the scale of the atom.

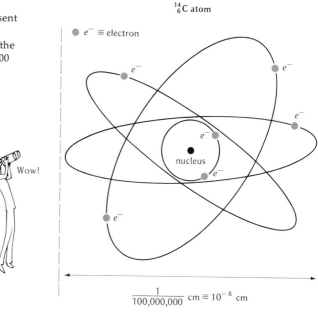

Wow!

orbits about 100 yd (yards) across (the length of a football field), the nucleus would only be as large as a grain of rice.

We find that each neutral atom of a given element (that is, in the uncombined state) has exactly the same number of electrons. This number of electrons, which equals the atomic number, determines the chemical properties of the element. It is because potassium has 19 electrons that it burns on contact with water whereas copper with 29 electrons sinks harmlessly to the bottom. The burning of fuels such as coal and oil is a chemical reaction that consists basically of a rearrangement of the electron shells of atoms. We thus have another way of describing an element. Instead of talking about the element **carbon** we could speak of the element with atomic number 6 (the letter Z is often used for atomic number) or instead of iron, the element $Z = 26$. When we learn more about the behavior of the electrons, this number becomes more descriptive of the way the element behaves than is its common name.

Scientists have found only 92 elements occurring naturally on the earth; in other words the number of electrons for elements in the uncombined state only ranges from 1 to 92 from the lightest element hydrogen with one electron to the heaviest element uranium with 92 electrons. As man's technical expertise has increased in this century he has been able to produce new heavier elements up to number 105, and he is now hoping to go even higher to make "superheavy" elements with atomic numbers as high as $Z = 114$.

2-3 Nuclei

It is now time to continue our adventure, to shrink even more and investigate the structure of the tiny but heavy central core of the atom—the nucleus. Let us begin to penetrate the shells of the six electrons of the carbon atom. At first nothing is visible, but finally the tiny dense core of the atom, the nucleus, begins to emerge. We will see in later chapters that it is possible to obtain enormous amounts of energy from certain of these unimaginably small nuclei. As the nucleus of this atom appears to grow bigger, we see that there are two different kinds of particles in the nucleus. One kind is called protons, which have a positive charge, the other kind neutrons, with no charge. We have now shrunk by another factor of 100,000. In this particular nucleus there are six protons and eight neutrons, the positive charge of six protons exactly balancing the negative charge of the six electrons moving around at what seems to us a very great distance away. The mass (heavyness) of both the proton and neutron are very similar so that we could write the total mass of the six protons and eight neutrons as 14 units of atomic mass.

If we looked at the nuclei of many carbon atoms we would find that all of them have exactly six protons. This is as characteristic as the number of electrons in the neutral atom and so could also be described by the atomic number, Z. However not all the carbon nuclei will have eight neutrons. A few will have seven neutrons and the majority will have six neutrons. In these cases, the mass of the nucleus will be 13 units and 12 units respectively. This number, which is the sum of the number of protons and the number of neutrons is called the **atomic mass** and is often written as A. These different carbon nuclei, with the same number of protons (six) but different numbers of neutrons (six,

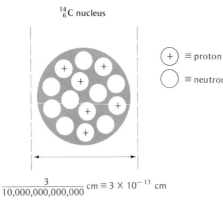

$^{14}_{6}C$ nucleus

$(+) \equiv$ proton

$\bigcirc \equiv$ neutron

$$\frac{3}{10,000,000,000,000} \text{ cm} \equiv 3 \times 10^{-13} \text{ cm}$$

Figure 2-3
A model of the $^{14}_{6}C$ nucleus. This nucleus of total mass 14, has six positively charged protons and eight neutrons, which carry no charge.

seven, or eight) are called different **isotopes** of the element carbon. These isotopes are usually written $^{12}_{6}C$, $^{13}_{6}C$, or $^{14}_{6}C$ where the superscript refers to the atomic mass A and the subscript to the atomic number Z. Of course the difference between these two numbers $(A - Z)$ is equal to the number of neutrons n, in that particular isotope.

I should stress again that the number of protons characterizes the element—six identifies carbon, but the same element can have many different isotopes with different numbers of neutrons. A model of the $^{14}_{6}C$ nucleus is shown in Figure 2-3. The element tin, for example, with $Z = 50$ has ten stable isotopes with neutron numbers ranging from 62 to 74. Notice that all the isotopes have the same chemical properties even though the nuclei may be different because the chemistry is determined by the number of electrons surrounding the nucleus, which always equals the number of protons in the nucleus, in a neutral atom.

2-4 Radioactive Decay

Standing near a ^{14}C nucleus, we may, if we were very fortunate, see another feature that is unique to the microscopic world. The $^{14}_{6}C$ nucleus with six protons and eight neutrons can change into a new nucleus called nitrogen-14, $^{14}_{7}N$, with seven protons and seven neutrons. The change is effected by one of the eight neutrons changing into a proton and an electron which speeds away from the nucleus. This process is called radioactive decay. For the ^{14}C nucleus (often the Z, which characterizes the element, is omitted when writing the isotope) this is a very unlikely event. If we had a sample of 100 equivalent ^{14}C nuclei, it would take 5730 years before 50 of them would have changed into ^{14}N. This time, 5730 years, which it takes for half of the nuclei to decay is called the **half-life** of the isotope and is very characteristic of the particular isotope. This long half-life for ^{14}C has made it very useful for determining the age of old artifacts containing carbon. The technique is called **carbon dating.**

There are very many of these unstable nuclei which can decay into other nuclei emitting a variety of particles. We saw that ^{14}C emits an electron exactly like the electrons whizzing around the nucleus in the atom. Other nuclei emit positively charged electrons, called positrons and often written β^+. In this kind of nucleus, a proton changes into a neutron and a positron. Others, especially heavier nuclei, emit an alpha (α) particle, which is just another name for a nucleus of the element helium, $^{4}_{2}He$, consisting of two protons and two neutrons. A final emission product might be gamma (γ) rays, which we will study in the next section. There are approximately 300 nuclei that are completely stable, 2000 others that are unstable, and estimates suggest 6000 other unstable nuclei that have yet to be discovered. Most of the unstable nuclei have half-lives of only a fraction of a second.

One should be cautious therefore with the use of the term isotope. This is commonly used to describe a nucleus that undergoes radioactive decay, emitting an α particle, β particle or δ ray. However we should remember that (fortunately) not all isotopes are unstable. Strictly **isotope** refers to the many possible nuclei of the same element (same Z) with different numbers of neutrons. Generally, some of these isotopes will be stable and some will decay.

Radioactive isotopes, that is isotopes that decay, can be either harmful or useful to man. Some isotopes, such as fluorine-18, ($^{18}_{9}F$) or technetium-99 ($^{99}_{43}Tc$) which have short half-lives, are used in medical diagnosis. The isotope cobalt-60 ($^{60}_{27}Co$) is used in some treatments of cancer. However other radioactive isotopes such as strontium-90, produced for example in testing nuclear weapons, may be absorbed by bone tissue and prove harmful. The effect of radioactive isotopes produced by nuclear reactors will be discussed in Chapter 11.

2-5 Electromagnetic Radiation

We saw in Section 2-4 that an unstable nucleus often emits a γ ray as it decays. A γ ray is a name for a particular kind of electromagnetic radiation. We are more familiar with other kinds of electromagnetic radiation, one of which we call light, another radio waves. You may also have heard of infrared (heat) lamps or ultraviolet lamps, or microwave ovens, or x rays. These are all examples of electromagnetic waves

Figure 2-4
The definition of wavelength. The distance between two equivalent points such as a and b or b and c or between x and y or y and z is called the wavelength. In this example the wavelength is 2 ft.

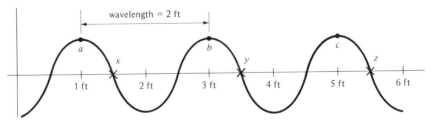

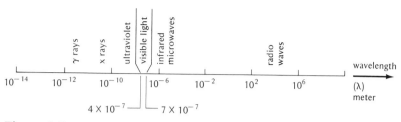

Figure 2-5

Electromagnetic radiation spectrum. The wavelength (λ) of electromagnetic radiation ranges from 10^{-14} m (meter) (one hundred million millionth of a meter) to 10^6 m (1 million meters). Radiation of various wavelengths is given different names. Visible light is only a very narrow band in the whole spectrum.

and are closely related to each other. All electromagnetic radiation consists of oscillating electric and magnetic fields. This radiation, which carries energy, can travel through a vacuum and sometimes through various materials. For example, light radiation goes through quite thick plate glass but not through even a thin sheet of copper.

Electromagnetic radiation is described as a wave motion caused by something, in this case electric and magnetic fields, vibrating. It is characterized by a **frequency of oscillation** (or in other words, the rate at which the fields vibrate) and a distance between two equivalent places on the wave, called the **wavelength.**

Suppose I take a piece of string and shake one end of it to make a wave as shown in Figure 2-4. The three points marked a, b, and c are equivalent as are those marked x, y, and z. The distance between any two successive equivalent points say a and b is called the wavelength.

All the different kinds of electromagnetic radiation, light, x rays, radio waves, infrared radiation, and γ rays are all described in the same way and travel with the same very high speed* through empty space. They differ only in their wavelength or, equivalently, their frequency. This is illustrated in Figure 2-5, which shows the huge range of wavelengths from very short for γ rays to very long for radio waves. Also marked is the very narrow band of radiation to which our eyes are sensitive and which we call light. Here again we notice how selective our senses are in accepting and using only a small fraction of the possible information available. The electromagnetic spectrum will be discussed further in Chapter 6 when the radiation from the sun is treated.

* This speed, usually called the speed of light, is approximately 186,000 mi/sec (miles per second). Therefore electromagnetic radiation can travel around the earth in a little over $\frac{1}{10}$ of a second.

2-6 Electricity

After discussing electromagnetic radiation, let me be careful to distinguish it from electricity which travels along the wires in our homes. Electricity consists of moving electrons that travel through metal conductors, such as copper or aluminum wire, rather like water flows through pipes. Because the electrons in the outer shells of metal atoms are free to move from one atom to another, metals can conduct electricity. Other materials like glass, where even the outer electrons are bound tightly to the nucleus, are called nonconductors.

The moving electrons produce an electrical **current** which is measured in **amperes**. The electrons are forced to move through the conductor by the application of an electromagnetic force or **voltage** measured in **volts**. The electrical resistance of the wire to the flowing current depends upon the length of the wire, its thickness, and the nature of the material of which the wire is made. **Resistance** is measured in **ohms**. For many simple electric circuits, there is a relationship between current flowing and voltage applied which is called **Ohm's Law.** This law states that *the current flowing is directly proportional to the voltage applied,* where the proportionality constant is the inverse of the resistance.

As an equation:

$$I = \frac{V}{R}$$

2-1

where I stands for the current flowing (in amperes);

V stands for the voltage applied (in volts);

and R represents the resistance of the circuit (in ohms).

Figure 2-6

A plot of voltage versus time for common household electricity, marked alternating current (ac). The voltage continually varies. The curve crosses the axis every 1/120 sec and exactly repeats 60 times per second. The dotted horizontal line marked direct current (dc) corresponds to a constant voltage, which would be obtained for example from a battery.

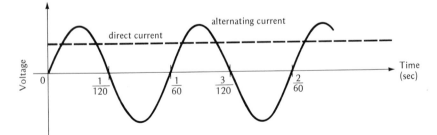

If the applied voltage is constant, for example from a battery, the current flows in one direction and is called **direct current** or **dc.** In the common household current, however, the applied voltage is continually changing its direction 60 times each second (Figure 2-6). Consequently the direction of current flow is also changing 60 times per second and this type of current is termed **alternating current** or **ac.** The reason that household current is ac is both because of the method of production and also because it is very easy to increase or decrease a changing voltage using a transformer.

A voltage difference, sometimes termed potential difference, is produced in a conductor that moves in a magnetic field. (A **magnetic field** is found around a permanent magnet like a compass needle or around an electromagnet made of iron and surrounded by a coil of wire through which current flows.) This fact is the basis of an electric generator used to produce electricity in a power plant. A schematic of the basic principle is shown in Figure 2-7. A loop or coil of wire is rotated in the magnetic field between the poles of a magnet, usually an electromagnet. As the loop crosses magnetic field lines, an ac voltage is produced between the ends of the loop. If the ends are connected to a continuous circuit, an ac current will flow.

A more complete schematic of a fossil fuel power plant is shown in Figure 2-8. The coil, containing many turns, is rotated in the magnetic field of a large electromagnet by means of a turbine. In the usual steam turbine, steam produced in a boiler causes the blades or the turbine to rotate. The shaft is connected to the coil of the generator so that the coil is also rotated. The output of the generator is hooked to the electric grid.

Figure 2-7

Schematic of the basic principle of the electric generator. A coil of wire rotates in the magnetic field (dotted lines) produced between the poles (labelled N for north and S for south) of a magnet. As the coil rotates, a voltage is produced between the ends of the coil of wire.

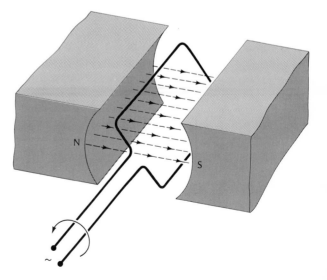

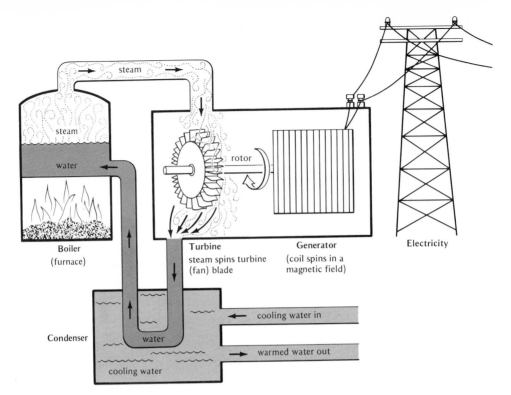

Figure 2-8

Schematic diagram of fossil fuel electric power plant. Coal, oil, or natural gas is burned to produce steam in the boiler. The steam rotates the blades of a turbine, rotating the coil in the generator and producing electricity.

At present fossil fuels, coal, oil, or natural gas, are the usual sources of heat that produce steam in the boiler. However, a very similar system is used in nuclear power plants where heat is produced by a controlled nuclear fission reaction instead of the chemical burning of coal, oil, or gas. These nuclear reactors are discussed in more detail in Chapter 11.

Questions

1. Which is larger in size, an atom of carbon or a carbon nucleus? By how much?
2. Does the nucleus contain (a) protons and neutrons, (b) protons and electrons, or (c) neutrons and electrons?
3. If the size of an atom can be determined, why cannot its color also be found?

4. Which of the following statements are true and which are false?
   (a) All isotopes are radioactive.
   (b) The element carbon has a number of isotopes.
   (c) The nuclide $^{14}_{6}C$ has 6 protons and 14 neutrons in the nucleus.
   (d) A radioactive isotope decays emitting α particles, β particles or γ rays.
   (e) The wavelength of γ rays is longer than the wavelength of light.
   (f) Light, radio waves, and x rays are all examples of electromagnetic radiation.
   (g) Electricity consists of moving protons.
5. Describe how steam is used to generate electricity.
6. What is the difference between ac and dc voltages?
7. Mark the correct answer. An alpha particle is the same as a nucleus of (a) hydrogen (b) helium (c) neon (d) lithium (e) carbon.
8. Find out some applications where radioactive isotopes are used in medicine or industry for beneficial purposes.
9. If an electric toaster has a resistance of 60 ohm, and the average voltage across it from the power mains is 120 volts, what average current does it draw, assuming it behaves according to Ohm's Law?

Bibliography

The concepts of atoms and nuclei are discussed in most basic physics textbooks. For example:
[1] R. K. Adair: *Concepts in Physics.* Academic Press, 1969, Ch. 23, 24, and 25.
[2] P. E. Highsmith and A. S. Howard: *Adventures in Physics.* Saunders, 1972, Ch. 9 and 10. (A text in a simple vein.)
[3] Clifford E. Swartz: *Microstructure of Matter.* U.S. Atomic Energy Commission, Division of Technical Information, April, 1965. (Another excellent book.)

CHAPTER

Energy, Work, and Power

3-1 Force

One of the first things to realize about physics is that familiar terms, for example, work, energy, force, are often used in a very particular, restricted, and defined way. It is very important for an understanding of what comes later to learn to use the words and to understand their definitions when they are used scientifically.

Let us look first at the word **force**. In this case the common usage is fairly accurate. We think of a force generally as a push or a pull. We experience forces as chairs pushing up on us, holding us up, or when we pull a load with a rope. (We also use the term about people as, "Mayor Daley exerts a lot of force around Chicago.") This idea of force as a push or a pull is basically true in scientific use also although it is also known that some forces or interactions do not need a material medium (like a rope) through which to act. One force of this kind which we take for granted is the gravitational force that generally keeps our feet firmly on the ground but also keeps hold of a spinning satellite circling the earth. Many of the common contact forces which prevent one from falling through the floor or passing through a solid wall are ultimately due to electrical forces between atoms produced basically by the charge structure discussed in Chapter 2.

So far, physicists have discovered what they believe to be four and only four basic kinds of forces in all of nature. These forces or interactions are responsible for all the phenomena we observe, even with very complex and sophisticated apparatus. The four fundamental forces are gravitational, electromagnetic, weak interaction (responsible for radioactive decay) and the strong interaction which binds protons and neutrons together in nuclei.

The famous English physicist and mathematician Isaac Newton, established a method for finding the force exerted on a body of mass m. The total force $\vec{F}$ is equal to the product of the mass, m, times the acceleration $\vec{a}$ of the body when the force is applied. Acceleration, which is familiar from automobile driving or watching space rockets take off, is a measure of the rate at which an object goes faster. The more quickly it reaches a high velocity, the greater is the acceleration. Newton's relation may then be written as the simple equation,

$$\vec{F} = m \times \vec{a} \qquad 3\text{-}1$$

Both force and acceleration are just two examples of physical quantities where direction is important. Such quantities, which are only fully defined when both their magnitude and direction are given, are called **vectors** and are often written with an arrow ($\rightarrow$) above the symbol. Other quantities, which do not require a direction for their specification, are called **scalars.** Mass is an example of a scalar quantity.

3-2 Work

There is another term, like force, which is commonly used but which also has a restricted "technical" meaning in science, namely work. To a physicist **work** means the product of a force times the distance over which the force acts (Figure 3-1).

If the work done is written as W, the force as $\vec{F}$ and the distance the force has acted as $\vec{S}$, then the definition of work can be written down in the form of a very simple equation

$$W = \vec{F} \cdot \vec{S} \qquad 3\text{-}2$$

where the arrows mean that the directions of the force and the distance moved are important and the dot simply means that the force $\vec{F}$

Figure 3-1
Work done = force × distance = $\vec{F} \cdot \vec{S}$.

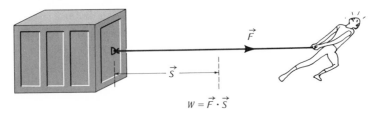

$$W = \vec{F} \cdot \vec{S}$$

must be multiplied by the distance $\vec{S}$ to find the work done, W. Distance moved, or displacement, $\vec{S}$ is another example of a vector quantity.

3-3 Units

There is another point beside the strict definitions of the terms that scientists find very important to stress to make communication easier. This is the question of **units.** Suppose I wish to measure the length of a table top. I could lay down an inch rule and find, perhaps, that the table measured 60 in. (inches). But if I used a centimeter rule I would find that the same table top measured 152 cm (centimeters). So it is with any physical quantity, length, mass, force, or work. The numerical amount of the particular physical quantity depends on the units we use. It is therefore important to know and use the *correct units* for the different quantities we discuss and to know the relation between them.

In the United States, we are used to working in a system where distances are measured in feet and yards and mass is measured in pounds. A system that is easier to use is based on metric units. In the **metric system** distances are measured in **m**eters, mass in **k**ilograms and time in **s**econds. Thus this system of units is called the mks system, after the initial letters of meter, kilogram, and second. In this book the mks system will be used almost exclusively. The mks units for some physical quantities discussed so far or that will be discussed in this chapter are listed in Table 3-1.

It may sometimes be necessary to convert other units into the mks system. Some useful conversion factors are therefore listed in Table 3-2.

Table 3-1
Units of Physical Quantities in the Metric System

Physical Quantity	Metric Unit	Abbreviation
distance	meter	m
mass	kilogram	kg
time	second	sec
force	newton	N
acceleration	meter per second per second	m/sec^2
work	joule	J
energy	joule	J
power	watt	w

Table 3-2
Conversion Factors to Metric Units

1 foot (ft)	= 0.3048 meter (m)
1 mile (mi)	= 1609 m
1 pound (lb) (mass)	= 0.4536 kilogram (kg)
1 ton	= 1016 kg
1 day	= 8.64×10^4 sec*
1 year	= 3.16×10^7 sec*

* NOTE: An easier way of writing large numbers such as 300,000,000 is 3×10^8 called three times ten to the eight. In this notation

100	would be	$10^2 = 10 \times 10$
1000	would be	$10^3 = 10 \times 10 \times 10$
10,000	would be	$10^4 = 10 \times 10 \times 10 \times 10$ and so on.

Also, $\dfrac{1}{1000}$ is written in this notation as 10^{-3}.

It is now possible to give some examples of finding the work done by a force. Note that the unit of work in the mks system is the *joule* (J) (See Table 3-1). In calculating the work done, all the quantities used should be expressed in mks units. The answer will then be given in joule (J).

EXAMPLE 3-1: *Suppose a heavy box lies on the floor and you find that a force of 60 N (newton) is required to slide it across the floor. If you move it 3 m (meters) across the room, how much work did you do on the box?*

Solution

From equation (3-2)

$$\text{work done} = \text{force} \times \text{distance}$$

$$= 60 \text{ N} \times 3 \text{ m}$$

And because 1 J = 1 N × 1 m

$$\text{work} = 180 \text{ J}$$

EXAMPLE 3-2: *Suppose a train carries 20 trucks each loaded with 75 tons of coal along a level track for 300 mi (miles). If the force exerted by the engine is 1000 N/ton (newton per ton) pulled, how much work has the engine done in pulling the train this distance?*

Solution

$$\text{total force exerted} = 1000 \text{ N/ton} \times \text{total tons}$$
$$= 1000 \text{ N/ton} \times 20 \times 75 \text{ tons}$$
$$= 1,500,000 \text{ N}$$
$$= 1.50 \times 10^6 \text{ N}$$

$$\text{distance travelled} = 300 \text{ mi}$$
$$= 300 \text{ } mi \times 1609 \quad (\textit{from Table 3-2, 1 mi} = 1609 \text{ m})$$
$$= 4.83 \times 10^5 \text{ m}$$

Therefore

$$\text{work done} = \text{force} \times \text{distance}$$
$$= 1.50 \times 10^6 \text{ N} \times 4.83 \times 10^5 \text{ m}$$
$$= 7.25 \times 10^{11} \text{ J} \quad (\text{because N} \times \text{m} = \text{J})$$

The force of gravity, called the **weight** of an object, can be written using equation (3-1) as

$$\text{weight} = \text{mass} \times \text{acceleration of gravity} \qquad \text{3-3}$$

We readily observe the acceleration due to gravity at the earth's surface when an object falls. This acceleration, usually written g has been measured as approximately 9.8 m/sec². It is now possible to calculate the work done against the force of gravity. Note that since weight is a force, the unit of weight in the mks system is the newton (N). As before in calculations, all physical quantities should be expressed in mks units.

EXAMPLE 3-3: *Suppose you are into weightlifting. What is the minimum amount of work done in lifting a 40-kg mass above one's head, a lift of 2.5 m, for 10 repetitions?*
   Solution
   Since you must apply a force at least as great as the weight force to lift the mass, let us take the minimum force to equal the weight

$$\text{weight} = \text{mass} \times \text{acceleration of gravity}$$
$$= 40 \text{ kg} \times 9.8 \text{ m/sec}^2 \quad (g = 9.8 \text{ m/sec}^2)$$
$$= 392.0 \text{ N} \quad (1 \text{ N} = 1 \text{ kg} \times 1 \text{ m/sec}^2)$$

$$\text{work done for 10 reps} = 10 \times \text{force} \times \text{distance}$$
$$= 10 \times 392 \text{ N} \times 2.5 \text{ m}$$
$$= 9800 \text{ J}$$
$$= 9.8 \times 10^3 \text{ J}$$

3-4 Energy

Now these examples seem to have taken us a long way from the questions about energy resources and pollution that were discussed in Chapter 1. But these thoughts are tied together by defining another physical quantity, **energy,** or the **energy in a body or system,** as the measure of the ability of the body or system to do work. This may seem rather vague at first and it is, deliberately so, as I will try to make clear shortly. Let me first point out that there are many different kinds of energy that can be associated with a body. (A **body** by the way is another of these technical terms meaning an "idealized" body—not Ursula Andress or Mr. America but more along the lines of a billiard ball. If you think of a red billiard ball for "body" I think you'll be close to the right idea.)

One of the very early ideas of energy was associated with **motion**—so called **kinetic energy** (literally motion energy). I think it is obvious that a moving body can exert a force on another body and cause it to move some distance. Imagine a bullet fired into a block of wood sitting on a table top. I think we can see that this causes an effect similar to pushing or pulling on the block with one's hand, only more dramatically. The bullet, in motion, is then said to have *kinetic* energy, which it loses as it does work on the block and itself comes to rest. The mathematical expression for kinetic energy is

$$KE = 1/2 \; mv^2 \qquad\qquad 3\text{-}4$$

where m is the mass of the moving object and v is its velocity (speed).

What are the units of energy? Following the definition you will not be too surprised to learn that they are the same as the units of work. However, the number of units used in measuring different kinds of energy is quite large and, because we will be using various kinds of units, a list is given in Table 3-3. These are all units of the same physical quantity (energy), so it must be possible to change from one kind of unit to another. Some of the factors for converting other energy units into joules are also given in Table 3-3.

EXAMPLE 3-4: *If a 1-ton piledriver is moving at a velocity of 10 m/sec just before it strikes the pile, what is its kinetic energy? Note that if all physical quantities like mass and velocity are written in mks units the answer will be given in the mks unit of energy, namely joule.*

Solution
From Table 3-2, 1 ton = 1,016 kg, and from equation (3-4)

$$KE = \tfrac{1}{2}\,mv^2$$
$$= \tfrac{1}{2} \times 1{,}016 \text{ kg} \times 10^2 \; (\text{m/sec}^2)^2$$
$$= 5.08 \times 10^4 \text{ J}$$

There is another very important kind of energy that can be associated with a body because of its position or particular situation or state, called therefore **potential energy.** Suppose I take my spent bullet out of the wooden block and attach it to the end of a spring which I now compress (Figure 3-2). I think it is clear that I can again move the block with the bullet, this time making use of the energy the bullet possesses due to its position on the end of the compressed spring.

Another example of potential energy is the energy possessed by a body raised above a surface. Such a body, for example, the piledriver in the previous exercise, can do work as it falls. The potential energy

Figure 3-2

Potential energy of bullet on a compressed spring. The bullet can do work on the block as the spring expands.

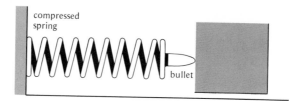

in this case can be written as

$$PE = mgh \qquad\qquad 3\text{-}5$$

where m is the mass of the body, g is the acceleration of gravity, and h is the height the body is raised. In the case of the gravitational force it is also possible to show that the work done on the body is equal to its gain in potential energy.

These are only two of the many different kinds of energy that exist. Other kinds of energy are chemical energy, electrical energy, or even "rest-mass" energy. This brings me back to my point about deliberate vagueness. Suppose the "body" that I knew had kinetic energy *also* turned out to be a bomb with a great deal of chemical energy, then I might get a lot more work done than I had bargained for. So sometimes we get more work out than we expect. If I find that I am getting more work out of a system than I can explain with the known sources of energy, then my tendency (or rather the bias of physicists) is to postulate (assume, make up) a new form of energy to explain this increase in work output. Perhaps the most famous example of this is the Einstein relation

$$E = mc^2 \qquad\qquad 3\text{-}6$$

which says that there is energy associated with the mass of an object and that this energy can be very large since c, the velocity of light $= 300{,}000{,}000$ (3×10^8) m/sec and so $c^2 = c \times c = 90{,}000{,}000{,}000{,}000{,}000$ (9×10^{16}) (m/sec)^2. The fact that mass is a form of energy was demonstrated most dramatically by the explosion of the atomic bomb. Nuclear reactors represent a use of mass energy spread out over a longer time.

3-5 Power

The final quantity I wish to discuss in this chapter is one that is commonly confused with energy, namely power. **Power** is defined as

Table 3-3
Units of Energy and Power

Energy	Expressed in Joules	Power
joule (J)		watt (W) = J/sec
erg	10^{-7} J	erg per second (erg/sec)
kilowatt-hour (kwh)	3.6×10^6 J	kilowatt (kw) = 1000 watts (W)
calorie (cal)	4.2 J	
kilocalorie (kcal)	4.2×10^3 J	
(large calorie, food calorie)		
foot-pound (ft-lb)	1.36 J	foot-pound per second (ft-lb/sec)
		horsepower (hp.) = 550 ft-lb/sec = 746 watt.
British thermal unit (Btu)	1.05×10^3 J	
electron volt (ev)	1.6×10^{-19} J	

the rate of doing work. In other words if two bodies do the same amount of work but one does it in half the time then the power generated by one body is twice that of the other. This can also be written as a simple equation:

$$P = \frac{W}{t} \qquad 3\text{-}7$$

where P refers to the power generated, W is the work done and t is the time taken to do the work.

By multiplying each side of equation (3-7) by t we can write down another important relation, namely that the work done by a body (which equals the energy given up by the body in doing the work) is equal to the power generated times the time taken to do the work. That is

$$W = E = P \times t \qquad 3\text{-}8$$

The units of power are also given in Table 3-3 alongside the appropriate units of energy. In particular one may look at the case of the kilowatt-hour. This is a product of a power unit (1 kilowatt = 1000 watt) times a time unit (hour) and is therefore a unit of *energy*.

Some examples of these units may help to make them less mysterious. If we leave two 100 w (watt) light bulbs burning for 5 hr (hours), we would have consumed 1 kwh (kilowatt-hour) of electric energy. An electric stove cooking dinner with two burners on for 1 hr uses about 3 kwh.

EXAMPLE 3-5: *A 180 lb. (pound) man climbs 5 flights of stairs in 30 sec. How much work has he done and what power level has he been working at? Express the answer in both watts and horsepower.*

Solution

Assume each flight of stairs = 10 ft. Then 5 flights of stairs means a total height climbed of 50 ft. From Table 3-2, 1 lb = 0.454 kg and 1 ft = 0.305 m. Therefore

$$180 \text{ lb} = 81.7 \text{ kg} \quad \text{and} \quad 50 \text{ ft} = 15.3 \text{ m}$$

From equation (3-5), the gain in the man's potential energy (which equals the work done) is given by,

$$PE = mgh$$

that is

$$\text{work done} = PE = 81.7 \text{ kg} \times 9.8 \text{ m/sec}^2 \times 15.3 \text{ m}$$
$$= 1.23 \times 10^4 \text{ J}$$

From equation (3-6),

$$\text{power expended} = \frac{\text{work done}}{\text{time}}$$

$$= \frac{1.23 \times 10^4 \text{ J}}{30 \text{ sec}}$$

$$= 408 \text{ W} \qquad (\text{w} = \text{J/sec})$$

From Table 3-3 1 hp (horsepower) = 746 watt

and

$$1 \text{ w} = \frac{1}{746} \text{ hp} = 1.34 \times 10^{-3} \text{ hp}$$

Thus

$$408 \text{ w} = 408 \times 1.34 \times 10^{-3} \text{ hp}$$
$$= 0.55 \text{ hp}$$

Answers

The man does 1.23×10^4 J of work. He is working at the rate of 408 w of power, which is equal to 0.55 hp.

EXAMPLE 3-6: If an electric appliance is rated to operate at 2.5 kw (kilowatt), how much will it cost to operate it for 12 hr if electricity costs 5¢ per kwh (kilowatt-hour)?

Solution

From equation (3-7)

$$\text{total energy expended} = 2.5 \text{ kw} \times 12 \text{ hr}$$
$$= 30 \text{ kwh}$$

Then

$$\text{cost} = 0.05 \times 30$$
$$= \$1.50$$

Questions

(Take $g = 9.8$ m/sec for problems below)

1. The Harvard Step Test consists of repetitive stepping up and down on a 0.5 m step at a rate of 30 step ups/min and then measuring your pulse rate. If you do this for 5 min: (a) How much work (in joules) have you done during the stepping up parts of the cycle? (b) What is your rate of working in watts?

2. Suppose your toaster is rated at 500 w. Estimate how much energy (in joules) it consumes in 1 year.

3. If a slice of pie contains 300 kcal of energy, how many Btu is this?

4. A man consumes about 2500 kcal/day. If 80% of this energy is used to provide heat for his body, at what power level is he producing heat? (*Answer:* 97 w. In other words, a human body acts rather like a 100-w heater. Can you think of some applications?)

5. How many joules of work can the man in question 4 do with the remaining 20% of the food energy he consumes, assuming he operates at 60% efficiency?

6. Find the least amount of work done in carrying a 30 kg trunk up a 20 m stairway.

7. Suppose the trunk slips over the stair rail at the top and falls to the ground. Just before it hits the ground its velocity is about 20 m/sec. Find the ke the trunk possesses at that point.

8. If electricity cost 2.5¢ per kwh (approximately the rate in Michigan in 1973) and if your average monthly electricity bill is $15, how much electricity do you use in 1 year?

9. If the annual per capita every use in the United States is 350×10^6 btu/year, what fraction of this is the electricity consumed in Question 8? (assume all the electricity is consumed by one person).

Bibliography

There are a large number of elementary physics texts which cover the material of this chapter in more detail. I have listed a few, approximately in order of increasing sophistication.

[1] P. Highsmith and A. Howard: *Adventures in Physics.* Saunders, 1972, Ch. 2.

[2] F. Bueche: *Principles of Physics.* McGraw-Hill, 1972, Ch. 2, 3, 4, and 5.

[3] K. Atkins: *Physics.* John Wiley, 1970, Ch. 6 and 9.

And for the more mathematically prepared reader:

[4] R. K. Adair: *Concepts in Physics.* Academic Press, 1969, Ch. 5.

[5] D. Halliday and R. Resnick: *Physics,* John Wiley, 1967, Ch. 6 and 7.

Conservation of Energy

4-1 Kinds of Energy

In the previous chapter, we noted that there were various kinds of energy such as kinetic (motion) energy and potential (position or state) energy. This list could be extended to include many different kinds of energy, although in a sense these different kinds are really examples of either kinetic or potential energy (see Table 4-1). For example heat or thermal energy possessed by a body ultimately arises from the motion of the molecules in the body. In "hot" bodies the molecules move faster; in "cold" bodies they move more slowly. Heat energy is thus a form of kinetic energy on a molecular scale. On the other hand, chemical energy stored, for example, in food or in gasoline is released by breaking chemical bonds in these materials rather like the cutting of coiled springs. These bonds arise from electrical forces within the molecules and represent a form of potential energy, rather like the spring with the bullet considered earlier.

33

Table 4-1
Kinds of Energy*

gravitational energy
electrical energy
chemical energy (contained for example in food and in fossil fuels)
heat energy (thermal energy)
nuclear energy
mass energy

* The list is not necessarily exclusive.

4-2 Transformation of Energy

One of the most important things to realize about different kinds of energy is that one kind can be changed into another. The world around us abounds in examples of such energy transformations. A very simple example of such a transformation is shown in the pendulum clock. Let me consider an ideal pendulum consisting of a light string tied to a support with a heavy bob at the end of the string. I can give the bob potential (gravitational) energy by raising it to position marked 1 in Figure 4-1, at a height h above its lowest point. The potential energy of the bob relative to the lowest point is mgh. If I then let the bob go, it will fall along the dotted arc gaining kinetic energy, which will reach a maximum at position 2. In other words, as the bob falls, it *loses* potential energy but *gains* kinetic energy; that is, an energy transformation is taking place.

Living plants are other examples of energy transforming systems. A plant absorbs energy from sunlight (electromagnetic waves—a kind of electrical energy) and changes it into chemical energy by manufacturing complicated molecules. If this plant, say a tree, is cut down and burned, it can release some of this chemical energy as heat energy. Rockets burn fuel, releasing chemical energy and converting it into potential gravitational energy (Figure 4-2).

Most of our homes have numerous appliances that convert electric energy to other forms. The flick of a light switch produces light energy and heat energy (mainly heat) from electric energy; electric stoves, toasters, and coffee pots convert electric energy into heat energy; electric motors in drills, can openers, or carving knives convert electric energy into kinetic energy of the moving parts. These and innumerable other energy transforming processes are now a part of our everyday experience which we take very much for granted.

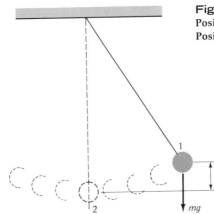

Figure 4-1
Position 1: potential energy (PE) $= mgh$; KE $= 0$
Position 2: kinetic energy (KE) $= \frac{1}{2}mv^2$; PE $= 0$

Figure 4-2

A rocket converts chemical energy contained in its fuel to
heat energy and to kinetic and potential energy as the rocket
rises above the earth.

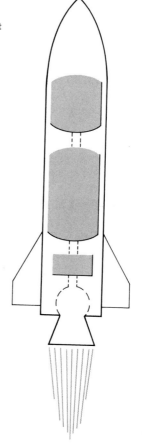

4-3 Conservation of Energy

We have seen that the various kinds of energy can be changed from
one kind to another. However, there is one additional element that
must be introduced, namely, that within one particular system, *isolated*
from the outside world, whenever energy is transformed *none is lost*,
no matter how many changes take place. Of course there is never any
completely isolated system, although many are approximately isolated.

As an example, consider the swinging bob in Figure 4-1. At the top
of its swing the bob is at rest and has no kinetic energy. It does, however, have gravitational potential energy and, as the bob swings down,
this potential energy is gradually changed into kinetic energy until, at
the bottom of the swing, all the energy is kinetic and the potential
energy is zero. If we neglect the rubbing of the string against its sup-

port and the air molecules bumping against the bob, then *all* the potential energy is changed into kinetic energy. We can see that this is so by watching the bob continue its swing and note that it goes as high on the other side as it was originally. In other words it has recovered all its initial potential energy.

Another everyday example of conservation of energy is observed when you throw a ball into the air. If you throw the ball with a certain velocity *v*, then, when the ball returns to your hand, it will have the same speed (neglecting again the effect of the friction of the air). This means that the ball has the same kinetic energy just after you let it go and just before you catch it again. However at the top of its flight, the ball is stationary for a brief instant as it stops rising and begins to fall. It therefore has zero kinetic energy but a maximum potential energy at that point. So, during its flight, the energy of the ball is changing from kinetic energy to potential energy and back to kinetic energy, but the total energy remained constant.

This principle of **total conservation of energy** is extremely important in the whole picture that physics has of the world. We may get some idea of how important this principle is if we consider the extraordinary lengths to which physicists have gone in order to preserve this concept in the face of apparently disastrous counterexamples. Consider the case of the neutrino. When a radioactive atom decays emitting an electron, the energy of the emitted electrons is found to vary. However, the principle of conservation of energy would imply that each electron must have the same energy in the same decay process, otherwise some energy would be missing. Rather than accept the varying electron energy as a breakdown of the principle of energy conservation, Wolfgang Pauli in 1931 postulated the existence of some other particle, tiny, neutral, and not detected in the radioactive decay experiment—the elusive neutrino—which he claimed was always emitted with each electron and accounted for the missing energy.

In spite of being such a bold, even seemingly reckless explanation, this view was taken seriously by physicists. Now with better measuring techniques, neutrinos have been directly observed, confirming once again the physicist's faith in the very basic law of the conservation of energy.

EXAMPLE 4-1: *If a piledriver of mass 4000 kg is lifted 10 m above a pile, what will be its kinetic energy just before it strikes the pile, neglecting air friction losses? (Remember that* g $= 9.8$ m/sec².)

Solution

If all quantities are expressed in mks units, the answer will also be in mks units, in this case joules (J)

$$PE = mgh$$
$$= 4000 \text{ kg} \times 9.8 \text{ m/sec}^2 \times 10 \text{ m}$$
$$= 3.92 \times 10^5 \text{ J}$$

From the principle of conservation of energy, this potential energy will be converted to kinetic energy again before reaching the level of the pile. Thus

$$\text{kinetic energy just before striking pile} = 3.92 \times 10^5 \text{ J.}$$

EXAMPLE 4-2: *If 5000 kg of water flows over a 20 m high dam each second, what is the maximum possible power produced by a generating station at the base of the dam (assuming 50% conversion efficiency)?*

Solution

The potential energy of 5000 kg of water at the top of the dam is

$$\begin{aligned}
PE &= mgh \\
&= 5000 \text{ kg} \times 9.8 \text{ m/sec}^2 \times 20 \text{ m} \\
&= 9.8 \times 10^5 \text{ J}
\end{aligned}$$

This energy is available each second, therefore the power producible, assuming 50% conversion efficiency is

$$\begin{aligned}
\text{power} &= \frac{PE \text{ available}}{\text{time}} \\
&= \frac{50\% \text{ of PE of 5000 kg of water}}{\text{time}} \\
&= \frac{9.8 \times 10^5 \text{ J}}{1 \text{ sec}} \times \frac{50}{100} \\
&= 4.9 \times 10^5 \text{ watt}
\end{aligned}$$

But (and in physics whenever things seem so beautiful, simple, and well ordered, there is nearly always another but) this is not the whole story about energy transformation.

The rest of the picture is also contained in the example of the swinging pendulum bob. As we know, this bob will *not* keep swinging indefinitely. Eventually it will run down. The reason is that some of the potential and kinetic energy is changed into heat energy mainly at the point of support as the bob swings. This problem of the loss of *useful* energy is extremely important and will be considered in detail in the next chapter.

Questions

1. Point out five examples of energy conversion taking place in the room you are sitting in.
2. If you drive your car to work and then on your return park it in the same spot in the driveway, you have used up some chemical energy from the gasoline in the gas tank. What has happened to this energy, because after you return home your car has zero kinetic energy and no change in potential energy?

3. Why was Pauli's hypothesis of the existence of a massless, chargeless particle taken so seriously be scientists?
4. A pendulum bob at the bottom of its swing has a velocity of 5 m/sec. How high will it rise above the lowest point on its swing? (Acceleration of gravity $= 9.8$ m/sec^2.)
5. A bullet of mass 10×10^{-3} kg moving at 200 m/sec strikes a large block of mass 20 kg which hangs from a string. If half of the ke of the bullet is transferred to the block, how high will the block rise as it swings on the string? What happened to the remaining 50% of the bullet's ke?
6. If 60% of the potential energy of the water flowing over a dam can be converted to electricity, find the maximum power output, in kw for a dam 50 m high where the water crosses at a rate of 300,000 kg/min.
7. A girl throws a ball of mass 0.5 kg straight up in the air with a velocity of 5 m/sec. How high will the ball rise? What will be its velocity just before it strikes the ground? (Neglect any air friction effects)

Bibliography

[1] D. Halliday and R. Resnick: *Physics.* John Wiley, 1967, Ch. 8.
[2] R. K. Adair: *Concepts of Physics.* Academic Press, 1969, Ch. 6.
[3] F. A. Kaempffer: *The Elements of Physics; A New Approach.* Blaisdell, 1967, Ch. 9.
[4] P. Morrison: The neutrino. *Scientific American,* January, 1956, p. 58.

Heat, Efficiency, and Entropy

5-1 Temperature and Heat

It is necessary first to distinguish clearly between heat and temperature. As noted in Chapter 4, heat is a form of energy that arises from the random translational motion (thermal motion) of the molecules of the body. Such motion exists in all bodies. The faster the molecules move, the "hotter" the body will be and vice versa. Temperature is a measure of how hot the body is, that is, how quickly or slowly the molecules are moving. The total amount of heat energy depends both on how fast the molecules are moving and on how many molecules there are.

We can sense the temperature of a body, for example, by touching it with our hand, but this is a rather subjective measurement and is not accurate enough for scientific use. There are more objective ways of measuring temperature by means of thermometers. As with other physical quantities, it is necessary to specify the units of temperature.

There are a number of scales for measuring temperature: the old fashioned Fahrenheit scale, which is still used in weather reporting in the United States, the common and convenient centigrade (or Celsius scale), and the more scientific Kelvin (or absolute) scale. Each of these scales uses a set of physical conditions, like the melting of ice or the condensing of steam to define two particular temperatures. The interval between the two fixed points is then divided into a number of

Table 5-1

Fixed Point	Fahrenheit	Centigrade†	Kelvin*
condensing steam	212°F	100°C	373K
melting ice	32°F	0°C	273K
salt and ice mixture	0°F	−17.8°C	255.2K
lowest temperature possible (absolute zero)	−460°F	−273°C	0K

* When temperature is written as T, it usually refers to the Kelvin scale.
† °C = 5/9(°F − 32).

equal intervals called degrees.* One can see the comparison of the three scales in Table 5-1. Note that temperature **differences** measured either in degrees Celsius (°C) or kelvin (K) are the same.

5-2 Heat and Work: First Law of Thermodynamics

As observed in Chapter 4, when discussing the decreasing size of the swing of the pendulum bob, the work done originally in raising the bob finishes up mainly as heat at the support. Many more dramatic examples illustrate the fact that work is often accompanied by heat. If you have ever pumped up a bicycle tire with a hand pump, you will remember how hot the pump became. Nails pulled quickly from a piece of hardwood can be almost too hot to touch. Or if we measured the temperature of a bucket of water and then swirled a paddle back and forth in the water we would see a small increase in the temperature of the water.

These observations are simply other examples of the principle of conservation of energy—emphasizing once again that heat is a form of energy and that we should also consider heat energy in any energy balancing. This principle is often called the **first law of thermodynamics.** It can be stated a little more formally as *the total gain in internal energy of a system is equal to the quantity of heat added minus the work done by the system.* As an equation

$$\Delta U = \Delta Q - \Delta W \qquad \text{5-1}$$

where ΔU represents the change in internal energy, ΔQ the quantity of heat added, and ΔW the work done by the system.

Consider for example, the piston and cylinder shown in Figure 5-1.

* The 13th General Conference on Weights and Measures in October 1967, agreed to change the unit of the Kelvin scale from **degrees kelvin** to simply **kelvin** (with the symbol, K). Thus no degree symbol (°) is needed for absolute temperatures. For example, 100°C is the same temperature as 373 K.

Figure 5-1

The first law of thermodynamics. When an amount of heat ΔQ is added, the gas expands and does work ΔW on the piston. The initial and final energy contents of the system are U_1 and U_2.

$$U_2 - U_1 = \Delta U = \Delta Q - \Delta W$$

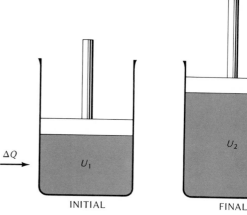

INITIAL   FINAL

The gas in the cylinder, which we can call "the system," initially has an energy content U_1. Heat energy ΔQ is added to the gas, and the gas expands doing work ΔW on the piston. The final energy content of the system is U_2. Thus, the change in internal energy ($U_2 - U_1$) is given by equation (5-1) as

$$U_2 - U_1 = \Delta U = \Delta Q - \Delta W$$

Because heat is a form of energy and because work and energy have the same units, there must be a relation between the units of heat and work. As noted in Chapter 3, the joule is a unit of work.

The common unit of heat is the calorie. The **calorie** is defined as *the amount of energy required to raise the temperature of 1 g (gram) [10^3 g equal 1 kg (kilogram)] of pure water by 1°C (degree Centigrade).* We have all heard of the Calorie describing the energy contained in food. This is really a "large calorie" or kilocalorie and is equal to 1000 small calories.

The relation between calories and joules was first established by James Joule, an amateur scientist from Manchester, England in the 1840s. The modern value is

$$1 \text{ cal (calorie)} = 4.18 \text{ J (joule)} \quad \text{or} \quad 1 \text{ kcal (kilocalorie)} = 4.18 \times 10^3 \text{ J}$$

5-3 Heat Transfer

Before discussing further the conversion of mechanical or chemical energy into heat energy and the inverse process, let us first consider

---

* Because the amount of heat required to raise the temperature of water depends upon the temperature of the water, the calorie is more accurately defined as the amount of heat required to raise the temperature of 1 g of water from 14.5°C to 15.5°C.

the transfer of heat from one place to another. There are three processes by which heat can be transferred, convection, conduction and radiation. In the last process, electromagnetic radiation with a wavelength slightly greater than visible light, called infrared radiation, carries heat energy from one body to another. This process will be discussed further in Chapter 6.

Convection, which is the common heat transfer process in liquids or gases *consists of the movement of hot fluid (that is, a liquid or a gas) from one place to another.* In a beaker of water placed over a flame, the hot water heated by the flame at the bottom of the beaker rises to the surface near the center and then, as it cools, returns to the bottom of the beaker to be heated again. A circulation or convection pattern is set up, which eventually heats all the water in the beaker. On a much larger scale, ocean currents carry heat from tropical regions near the equator to more temperate regions of the earth. Winds also are a type of convection carrying masses of warm or cool air from one region to another. Convection currents either in the air or in the oceans have a significant effect on climate.

Conduction involves the transfer of the random kinetic energy of molecules without the overall transfer of materials. Moving molecules strike neighboring molecules, causing them to move faster and thus transferring heat energy. Conduction is the primary heat transfer mode in solids, and an understanding of this process is important in considering insulation of buildings or appliances. Consider the block of material in Figure 5-2 separating two regions at temperatures t_2°C and t_1°C where t_2 is greater than t_1. Heat will flow from the hotter region to the cooler through the block of thickness S and area A. The rate of heat flow, that is, the number of calories that flows across the block per second Q/t can be written as an equation

$$\frac{Q}{t} = \frac{KA(t_2) - t_1)}{S},$$

5-2

where K is a constant, called the **thermal conductivity** of the particular material of the block. The greater the value of K, the more quickly will

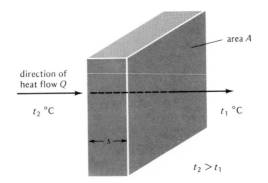

direction of heat flow Q

t_2 °C

t_1 °C

— S —

$t_2 > t_1$

Figure 5-2
Heat conduction across a slab of material of thickness S, area A inserted between two regions at temperatures t_1°C and t_2°C.

area A

Table 5-2
Thermal Conductivities

Material	Thermal Conductivity, cal/(sec)(m)(°C)
copper ⎫	95.1
aluminum ⎬ *metals* are good thermal conductors	56.6
iron ⎭	19.2
kapok between paper ⎫	8.3×10^{-3}
sawdust ⎪	14.0×10^{-3}
charcoal ⎬ *insulators* are poor thermal conductors	12.0×10^{-3}
corkboard ⎪	8.6×10^{-3}
insulite (wood pulp) ⎭	11.7×10^{-3}

heat be transferred. Metals have large values of K and insulators have small values as shown in Table 5-2. Similarly the greater the temperature difference $(t_2 - t_1)$, the faster will heat flow from region 2 to region 1.

This has clear implications for heating a house in winter. If the thermostat is set to keep the home a little cooler, the temperature difference between inside and outside will be decreased and less heat will be conducted from inside the house to the outside.

EXAMPLE 5-1: *Find the percentage increase in the heating bill for your house if the outside temperature is 5°C (41°F) and you keep your home at 23°C (about 73°F) instead of 20°C (68°F), assuming the main heat losses are from conduction through the walls and windows.*

Solution

The increase in the heating bill will depend upon the different heat losses in the two cases. If your home is at 23°C, the heat flow (Q_2/t) is given by equation (5-2)

$$\left(\frac{Q_2}{t}\right) = \frac{KA(23-5)}{S} = \frac{KA(18)}{S}$$

where A, S, *and* K *refer to the size, thickness, and composition of the insulation of your home, which are not altered by simply changing the thermostat. If your home is kept at 20°C instead, the heat loss (Q_1/t) is*

$$\left(\frac{Q_1}{t}\right) = \frac{KA(20-5)}{S} = \frac{KA(15)}{S}$$

because A, S, *and* K *remain the same.*

$$\frac{(Q_2/t)}{(Q_1/t)} = \frac{18}{15}$$

or

$$\frac{Q_2}{Q_1} = \left(\frac{18}{15} \times \frac{100}{1}\right)\% = 120\%$$

Answer

Thus 20% more heat is lost if the thermostat is set at 23°C (73°F) rather than 20°C (about 68°F). This increased heat loss will mean a 20% increase in heating requirements and your fuel bill.

5-4 Entropy: The Arrow of Time

Before returning to the conversion of heat energy, it is useful to introduce a new concept called entropy. **Entropy** means *the amount of disorder in a system.* The greater the degree of disorder or randomness in a system, the greater is the entropy of the system. More-ordered systems have smaller entropy than less-ordered ones. A new pack of cards is usually arranged in numerical order and by suits; it has a high degree of order and a low entropy. If the pack is shuffled, the pack rapidly becomes disordered and its entropy increases. Or consider a more homely example: Suppose I had one drawer containing only white socks and one containing only black socks, a well-ordered system. If I now mix the two drawers of socks I will have a more disordered system. I could describe this also by saying that the entropy of the system, consisting of the two drawers and the socks, has increased.

Children are sometimes given a series of pictures and asked to order them in a time sequence. Figure 5-3 represents such a sequence where the house is destroyed by a storm. The final state is one of greater entropy. Likewise if I drop my new pack of cards and pick up the spilled cards with my eyes shut, I will have a more disordered system and therefore one with greater entropy. These examples illustrate an important property of processes in the real world, namely that entropy tends to increase. Although it is not impossible that I could spill a disordered pack and pick up a more ordered one, it is extremely

Figure 5-3
In which direction does time flow?

(1)

low entropy

(2)

(3)

high entropy

unlikely. Nor does it violate the physical laws we have discussed so far for the energy of a storm to be concentrated on the wreckage of a house in just such a way as to rebuild the house—it just isn't very likely.

R. K. Adair makes this point in his book *Concepts in Physics* [2]* by considering pool balls on a pool table. Initially all the colored balls are arranged in a triangle and one ball approaches them. After impact the balls scatter. If a film were made of this process and then the film were run backwards, physical conservation laws would apply. The pool balls could all collide in such a way that all the kinetic energy is concentrated in one ball and all the others come to rest in a tight triangle, *but* this is an extremely unlikely process. After viewing films of such processes, it is possible to determine when the film is being run forward and when backwards, because entropy tends to increase as time passes. Entropy is time's arrow and determines the direction of time moving forward. These considerations lead to one expression of the **second law of thermodynamics,** namely that *in any process in a completely isolated system, the entropy of the total system must increase.*

This does not mean that we cannot decrease the entropy of a system—we could in principle rearrange the deck of cards into its original highly ordered state—but we would have to do external work on the system and it would not be isolated. It is possible to decrease the entropy of part of a system, but only at the expense of an even greater increase in entropy in some other part of the system.

5-5 Heat Engines and Thermal Efficiency

We have noted earlier in this chapter that in almost any process some of the energy finishes up as heat. It is also true that heat energy can be converted into other forms of energy such as electrical, kinetic, or potential energy (kinetic and potential energy are sometimes called mechanical energy). A device for making such a conversion is called a **heat engine.** Electrical generators, steam engines, and internal combustion engines are examples of practical heat engines. We will not discuss the details of such practical engines but instead discuss an idealized heat engine. In such a heat engine, a quantity of heat Q_{hot} is absorbed from a hot reservoir.† This heat is used to extract useful work

* Numerals in square brackets refer to citations in the Bibliography at the end of the chapter.

† A heat reservoir is again an idealization and describes a system that can release or absorb heat without changing its own temperature. A large lake is a fairly good approximation to a heat reservoir. The lake can absorb heat without the overall temperature changing greatly.

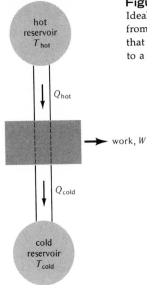

Figure 5-4

Ideal heat engine. A quantity of heat energy Q_{hot} flows from a reservoir at temperature T_{hot} K into the engine that does work W. An amount of heat Q_{cold} is passed to a cold reservoir at temperature T_{cold} K.

W, and waste heat Q_{cold} is vented to a cold reservoir (Figure 5-4). The thermal efficiency of such a heat engine is given by

$$\text{thermal efficiency} = \frac{\text{work done by engine}}{\text{heat absorbed}} = \frac{W}{Q_{hot}}.$$

If there are no other energy transfers, the principle of conservation of energy (first law of thermodynamics) implies that the work done by the engine, W, equals the heat given up in the process, $Q_{hot} - Q_{cold}$.

That is

$$W = Q_{hot} - Q_{cold}.$$

Therefore

$$\text{thermal efficiency} = \frac{Q_{hot} - Q_{cold}}{Q_{hot}}. \qquad 5\text{-}3$$

As heat is absorbed from the hot reservoir or vented to the cold reservoir, the entropy of these systems change. The change in entropy depends upon both the quantity of heat transferred and inversely on the absolute temperature. Using the dependence of entropy change on absolute temperature and the second law of thermodynamics, we can show that the expression for the thermal efficiency depends upon the temperatures of the two reservoirs as follows:

$$\text{thermal efficiency} \leq \frac{T_{hot} - T_{cold}}{T_{hot}}$$

where T_{hot} and T_{cold} refer to the temperatures of the hot and cold reservoirs *in Kelvin.* In other words, the maximum possible efficiency for any real heat engine, is given by,

$$\text{maximum thermal efficiency} = \frac{T_{hot} - T_{cold}}{T_{hot}} = 1 - \frac{T_{cold}}{T_{hot}} \qquad \text{5-4}$$

and is therefore always less than 1. Waste heat is thus an inevitable result of the operation of any real heat engine and of any energy conversion process.

The larger the temperature difference between the hot and cold reservoirs, the greater will be the maximum possible efficiency of the heat engine. It therefore pays to operate an engine at the highest possible temperature and to vent the heat to the coldest reservoir available.

EXAMPLE 5-2: *Suppose a power plant operates at 227°C and dissipates its waste heat in a condenser at a temperature of 27°C, what is the maximum possible efficiency of the plant? If 10^{12} J of energy (equivalent to about 30 tons of coal) are used as fuel each hour in the plant, what is the maximum number of kilowatt-hours of electrical energy the plant could produce each day?*

Solution

$$T_{hot} = 227°C = (227 + 273)\ K = 500\ K$$
$$T_{cold} = 27°C = (27 + 273)\ K = 300\ K$$

From equation (5-4)

$$\text{maximum thermal efficiency} = \frac{T_{hot} - T_{cold}}{T_{hot}}$$

$$= \frac{500 - 300}{500} = \frac{200}{500}$$

$$= 0.4$$

that is, the maximum efficiency of the plant is 40%. (In practice a real plant operating under these conditions would probably be less than 30% efficient.)

Maximum energy available for energy production each hour $= 0.4 \times 10^{12}$ *J, so that*

$$\text{Maximum energy available each day} = 24 \times 0.4 \times 10^{12}\ J$$
$$= 9.6 \times 10^{12}\ J$$

From Table 3-3, 1 kwh (kilowatt-hour) $= 3.6 \times 10^{6}$ *J. Therefore*

$$\text{maximum kwh/day} = \frac{9.6 \times 10^{12}}{3.6 \times 10^{6}} = 2.67 \times 10^{6}\ \text{kwh}$$

Thermal efficiencies are an important difference between present fossil fuel and nuclear power plants. Boiler design in modern fossil fuel plants allows them to operate at higher temperatures than present nuclear plants so that fossil fuel plants operate at higher thermal efficiencies than their nuclear counterparts. Thus, a nuclear plant with the same capacity as a fossil fuel plant produces more "waste" heat and is therefore a greater local thermal pollutor than the fossil fuel plant. Local thermal pollution by nuclear power plants will be discussed in more detail in Chapter 11.

Questions

1. Are heat and temperature the same physical quantity? Do they have the same units?
2. Clearly distinguish between the first and second laws of thermodynamics.
3. For the same power output, is the local thermal pollution increased or decreased by a higher operating temperature, assuming the same temperature of cooling water? Explain.
4. Find the maximum possible efficiency of a power plant operating at 270°C with input cooling water of 12°C. How does this efficiency compare with that of a typical nuclear or fossil fuel plant?
5. If your body is 20% efficient in converting food intake to useful work, how many kcal of food must you eat in 1 day to do 25×10^5 J of work without tapping any of your body's energy reserves?
6. A geothermal power plant operates at an efficiency of 0.33, using a steam geyser and a stream with a water temperature of 27°C. What is the minimum possible steam temperature of the geyser?
7. During the summer, on a day when the outside temperature is 92°F, you decide to save electricity by running your air conditioner at 78°F instead of 70°F. Assuming the heat input to the house comes predominantly from conduction through the walls, find the fractional saving you realize.
8. If your heating bill is $200 per year and half of your heat loss comes from conduction through the walls and ceiling, how much smaller will your bill be if you triple the insulation thickness on the ceiling and walls?

48
Heat, Efficiency, and Entropy

Bibliography

[1] D. Halliday and R. Resnick: *Physics.* John Wiley, 1967, Ch. 21, 22, and 25.
[2] R. K. Adair: *Concepts of Physics.* Academic Press, 1969, Ch. 16 and 18.
[3] W. B. Phillips: *Physics for Society.* Addison-Wesley, 1971, Ch. 10.
[4] D. E. Tilley and W. Thumm: *College Physics.* Cummings Publishing Co., 1971, Ch. 15 and 16.

CHAPTER

The Earth's Energy Balance

6-1   Fragility of Earth

Perhaps one of the concepts that has had the greatest impact on environmental thinking has been the idea of the "finiteness" of the earth. This is seen very clearly in the writings of R. Buckminster Fuller who speaks of "spaceship earth," thus emphasizing the limited nature of our resources and the fragility of our survival. Nowhere is this fragility more evident than when we consider the very delicate energy balance of spaceship earth. The earth is approximately a sphere 8000 miles in diameter situated about 93,000,000 (93×10^6) miles away from the sun—by far the main source of energy for our planet.

The earth must retain just the right amount of this energy to remain comfortable for living organisms. If too much energy is retained it may become too hot to support life as we know it, as the plant Venus is now; if too little is retained, the earth may return to a new ice age.

The earth's energy balance can also be disturbed by tapping other sources of energy already available on the earth. For example there is heat energy (geothermal energy) stored in the earth's core. This energy has been tapped in some regions where the heat was vented at or near the earth's surface. During the last century, man has also begun extensive use of the chemical energy stored in fossil fuels (coal, oil, and natural gas) and even more recently has released the energy from within the nucleus of the atom. Nevertheless, the major portion of the energy that reaches the surface of the earth is in the form of electromagnetic radiation (light, heat) from the sun.

49

6-2 The Sun as an Energy Source

The sun is pouring out this electromagnetic radiation by gradually "burning" (more precisely, fusing, as discussed in Chapter 12) its hydrogen and changing it into helium. This process has been going on for at least 4.5 billion (4.5×10^9) years and the sun probably has enough hydrogen to last another 4.5×10^9 years—so we have little worry on that account. Most of this radiation streams out of the solar system, but here and there one of the nine planets intercepts a small fraction of the light and heat which then serves as "food" for the planet, similar to a plant using sunlight. At the outer limits of the earth's atmosphere this radiation amounts to 2.0 cal/(min)(cm²) calories per minute per square centimeter) or about 1400 w/m² (watts/meter²) perpendicular to the direction of the incoming light. The radius of the earth r is approximately 4000 miles or 6.4×10^6 m and its effective cross section area is πr^2, namely 1.24×10^{14} m². Therefore the total power input is $1400 \times 1.24 \times 10^{14}$ w or about 1.74×10^{17} w.

Not all the radiation that falls on the planet is absorbed. Some of it is reflected back from clouds or dust particles in the atmosphere. Likewise, part of the radiation that does reach the surface of the earth is also reflected back by the surface, similar to the way a mirror reflects light. The amount of reflection depends upon the nature of the surface and is described by the term **albedo**, which measures the fraction of light that is simply reflected. On the average over the whole earth about one third of the incident radiation is reflected; the measured average albedo is about 0.36. For forest regions the fraction reflected would be smaller, but for the polar ice caps the albedo is very close to unity. For these areas most of the incident radiation is reflected and, therefore, there is very little warming effect.

The situation is illustrated in Figure 6-1. This figure shows dramatically how dependent we are on the sun for energy. The tidal energy from the moon, earth, and sun gravitational system is about 50,000 times less than the solar energy input. The geothermal energy from the heat stored in the earth's core, although 10 times larger than the tidal energy, is still 5000 times smaller than the amount from the sun. In discussing the earth's energy balance therefore, we will consider only the sun's energy input, although in specific regions other sources may be useful.

A large fraction (about 42%) of the energy from the sun goes into heating up the earth and making it warm enough to support life. Another large fraction (22%) produces evaporation of the oceans and lakes, which then brings rain to replenish the earth's fresh water supplies. Only a very small fraction, less than 0.1%, goes into pho-

Figure 6-1
The earth's energy balance. The circle represents the surface of the earth, with main energy inputs coming from solar, tidal, and geothermal energy (the last from inside the earth).

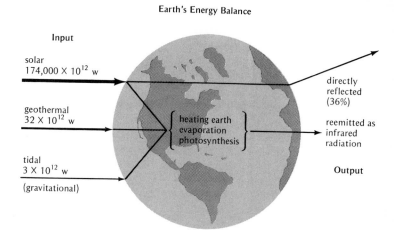

Earth's Energy Balance

Input

solar
$174,000 \times 10^{12}$ w

geothermal
32×10^{12} w

tidal
3×10^{12} w
(gravitational)

heating earth
evaporation
photosynthesis

directly
reflected
(36%)

reemitted as
infrared
radiation

Output

tosynthesis to make the earth green and provide us with fresh oxygen to breath and with food to eat.

6-3 Photosynthesis and Fossil Fuels

Photosynthesis is the process that occurs in green plants, including organisms near the surface of the oceans, in which the gas carbon dioxide and water are converted into carbohydrates, releasing oxygen. This process requires energy (solar radiation), and some of the energy is stored as chemical energy in the molecules in the plant. This chemical energy can be released by simply burning the plant, as in a campfire, or in a more complex way through some biological cycle, for example, decay.

Another extremely important area in which the chemical energy produced in photosynthesis has been stored is in fossil fuels. Certain kinds of plants under unusual conditions of temperature and pressure were packed together in a state of incomplete decay and have formed the earth's deposits of coal, oil and natural gas over periods of hundreds of millions of years. The rapid depletion of this rich legacy is one of the issues that we will take up in later chapters.

6-4 Emission and Absorption of Radiation

As noted above, about 64% of the radiation from the sun that reaches the earth is absorbed, the remainder being reflected just as a mirror reflects most of the light that falls upon it. However, if all the solar energy that was absorbed by the earth stayed here, it would fairly quickly make the earth too hot to support life. This has not happened, so we conclude that most of this energy must be emitted again from the earth. This equilibrium situation of continual absorption and reemission of energy determines the temperature of any body.

If the amount of energy absorbed equals the amount emitted, then the temperature of the body will remain constant. Such a body is said to be in **thermal equilibrium.** If more energy is absorbed than is emitted, then the temperature of the body will rise and vice versa.

There is an interesting property of the radiation emitted which depends upon the temperature of the body. In Chapter 2 we discussed electromagnetic radiation and noted that light, radio waves, ultraviolet light and x rays were all examples of electromagnetic radiation. They have very similar properties except for the frequency* and, therefore, the wavelength of the radiation.

In other words, light is just the same kind of thing as x rays, except that the wavelength of light is 5×10^{-7} m and for x rays the wavelength is only about 5×10^{-11} m, that is, much smaller. Radio waves are also similar, only they have longer wavelengths.

For some body at a temperature of T kelvin (Chapter 4), the maximum energy is emitted at a wavelength λ_{max} such that

$$\lambda_{max} T = \text{constant} = 2.9 \times 10^{-3} \text{ meter kelvin} \qquad 6\text{-}1$$

This relation is called **Wien's displacement law.** The hotter the body (larger T), the smaller λ_{max} will be. In other words, cooler bodies preferentially emit radiation with a longer wavelength. This is seen very clearly when we compare the radiation emitted by the sun and the earth. Figure 6-2 illustrates Wien's law, showing a plot of energy emitted by the sun and the earth at different wavelengths. The wavelength at which most radiation is emitted from the earth (λ_{max}) is much greater than the wavelength at which most radiation is emitted from the sun.

Thus, whereas the earth absorbs radiation from the sun at fairly short wavelengths, it emits at a much longer wavelength in the infrared. As we will see later, absorbtion and reemission of this long wavelength radiation in the atmosphere has an effect on the earth's equilibrium temperature.

Not only is the wavelength distribution of the radiation emitted by the sun different from the earth but also the total amount of radiation is much greater. Partly this is because the sun has a much greater surface area (about 12,000 times greater) than the earth, but also the amount of radiation emitted from any body depends very strongly on the temperature of the body and, of course, the sun is much hotter

---

* Frequency refers to the number of vibrations per second which characterize the wave. Wavelength is the length of one repetitive cycle. See Figure 2-4.

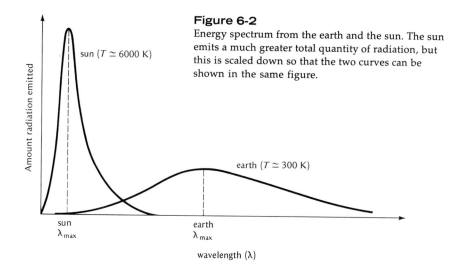

Figure 6-2
Energy spectrum from the earth and the sun. The sun emits a much greater total quantity of radiation, but this is scaled down so that the two curves can be shown in the same figure.

than the earth. We will use the temperature dependence of the emitted radiation from the earth to calculate the earth's equilibrium temperature at the outside of the atmosphere in the next section.

6-5 Stefan-Boltzmann Law and the Earth's Equilibrium Temperature

The relation between the amount of radiation emitted per second per square meter by some body and the temperature of the body is called the Stefan-Boltzmann law and can be written as an equation, namely,

$$S = \sigma\, T^4 \qquad\qquad 6\text{-}2$$

where S is the energy radiated per second per square meter, T is the temperature in kelvin, and σ is a constant called the Stefan-Boltzmann constant which has the value

$$\sigma = 5.67 \times 10^{-8}\ \text{w/(m}^2)(\text{K}^4)$$

Strictly this law only applies to bodies that are perfect absorbers (or emitters) of radiation. Such perfect absorbers are called **black bodies.** A small hole in a solid block of metal is an example of a black body.

Equation (6-2) shows that the amount of radiation emitted per square meter is extremely sensitive to the temperature of the body. This relation can now be used to calculate the equilibrium temperature of the earth, or at least the temperature at the top of the atmosphere. The surface temperature, which includes allowing for the effect of the atmosphere, will be discussed further in Chapter 16.

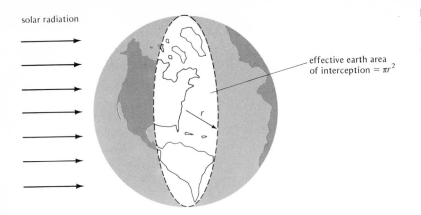

solar radiation

effective earth area
of interception $= \pi r^2$

r

Figure 6-3
Effective cross section of the
earth. The earth is a sphere
but presents a circular cross
section or target for incident
radiation from the sun of area
πr^2 where r is the earth's
radius. The surface area of the
earth, assuming it to be a
perfect sphere, is $4\pi r^2$.

The amount of radiation falling on the earth's upper atmosphere perpendicular to the direction of the radiation is 1400 w/m². The effective area of the earth is a circle of area πr^2 where r is the radius of the earth in meters (Figure 6-3). Because the earth's albedo is 0.36, only 64% of the incident radiation is actually absorbed by the earth. Thus,

$$\text{total radiation absorbed/sec} = 0.64 \times 1400 \text{ w/m}^2 \times \pi r^2.$$

Because the earth is at some equilibrium temperature (T kelvin), the amount of radiation emitted must equal the amount absorbed. The surface area of the earth assuming it is perfectly spherical, is $4\pi r^2$ where r is again the radius of the earth in meters. Therefore,

$$\text{total radiation emitted/(sec)(m}^2) = \frac{0.64 \times 1400 \text{ w/m}^2 \times \pi r^2}{4\pi r^2}$$
$$= 224 \text{ w/m}^2$$

Now we may use the Stefan-Boltzmann law, equation (6-2), to find the earth's temperature T kelvin. To do this we set the total radiation emitted per square meter per second equal to σT^4. That is,

$$224 \text{ w/m}^2 = 5.67 \times 10^{-8} \ T^4$$
$$T^4 = 39.5 \times 10^8 \text{ K}$$
$$T = \sqrt[4]{39.5 \times 10^8} \text{ K } *$$
$$= 251 \text{ K} = -22°C$$

Thus the temperature of the earth from these simple considerations is −22°C. This calculation strictly refers to the temperature at the edge of the earth's upper atmosphere, and we shall show in Chapter 16 how this temperature is modified by the atmospheric blanket.

* $\sqrt[4]{}$ simply means take the square root twice or $\sqrt{\sqrt{}}$.

6-6 Atmospheric Carbon Dioxide

There are a number of factors that can affect the balance between incoming and outgoing energy. One is the addition of carbon dioxide (CO_2) to the atmosphere. The carbon dioxide molecules along with the water vapor (H_2O) and ozone (O_3) molecules in the atmosphere have the property of preferentially absorbing in the infrared or long wavelength region. Thus the short wavelength radiation from the sun passes through the earth's atmosphere, but the long wavelength radiation emitted by the earth is absorbed by CO_2, H_2O and O_3 molecules in the atmosphere and then reradiated in all directions. Therefore these molecules inhibit the escape of the long wavelength radiation and are responsible for additional heating of the earth's atmosphere. This phenomenon is called the "greenhouse effect" because the same principle works in a greenhouse where the glass roof and sides transmit short wavelength radiation from outside but inhibit the loss of long wavelength radiation from inside. The effect is readily observable also in a car left in the sun with the windows closed. The short wavelength radiation (sunlight) streams in and is absorbed in the car's interior. The long wavelength radiation however is reflected by the glass windows which prevents its escape so that the interior of the car warms up. On a cold winter's day this can be a pleasant surprise but in summer it can be an unwelcome nuisance. The carbon dioxide in the atmosphere has an effect similar to the closed glass windows since it prevents the escape of long wavelength (heat) radiation from the earth's surface.

Beginning in the first International Geophysical Year (1958), the amount of carbon dioxide in the atmosphere has been monitored in a number of areas, but most extensively at a station on Mauna Loa in Hawaii. These observations indicate a steady increase of 0.2%/year up to the 320 ppm (parts per million) carbon dioxide presently in the atmosphere. This increase is presumably due to the increased burning of fossil fuels and, perhaps, to a smaller extent to the diminishing of forest areas around the globe. Approximately half of the increased input of carbon dioxide remains in the atmosphere; the remainder is absorbed by the oceans and the biosphere (plants).

The effects of this increased carbon dioxide concentration have been calculated (see the bibliography for this chapter), but the authors admit that, because they neglect complex interaction processes, these calculations are somewhat uncertain. The best estimate of the effect of adding carbon dioxide is that an increase of the carbon dioxide concentration in the atmosphere to 379 ppm would increase the earth's surface temperature by 0.5°C. A doubling of the carbon dioxide concentration would produce a temperature rise of 2°C.

Two points of concern should be noted. Although the likely increase of carbon dioxide in the atmosphere by the year 2000 will probably be about 20%, to around 380 ppm, if all the present reserves of fuel were consumed (see Chapter 10) there would be an increase of a factor of 4 in the carbon dioxide concentration. Secondly any warming trend could quickly be accelerated by a simple positive feedback mechanism. The oceans can hold less carbon dioxide if they are warmed. Therefore an increase in temperature that warms the ocean will release more carbon dioxide into the atmosphere, increasing the temperature of the atmosphere, and so on. The planet Venus, which has approximately the same outer atmosphere temperature as the Earth, has an atmosphere rich in carbon dioxide and has a surface temperature far too hot to support life as we know it. One wonders if it was always this way!

6-7 Particle Concentrations

A potentially even more dangerous effect may be the amounts of small solid particles or droplets with radii greater than 0.1 μ (micron, 10^{-7} m) being added to the atmosphere. These particles may cause a change in the earth's average albedo and thus change the temperature. The particles may come from a number of sources both natural and man made. Natural sources include dust storms, oceanic evaporation, and volcanic eruptions. The eruptions of Mount Krakatoa (1883) and Mount Agung (1963) had noticeable cooling effects on the atmosphere for many years.

Man-made sources include smoke, automobile exhausts, and large scale farming and mining operations. The man-made contribution is at present about 20% of the total on a global basis, but this fraction is steadily increasing. Over more industrially active regions the fraction is much higher. Very little detailed study has been done in this area although it is obviously a problem that merits close attention.

The effects of particulate matter on climate will be further discussed in Chapter 16.

Questions

1. Although 5.4×10^{25} J of energy from the sun fall on the earth each year, the temperature of the earth stays fairly constant. Explain.
2. On an average summer day, assume 40% of the solar constant (1.4×10^3

w/m²) falls on the city of Detroit (area 10^9 m²). How many joules fall on Detroit in 8 hr?

3. Assuming a reasonable rate of increase of atmospheric carbon dioxide, how much might this affect the global temperature by the year 2050? Try pressing your assumption to a reasonable limit and find the possible temperature change.

4. How can the addition of dust to the earth's atmosphere lead to a change in the earth's average temperature?

5. If the earth's albedo was 0.50 instead of 0.36, what difference would there be in the earth's average temperature?

6. Mark the best answer.

The explosive eruption of the volcano Krakatoa in the 1880's
(a) did not influence the weather at all.
(b) heated up the planet.
(e) increased Mexican corn crops.
(d) cooled the planet.
(e) none of the above.

7. Mark the best answer.

The earth has been cooling slightly in the last 25 years. This could be due to
(a) increased carbon dioxide in the atmosphere.
(b) increase in the amount of waste heat from fossil fuels.
(c) increased dust in the atmosphere.
(d) increased use of geothermal energy.
(e) decreased use of windmills.

8. Use Wien's displacement law, Equation 6-1, to calculate λ_{max} for the sun (T = 6000 K) and the earth (T = 300 K) as shown in Figure 6-2.

Bibliography

[1] R. Buckminster Fuller: *Operating Manual for Spaceship Earth*. Simon and Schuster, 1969.

[2] M. K. Hubbert: Energy resources. In W. W. Murdoch (ed.): *Environment*. Sinauer Associates, 1971.

[3] A good discussion of the effect of carbon dioxide and dust on the temperature of the atmosphere is given in *Man's Impact on the Global Environment; A Report of the Study of Critical Environmental Problems*. Massachusetts Institute of Technology Press, December, 1970.

PART TWO

ENERGY USE: PAST, PRESENT, AND FUTURE

CHAPTER **7**

Energy and Power Demands

7-1 Introduction

For nearly all the time man has spent on earth, most men have either had to hunt in the forests or toil in the fields to supply food, clothing, and shelter for themselves and their families. Although it is debatable whether or not men were happy with this situation, one thing is clear: they really had no choice. Progress from this state to one where more men do have choices can be described as largely coming about by the increased mastery of energy sources. For many centuries man was limited to manpower (literally) and animal power. Then came steam and chemical power, electricity, and now energy from the nucleus to help raise the burden from man's own shoulders. It is now possible, and I believe more rewarding, for many of us to spend time in varied pursuits such as the arts, sciences, or social experiments. Certainly in the United States only a small fraction of the population is directly involved in providing food and housing for the rest.

This revolution (or succession of revolutions) has not reached all men at the same time. Some countries obtained these advantages more quickly and developed at an accelerated pace, whereas many other countries were left behind at a more primitive stage. At present, there remains a large and growing disparity between the industrial and the underdeveloped nations. For example the United States with about 6% of the world's population uses approximately 35% of the world's resources of minerals and oil.

61

7-2 Energy Use and Gross National Product

There is a very interesting correlation between gross national product (GNP, a measure of the total value of all the goods and services produced by a country in a year) and the energy use of that country. One can see this by examining Figure 7-1. The United States stands out in the upper right hand side of the plot with both a high energy consumption and a high GNP per capita. In contrast, countries like India and Brazil both use very little energy per capita and have a very

Figure 7-1
A rough correlation is seen between per capita consumption of energy and GNP when the two are plotted together. High per capita energy consumption is a prerequisite for high output of goods and services. [Information from Earl Cook: The flow of energy in an industrial society. *Scientific American*, September, 1971.]

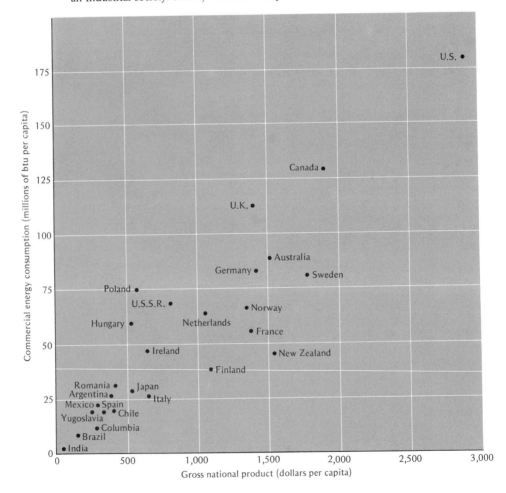

Figure 7-2
Energy use and GNP. This graph shows for the United States the general relationship of energy consumption to economic growth as measured by GNP. It appears to imply that the growth of energy is essential to continued national economic growth. GNP is expressed in 1958 dollars. [From *Energy — The Ultimate Resource, 68-184-0*. A study submitted to the Task Force on Energy, 92nd Congress, October, 1971.]

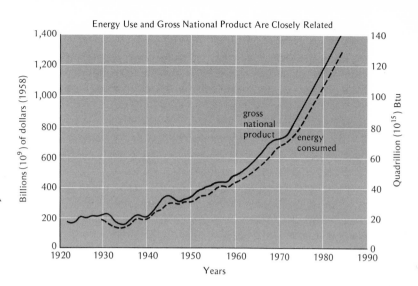

Energy Use and Gross National Product Are Closely Related

low GNP. Even countries like Australia, Germany, and Sweden, which we think of as having a high standard of living, consume less than half the energy per capita consumed in the United States. It is also interesting to compare Australia and New Zealand or Germany and France, all of which have approximately the same GNP per capita. Australia, more industrialized than New Zealand, used twice the energy per capita of her more agricultural sister. A similar but less dramatic effect is seen between Germany and France.

Of course these figures are for commercial energy production; if total energy use were considered, a somewhat different picture might emerge. In particular, in many of the underdeveloped countries, sources of energy (like animal dung and man himself) are used that are not usually tallied (or are impossible to tally), and this would change the picture slightly. Nevertheless, the overall picture is still undoubtedly true. The industrialized nations, and the United States in particular, consume far more than their share of the world's energy resources.

The correlation between energy use and GNP can also be noted by plotting the growth of both of these quantities with time in the United States. Figure 7-2, taken from the *Briefings before the Task Force on Energy* [4],* shows the close relationship between energy consumption and GNP plotted in 1958 dollars. This figure also shows the projected growth of both these quantities running closely parallel until 1985. Such correlations are usually used to argue that economic growth, as measured by GNP, requires a rapid growth in available energy.

* Numerals in square brackets refer to citations in the Bibliography at the end of the chapter.

7-3   Sources of Energy

As discussed in the introduction to this chapter, the sources of energy have been changing over the years. This change has been influenced by new scientific discoveries, by the development of new resources, and by more complex economic and political factors. If we look at the breakdown of the United States energy consumption in this century given in the *Briefings before the Task Force on Energy* (Figure 7-3), we see that around 1900, coal dominated the energy scene. By 1920 oil and natural gas had taken over a small but growing fraction of the total United States consumption. This trend has continued to the present; most of the increase in the use of energy has been taken up by oil and natural gas so that each of these contribute approximately one third of the total.

Two other features are noticeable from Figure 7-3. One is the small, albeit growing, fraction of energy obtained from hydroelectric power. Although this is a rather clean form of energy and is generally rather cheap to produce, there are not sufficient sites in the United States for the fraction contributed by hydroelectric power to change substantially. Other countries, for example Sweden, do have significant hydroelectric resources that play a major role in their energy picture, but this is not true of many countries.

The other feature to note from the graph is that, in spite of the considerable effort to develop nuclear energy since it was first recognized

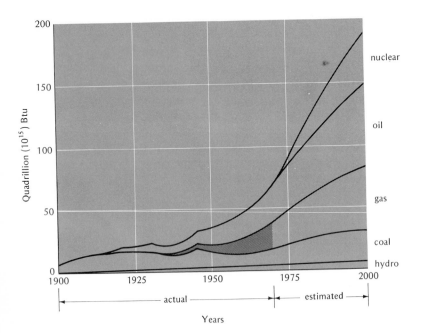

Figure 7-3
United States energy consumption in the twentieth century. This graph illustrates the historical dependence on fossil fuels and the relative contribution of the specific fuels to total energy consumption. [From *Energy—the Ultimate Resource, 68-184-0*. A study submitted to the Task Force on Energy, 92nd Congress, October, 1971.]

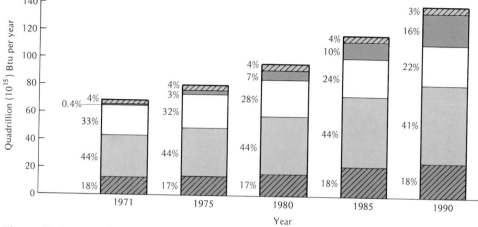

Figure 7-4

United States energy use, major sources. These are projections by the U.S. Department of the Interior from 1971 through 1990. [Courtesy U.S. Department of the Interior.]

as a power source in the early 1940s, it plays an insignificant role in the United States' energy economy at the present time. There are countries, in particular Great Britain, that have made rapid progress in nuclear power generation, but in the United States nuclear power has been introduced more slowly.

A rather similar projection of the breakdown of United States major energy sources from 1971 to 1990 is given in Figure 7-4 taken from the Staff Study by the Office of Emergency Preparedness [5]. Figure 7-4 predicts that through this period coal and hydroelectric energy resources are expected to stay at a fairly constant percentage of the total. Petroleum should fall slightly, from 44% to 41%, and natural gas is expected to suffer the greatest percentage decline, from 33% to 22% in 1990. Nuclear energy is anticipated to grow rapidly from the present tiny fraction (0.4% in 1971) to 16% by 1990. Whether these projections will in fact be realized depends on many factors, both political and technical. Any very significant alterations would require huge capital investments so that these predictions are probably fairly reliable through 1990.

7-4 Who Uses Energy?

So far we have noted the large and growing size of the United States' energy consumption and its changing nature. We now ask the

Table 7-1
Consumption of Energy Resources, by Major Consumer Group: 1963, 1965, and 1967 (in 10¹² Btu)

Consumer Group	Energy Inputs		
	1963	1965	1967 (prel.)
household and commercial	11,059	11,867	13,025
industrial	16,225	17,550	18,634
transportation	11,964	12,715	14,021
electrical generation, utilities	9,663	11,104	12,875
miscellaneous	738	549	298
Total	49,649	53,785	58,853

question, "In what areas of the economy is all this energy used?" The figures for the years 1963, 1965, and 1967 are shown in Table 7-1 and Figure 7-5. We see that the use breaks down into four more or less equal divisions:

1. Electric generation by the power companies.
2. Transportation.
3. Industrial (a somewhat great fraction).
4. Household and commercial.

The breakdown into these categories has remained comparatively stable during this period and continues to be true through 1972.

electric generation, utilities

transportation

industrial

household and commercial

Figure 7-5
Major energy consuming sectors. Historical use of energy by major sectors from 1963 to 1967. [From *Energy—the Ultimate Resource*, 68-184-0. A study submitted to the Task Force on Energy, 92nd Congress, October, 1971.]

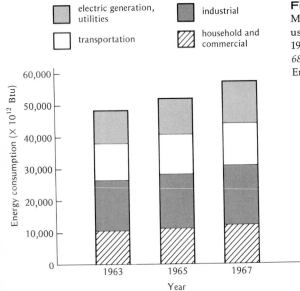

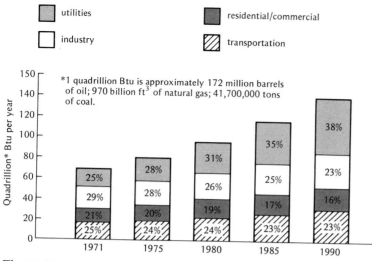

Figure 7-6

United States energy consuming sectors—projections from 1971 to 1990 by U.S. Department of the Interior. [Courtesy U.S. Department of the Interior.]

The projections from 1971 to 1990 given in Figure 7-6 suggest that the percentage of energy use by the electrical utilities will grow at the expense of small changes in the other three sectors. Utilities are expected to use 38% of total energy in 1990 compared to 25% in 1971. The percentage used by industry should drop from 29% in 1971 to 23% in 1990. Residential/commercial and transportation are both expected to show small decreases.

It is important to bear these numbers in mind when considering conservation proposals. Since household and commercial uses are only one quarter of the total, dealing with this sector alone will not make too significant an impact. For example, even if energy use in the home was reduced by 50%, this would still only make a 10% or 12% effect on the whole pattern of energy consumption.

On the other hand, it is also important to realize that the different sectors interact. Reduced energy use in the household and commercial sector would create less demand for electricity and the utilities would produce less, thus reducing their energy use. There might also be less demand for certain industrial products so that the energy used by the industrial sector would be lessened. The main effect would be on attitudes. For example, an oil company, in making the best extrapolations to 1985 for the transportation sector, points out that, with the antipollution devices now required and projected, oil consumption would probably double by 1985. However if everyone drove a *compact* car (not a mini car) the consumption in 1985 would be the same as today's.

7-5   Present Energy Crisis

What then is the cause of our present energy crisis? This is a very complex issue and a historian will probably be best qualified to write a book on this one subject some years hence. However it is interesting to examine for a few moments the shortages in electrical energy that have been common in the last few years. These have come about not because of a real shortage of world wide energy resources at the present time but from a lack of sufficient planning plus some mistakes in judgement. (One good aspect of the present "crisis" may be to focus attention on the possibility of a real shortage of resources some decades hence if the growth of energy use continues at present rates.) The Atomic Energy Commission pushed very hard to implement the use of nuclear energy and was able to convince the power companies that nuclear plants would be a solution to the growing energy demand. As a result the power companies, feeling the impact of the early environmental attack on air pollution, were glad to let their coal contracts lapse and to rest their hopes on nuclear power.

Concerned ecologists, however, did not limit their interest to coal fired plants. They were also critical of many aspects of the new nuclear power plants. Their efforts were rewarded among other things by section 102 of the National Environmental Policy Act of 1970, which required that the management of a nuclear plant prepare an environmental impact statement before the plant came into operation. This took the power companies by surprise, caused a tremendous slowdown of plant construction, and greatly increased the cost. Finally the electrical industry was able to convince Congress to delay implementation of section 102 during 1972 to help alleviate expected power shortages.

Another aspect of the problem was that, with new and larger equipment, both nuclear and nonnuclear (but especially nuclear), the utilities ran into delays due to poor quality in manufacturing. The technical problems, particularly radiation damage in materials, have been greater than expected and have also caused delays. The large nonnuclear Con Edison generator for New York City had many problems in starting up, and this is a lesson that probably will be relearned a number of times as the scale of generators increases. Larger sizes have their attendant larger problems.

The problems of the electrical industry have also had an impact on the oil shortages experienced during the early 1970s. As coal became difficult to use, the electrical power companies turned to oil as a fuel for generating stations, particularly low sulphur oil from the Middle East. This rapidly increased demand for oil taxed the available refinery capacity thus restricting the production of gasoline. Whether this increasing demand should have been anticipated by the oil companies or whether they were willing to let shortages develop as a means of raising prices, will be debated for some time. It is interesting to note that oil company profits did rise dramatically in 1973–74, which is not usually the reward in business for bad planning.

7-6 Power Crisis

Dr. George Szego writing in the Intertechnology Corporation report to the National Science Foundation [1] stated that there was not only an energy crisis but a power crisis. By this he meant that not only was there a problem of total energy available but an even more critical one of the time dependence of the demand. There are large changes in the demand for energy by as much as a factor of 3 at various times during the day as well as seasonal variations from summer to winter.

The power companies have responded to these seasonal demands by selective advertising. Some years ago the demand for electricity (for heating) was far greater in the winter than in the summer. The utilities then began a campaign advertising air conditioning to increase summertime use. This was so successful that in most cities now the peak demand comes in the summer. This response of stimulating a use to balance a gap will of course only result in an ever increasing spiral of use and will increase rather than solve the general problem.

An alternative approach has been taken in the case of the daily variation where the concept of pumped storage has become popular. Here excess capacity, say during the night, is used to pump water into a storage reservoir. During the higher demand period, the water is released to help turn generators and supplement the supply of electricity. Although the efficiency of this system is not very high (50%), it is still very advantageous. Consumers Power Company of Michigan has built the largest pumped storage facility in the world at Ludington on the shores of Lake Michigan. When completed in 1973 the reservoir had a capacity of 27×10^9 gal (gallons).

One problem with a hydroelectric system is the lack of suitable sites for such facilities. A hilltop near a large source of water is required, and such sites are becoming prime real estate to the electric industry. There is also the disadvantage that the cycling of the water leaves a very ugly hole in the ground for much of the time and denies the use of the reservoir and adjacent land for other purposes.

To help alleviate these difficulties an alternative storage technique has been suggested which uses compressed air in large underground caverns as its source of energy storage. This would alleviate the site problem because the caverns could, if necessary, be artificially created with explosives and the ground above them used for other purposes.

An additional advantage is that with a little heating of the compressed air this system could be made much more efficient than the 50% obtainable with water storage.

In the United States there is another possibility for minimizing the power demand. Because the country is large enough, the peak load occurs in different areas at different times during the day. With an efficient transmission system it should be possible to drain power from one part of the country to meet peak demands elsewhere. So far such long distance transmission lines are not available and this is one of the areas which require additional research effort. One possibility for such low-loss long distance transmission lines is the superconducting metals which, at very low temperatures (a few kelvin), can carry very large currents with minimum resistive losses. One of the problems is to find a material that would become superconducting at a temperature of 20 K or higher so that liquid hydrogen (which boils at 20 K) could be used as the coolant instead of the much more expensive liquid helium (boiling point 4 K). The metal niobium is one of the more promising cases; it becomes superconducting at 9 K.

Power transmission and other alternatives to the power crisis will be discussed in more detail in Chapter 15.

Questions

1. Discuss some reasons why the United States uses much more energy per capita than even the industrialized nations of Western Europe.
2. It is suggested in this chapter that there is a close correlation between energy use and GNP. Is this likely to remain true, or can you suggest methods of separating energy use from GNP increase?
3. Projections of energy use suggest an increase in the fraction of total energy supplied by electricity. How might this affect other consumption patterns for example in the home, in transportation or in industry? Suggest reasons why you think these projections might or might not come true.
4. One major component of the energy crisis in the early 1970s is a petroleum shortage. Give reasons why the United States is short of gasoline and heating oil at this time.
5. What is meant by a power crisis as opposed to an energy crisis?

Bibliography

[1] G. C. Szego (ed.): *Intertechnology Corporation Report C645.* National Science Foundation, November, 1971.

[2] *Energy — The Ultimate Resource, 68-184-0.* A Study submitted to the Task Force on Energy, 92nd Congress, October, 1971.

[3] D. D. Moore, G. B. Gaines, and D. Hessel: Getting energy to the user. *Batelle Research Outlook,* Vol. 4, No. 1, 1972.

[4] *Briefings before the Task Force on Energy.* 92nd Congress, 1971.

[5] *The Potential for Energy Conservation, A Staff Study.* Office of Emergency Preparedness, October, 1972.

[6] *Patterns of Energy Consumption in the United States.* Office of Science and Technology, January, 1972.

CHAPTER

Growth and Extrapolation

8-1 Population Growth

Many people have been introduced to ecological issues by considering the question of population growth. This is a problem first posed by Thomas Malthus, an English economist, in 1798. He pointed out that, if the population grows faster than the food supply, in some comparatively short time the human race will be faced with widespread starvation. Malthus' predictions have not yet come to pass on a very large scale, mainly because of an amazing increase in our agricultural output. We have seen more limited cases of population-caused disasters, including the 1971 flood in East Pakistan which claimed many lives because people were forced to live in flood areas due to population pressure. An even more widespread problem is the chronic protein deficiency that affects many people in Asia and Africa today.

The basic problem Malthus posed of runaway growth still has validity both for population increase and for many other quantities as well. We will consider such issues many times in this book, dealing both with increasing demands for energy and with dwindling resources. It is therefore important to discuss the problem quantitatively and try to generalize the ideas so that we can apply them in different contexts.

73

8-2 Powers and Logarithms

We already noted in Chapter 2, that we could write large numbers like 100,000,000 as 10^8, called ten to the eighth, or, more exactly, ten to

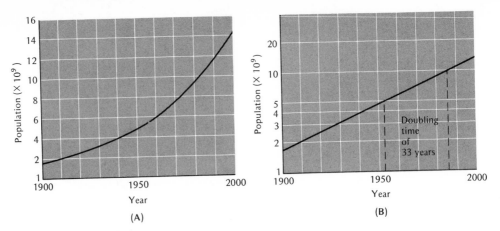

Figure 8-1
Population growth as a function of time. **(A)** The vertical scale is linear. **(B)** The vertical scale is logarithmic. This plot is called a semilogarithmic graph because one axis is logarithmic and one linear. The time to increase the population from 5 billion to 10 billion (doubling time) is concluded from the graph to be 33 years.

the power eight, meaning $10 \times 10 \times 10 \times 10 \times 10 \times 10 \times 10 \times 10$. This notation can be used for any number, not just 10. For example, we could write 8 as 2^3 meaning $2 \times 2 \times 2$, where the 3 is called the **power** to which the number 2 is **raised**. Another useful concept is that of the logarithm of a number. For example if $8 = 2^3$, then $3 = \log_2 8$, which is said in words as, 3 is the **logarithm** of 8 to the **base** 2.

Most times we take logarithms to the base 10. For example, if $100,000,000 = 10^8$, then we could write $8 = \log_{10} 100,000,000$. Usually the subscript 10 is suppressed so that we write simply

$$8 = \log 100,000,000 \qquad\qquad 8\text{-}1$$

An example will illustrate some of the advantages of using logarithms. Suppose we wish to plot the world's population growth curve between 1900 A.D., when the world's population was approximately 1.7 billion, and 2000 A.D., assuming the present growth rate of 2.1%/year.* In Figure 8-1A, the plot is made with both axes linear. The curve rises ever more rapidly as time passes and the population numbers quickly become larger and larger. In Figure 8-1B the same information is plotted on a **semilogarithmic** graph, where the population is plotted on a logarithmic axis and the time scale remains linear. We find it easier to accommodate larger numbers on a graph of this type. In addition the plot is a straight line and, therefore, is easier to extrapolate. Such extrapolation of course can be misleading because it

* Note: In fact the growth *rate* was smaller in the first part of this century and has been steadily increasing to the present 2.1% per annum. Therefore the population numbers are not accurate but simply illustrate the effect of a *constant* growth rate.

implies a continuation of the conditions that produced the present graph, which at some point may no longer be valid, as we shall see later in this chapter.

8-3 Exponential Growth

The property of having a straight line plot on semilogarithmic paper is characteristic of a certain type of growth called **exponential growth.** This type of growth pattern is true of many rapidly growing systems, such as bacteria with an ample food supply or of a savings account left undisturbed in a bank. Some decay processes are also characterized as exponential. The decay of radioactive nuclei is an example of exponential decay.

The defining feature of exponential growth is that the increase depends upon the amount of the quantity present. It can be described by equation (8-2) representing the increase of the quantity Q, such that

$$Q_t = Q_0 e^{\lambda t} \qquad\qquad 8\text{-}2$$

where Q_t is the value of the quantity after time t has elapsed, Q_0 is the initial value when $t = 0$ and λ is a constant called the **growth or decay constant** which specifies the rate of growth or decrease of the quantity Q. The letter e stands for the constant 2.72.*

An example may make this concept clearer. Suppose we have a magic orange tree that has an exponentially growing number of oranges with $\lambda = 2$ per year. The first year ($t = 0$) we observe the orange tree, we notice that it produces 10 oranges only. From our equation the number of oranges after t years equals $10 \times e^{2t}$. The results for various years t are shown in Table 8-1.

Table 8-1

	Number of Years (t)	Number of Oranges
	0	10
$10 \times 2.72^2 = 10 \times 7.4$	1	74
$10 \times 2.72^4 = 10 \times 54.6$	2	546
$10 \times 2.72^6 = 10 \times 404$	3	4040
$10 \times 2.72^8 = 10 \times 3000$	4	30,000

So in only 4 years, our exponentially growing orange tree has multiplied our 10 oranges into 30,000. Of course our assumed value of λ was rather high.

---

* More precisely $e = 2.71828$

It is this property of extremely rapid growth that makes population increase so explosive and likens it truly to a population bomb. Likewise the growth of energy use in the United States has been exponential, giving rise also to a potentially dangerous situation.

8-4 Doubling Time

One further important concept that is used in discussions of growth is that of **doubling time.** This is the time for a quantity to increase to twice the present amount. Such a number could be easily read off a straight line graph such as Figure 8-1B, where the doubling time for the world's population is about 33 years. If we go back to our exponential growth equation

$$Q_t = Q_0 e^{\lambda t}$$

and ask when will $Q_t = 2Q_0$, that is, when will Q have doubled, we find a very simple relation

$$2Q_0 = Q_0 e^{\lambda t_D}$$

where t_D is called the doubling time. If we divide each side of this equation by Q_0 and take logarithms to base e of each side

$$\log_e 2 = \lambda t_D.$$

Now $\log_e 2$ is usually written ln 2 and has a value of 0.693. Therefore

$$\lambda t_D = 0.693$$

and,

$$t_D = \frac{0.693}{\lambda} \qquad\qquad 8\text{-}3$$

Thus if we know λ, we can immediately find the time for the quantity Q to double.

What may seem like a comparatively modest increase in growth rate, can lead to a rather short doubling time. For example, a 5% growth

Table 8-2

Annual Growth Rate (% per annum)	λ	Doubling Time (years) (approx.)
1	0.01	69
2	0.02	35
3	0.03	23
4	0.04	17
5	0.05	14
10	0.10	7

Table 8-3

Present Depletion (or saturation) (%)	Years for Complete Depletion for Doubling Time of 10 years (7fi/annum increase)
100	0
10	33
1.0	66
0.1	100
0.01	133
0.001 $\left(\dfrac{1}{100,000}\right)$	166

rate per year, which means a λ of 0.05, leads to a doubling time of only 14 years. Table 8-2 lists the doubling times corresponding to various annual growth rates.

The speed with which quantities can grow when they have a short doubling period is staggering. In a single doubling period, the quantity grows by an amount equal to its total size up to that time. A few examples may make this clear. The total energy growth rate in the United States in the past 50 years has been 3% per annum leading to a doubling time of 23 years. That is, at this rate we will have used again as much energy as we have used up to 1972 between now and the year 1995. But if we only take the growth rate over the past 10 years (approx. 5%), with a doubling time of only 14 years, by the year 2000 we will have used three times the total amount used up till now.

If one now looks to the diminution of our resources, another feature of the problem is illustrated. It makes very little difference how much of our resources we have used now, if the doubling period is short enough, the time at which our resources are completely depleted is only slightly delayed. This is illustrated in Table 8-3.

So, whether we have used 0.1% or only 0.01% of our fuel resources, *if* the doubling time is 10 years, we have only an extra 33 years before *all* the resource has vanished.

8-5 Alternative Method of Estimation of the Duration of Resources

Some of the mathematics in the previous section may be a little difficult if you are unfamiliar with exponentials and logarithms. Using the concept of doubling time, the time to double the use of a particular resource, there is a rather simple procedure for estimating the depletion time of a resource. Let us illustrate the method with an example.

Suppose I have $64 and that, at present, my rate of spending is 25¢

every 6 hr or $1 per day. Suppose the doubling time for my rate of spending is 1 day. Therefore tomorrow I shall be spending money at the rate of 50¢ per 6 hr or $2 per day. Let me write down the number of dollars I shall spend on successive days and add them up.

1st day	amount spent =	$ 1
2nd day	amount spent =	2
3rd day	amount spent =	4
4th day	amount spent =	8
5th day	amount spent =	16
6th day	amount spent =	32
	Total spent =	$63

Therefore my $64 dollars will last just a little over 6 days if the doubling time of my rate of spending is 1 day.

Note that $2^6 = 2 \times 2 \times 2 \times 2 \times 2 \times 2 = 64$, and

$$\frac{\text{the total amount of money I had}}{\text{amount spent in the first doubling}} = \frac{\$64}{\$1} = 64$$

This is the basic technique for determining the time a resource will last with a constant doubling of its rate of use. The method can be summarized as follows:

1. Find the doubling time for the use of the resource. If the annual growth rate is known, the doubling time can be found from Table 8-2.
2. Compute the amount of resources used in one doubling time at present. This is obtained by multiplying the amount consumed in 1 year by the doubling time in years.
3. Divide the total amount of the particular resource available, by the amount used in one doubling time (as was found in item 2), and set this equal to 2^{n*}

$$\frac{\text{total amount of resource available}}{\text{amount of resource used in one doubling time at present}} = 2^n \qquad \text{8-4}$$

4. Find n by examining Table 8-4 where values of 2^n are listed.† The value of n is the number of doublings till the resource is exhausted. In the example discussed n was equal to 6.
5. Multiply n times the doubling time to find the total time before the resource will be completely depleted.

EXAMPLE 8-1: *Suppose the total United States coal reserves are 1.6×10^{12} tons and that our present annual use is 6.0×10^8 tons/year. The present*

---

* Note: $2^{10} \approx 1000 \approx 10^3$.

† Note that n will not always be close to an integer value but can be found approximately by interpolating between integer values.

Table 8-4
Powers of 2

n	1	2	3	4	5	6	7	8	9	10	11	12
2^n	2^1	2^2	2^3	2^4	2^5	2^6	2^7	2^8	2^9	2^{10}	2^{11}	2^{12}
value	2	4	8	16	32	64	128	256	512	1024	2048	4096

* Note: $2^{10} \approx 1000 \approx 10^3$.

† Note that n will not always be close to an integer value but can be found approximately by interpolating between integer values.

growth rate of coal use is 3% per year. How long will it take to deplete the United States coal reserves?

(a) If the present annual use stays constant, that is, there is no growth in the amount of coal used per year.

(b) If the present growth rate of 3% per year stays constant.

Solution

(a) For this part, because the growth rate is zero, we can find the time for depletion simply by dividing the total amount of coal by the amount used per year. That is

$$\frac{1.6 \times 10^{12}}{6.0 \times 10^8} = 2.7 \times 10^3 \text{ years}$$

Answer

Thus with constant use, the United States coal reserves would last 2700 years.

(b) With a growth rate of 3% per year, let us use the procedure outlined in the list.

1. From Table 8-2, the doubling time for a 3% annual growth rate is 23 years.
2. Since 6.0×10^8 tons of coal are used per year, the amount used in one doubling time (23 years) equals.

$$6.0 \times 10^8 \times 23 = 1.38 \times 10^{10} \text{ tons}$$

3. $\dfrac{\text{total U.S. coal reserves}}{\text{amount used in one doubling}} = \dfrac{1.6 \times 10^{12}}{1.38 \times 10^{10}} = 116 = 2^n$

4. From Table 8-4

$$2^7 = 128 \approx 116$$

Therefore $n = 7$. Therefore the coal will be depleted in seven doubling times.

5. Total time to deplete coal reserves equals n times doubling time. Thus

$$\text{depletion time} = 7 \times 23$$
$$= 161$$

79

8-5 Alternative Method
of Estimation of
the Duration of
Resources

Answer

Therefore with a 3% per year growth rate, the United States coal reserves would be depleted in about 160 years.

8-6 Getting off the Growth Curve

One might consider various ways of getting off the growth curve. For example if the consumption at any one time were halved (say by some new technical breakthrough) but the growth rate remained the same, we would only gain a single doubling period. The only way that any significant change can be made is to alter the annual growth rate.

I think it is important to realize that these numbers are irrefutable. There is no room for opinion or discussion about these facts — *provided the growth rate stays the same,* and this is a very significant provision. We know that eventually all such growth curves must turn over. This point is shown graphically in Figure 8-2. The solid, bell-shaped curve illustrates what must happen to the use of a resource if exponential use continues. Eventually the resource is depleted and its use diminishes catastrophically. Examples of such curves are known in nature when an animal population expands too rapidly. Eventually the food supply becomes too small to support the population, widespread starvation results, and the population plummets. The dashed curves repre-

Figure 8-2
Resource depletion. The solid curve assumes continued exponential growth to depletion. The dashed curve represents a decreased growth rate.

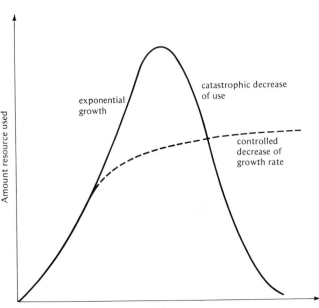

exponential growth

catastrophic decrease of use

controlled decrease of growth rate

Amount resource used

Time

sents a situation where the growth rate is slowed before the resource is close to depletion so that it lasts a much longer time.

Exponential growth cannot be maintained indefinitely. That is why projections that cover the United States with power plants in the year 3000 or the earth with people jammed shoulder to shoulder are ridiculous. Many other factors will limit the growth curve before then.

The important question is what that factor will be. Will we consciously limit the growth rate in some ordered and organized way, or will it take some catastrophic event over which we will have no control to limit our growth? As mentioned previously such catastophic examples are known, though not common, in nature where checks and balances have usually grown up through trial and error over millions of years. The time scale of probable resource depletion of 100 to 150 years seems like a dangerously short time when one looks at the history of man, and we must be careful that we do not wait too long before taking action. The question of growth will also be discussed in Chapters 9 and 18.

Questions

1. How long will the world's coal supply last if the time for doubling its use is 20 years and if about 1.9×10^8 tons are used each year at present? (Assume world total coal resources $= 7.6 \times 10^{12}$ tons.)
2. If the use of oil in the United States stays constant at its present rate of use, how long will United States resources last?
3. If the rate of growth of the use of oil increases at 5%/year, estimate how long United States resources will last.
4. How much longer would United States oil resources last if the growth rate of use was temporarily halted for 10 years and then allowed to continue growing at 5%/year?
5. "Now that the Arab oil embargo of 1973–74 is over, there is no further energy problem and the United States can resume its historic growth pattern of energy use." Defend or attack this point of view.

Bibliography

[1] D. Meadows, D. Meadows, J. Randers, and W. Behrens: *The Limits to Growth.* Universe Books, 1972, Ch. 1.
[2] A. Turk, J. Turk, and J. Wittes: *Ecology, Pollution, Environment.* Saunders, 1972, Ch. 8.
[3] C. M. Summers: The conversion of energy. *Scientific American,* September, 1971.

CHAPTER

Future Use

9-1 Introduction

One of the most difficult things to do is to predict the future. Ancient kings had soothsayers who examined the entrails of chickens to decide whether a local war would be successful or whether next season's crops would prosper. Our methods are now more scientific and hopefully more reliable. They are based mainly on extrapolating what has happened in the past after taking account of changes we can foresee. However, the reason for indulging in this exercise is the same as always. If we can predict reasonably well what is going to happen in the future, this will help us to make more sensible decisions right now.

One of the central elements of the energy crisis is very closely related to our predictions of the future. I mentioned before that our present blackouts and powerouts occur partly because of the lack of accurate planning on the part of the power companies and not because of a basic lack of resources at present. However if the growth rate of energy use continues, more serious problems are likely to arise. We will now examine the growth of energy use in the United States.

9-2 Predictions of Energy Use

In Chapter 7 we mentioned some projections made by the U. S. Department of the Interior of total energy use which suggest a total energy use in the United States of about 140 to 150×10^{15} (British thermal units) by 1990. This is approximately double the 1971 total consumption of 70×10^{15} Btu, and thus assumes a doubling time of about 20 years. The growth rate associated with a 20-year doubling time is a little over 3% (see Table 8-2).

From 1961 to 1968 the average annual growth rate of energy consumption has been 4.3% per year (Figure 9-1). A report from the Office of Science and Technology in January, 1972, breaks down this growth by consuming sectors. Residential consumption has been growing at 4.8%, transportation by 4.1%, and industrial growth has been 3.9%. Thus, the projections of a growth rate of energy consumption of about 3% by the Department of the Interior, imply a somewhat reduced growth rate over the next 20 years than has been true over the last 10 years.

There have been a number of predictions of the growth of energy use in the United States. Among the most recent is a compilation from 56 separate forecasts prepared by the Intertechnology Corporation and presented to the National Science Foundation. Of the 56 forecasts, 30 make projections beyond 1980 and only 7 project beyond the year 2000. Most projections estimate a total United States consumption between 100 and 200×10^{15} Btu in the year 2000. Beyond this date the estimates diverge even more, ranging between 440 and 1100×10^{15} Btu by 2050. The Intertechnology Corporation report estimates a total energy growth rate of 2.8% per year, implying a doubling time of 25 years.

However, the same report also presents an estimate of the electrical industries' growth pattern: 35 projections are presented, 21 going beyond 1980. Only two estimates are given beyond the year 2000. The predictions of total electrical energy use in 2000 range from about 6000 to 9000×10^9 kwh (kilowatt-hours) per year. The Intertechnology Corporation report predicts a 5.5% increase in electrical consumption per year, implying a doubling time of only 13 years.

Unfortunately it is not possible to take these predictions too literally.

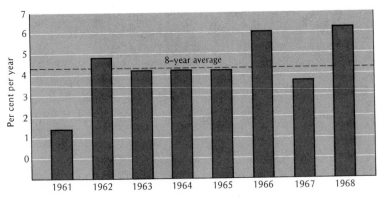

Figure 9-1

Annual growth of energy consumption from 1961 to 1968. [From *Patterns of Energy Consumption in the United States*, Office of Science and Technology, January, 1972.]

Figure 9-2

Comparison of annual United States total energy (E_T) input and total electrical energy (E_E) output forecasts with required energy input to electrical utilities (1970–2040). [From *Intertechnology Corporation Report C645*. National Science Foundation, November, 1971.]

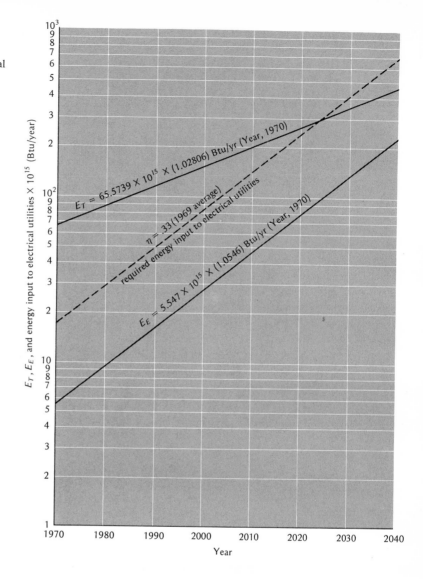

$E_T = 65.5739 \times 10^{15} \times (1.02806)\ \text{Btu/yr (Year, 1970)}$

$\eta = .33 (1969 \text{ average})$
required energy input to electrical utilities

$E_E = 5.547 \times 10^{15} \times (1.0546)\ \text{Btu/yr (Year, 1970)}$

E_T, E_E, and energy input to electrical utilities $\times 10^{15}$ (Btu/year)

Year

For example, in Figure 9-2, taken from this report, where an optimistic assumption of a conversion efficiency of 0.33 is made, the energy use curves are seen to cross at the year 2023. Thus, either the total energy extrapolation is too low or the electrical use is too high. In fact, over the last 10 years or so the electrical use has been growing at a higher rate than predicted, closer to 10% per year, with only a 7 year doubling period. The percentage conversion efficiency used in this figure is also optimistic because nuclear reactors will presumably account for a growing percentage of electrical consumption and, because these operate at a lower water temperature, their efficiency is less, as explained in Section 5-5.

Although detailed forecasts are difficult to make, they are important for future planning. A linear extrapolation of a semilogarithmic plot is clearly an oversimplified picture. The predictions should also include anticipated alterations in demand. For example, if pollution control devices are installed in automobiles and in power plants, we can anticipate increased energy consumption for the same output. Nevertheless, historical growth patterns suggest that a constant growth rate is a reasonable first approximation in predicting future consumption. In the past, most estimates have erred in predicting growth rates that were smaller than the actual growth which did take place.

9-3 Saturation?

An important question that arises immediately is how we will get off this exponential growth curve. It is clear that we will get off eventually one way or another—perhaps by depleting available energy resources or by a significant alteration of the biosphere, either of which could cause widespread loss of life. The general growth curve rises and then tapers off. This is seen for example in bacterial growth which finally stops after the food has run out. We will eventually reach a limit in the amount of energy we can consume. If this limit is reached in an unplanned and uncontrolled way, we are very likely to overshoot the safe limit with catastrophic consequences.

The question is whether, without any controls, we will reach a saturation level with a zero or very small growth rate. So far there are no figures to support this fond hope. It is possible that the large increases in consumption we have seen in the last few decades have been due to the poorer segments of society reaching towards the more affluent. It would be interesting to study the electric and total energy consumption of a few suburbs with different income ranges over a period of time to see whether the wealthier sections of our society are reaching "saturation." My suspicion is that this is not the case. Any hope for a saturation effect underestimates the persuasive powers of the advertising agencies.

Even if the more affluent members of society are satisfied with their present share of goods and services, there are still large numbers of people who will be increasing their income, and therefore their energy use, for some time to come.

One thing that seems clear is that the society as a whole is going to become more energy intensive as our resources diminish. In other words, as we are forced to use mineral deposits that are less accessible, we will require more energy to mine and refine them. Likewise, stopping the growing pollution, which is threatening to turn our world into one enormous sewer will also require more energy. One example is the more complete treatment of garbage. This can be done, but in most cases only at the expense of increased energy use. (This problem might be alleviated by the recovery of metals especially aluminum from the waste and by making use of the heat content of the waste.) Similarly, to stop the air pollution in our cities requires more control devices on our automobiles and on the smoke stacks of utility companies. These control measures produce an increase in the gasoline consumption per mile travelled as well as an increase in the amount of coal burned for the same electrical output.

A final extremely important problem is the availability of fresh water. At present we are using up our fresh water supplies at an alarming (and ever increasing) rate. To produce fresh water by some other means will also require an increase in energy consumption. Clearly from these examples it seems unlikely that there is going to be a natural turnover in energy use in the near future.

9-4 Population Growth

I suppose everyone is very aware of the extremely important problem of population growth. The present world population is 3.6×10^9 (3.6 billion) people and is growing at a rate of about 2% per year. In other words, the doubling time is about 35 years (Figure 8-1). At this rate the world's population would reach 14×10^9 before the year 2040 (see Table 9-1). While birth control measures and increasing industrialization are expected to slow the population growth rate, some agricultural and demographic experts believe that a maximum acceptable world population is 12×10^9, which will probably be reached around the year 2070. Here in the United States this problem is beginning to be tackled, and an active educational program is having an effect. The growth rate is beginning to slow in the United States, although our population will probably continue to increase for at least 70 years because of the present young average age of the population.

But, even if the population problem is successfully solved, the energy problem will not necessarily also be solved. There is a correlation between the two, and approximately half of the total growth rate in

Table 9-1
Population Growth Rate at 2% per Year (35-Year Doubling Time)

Year	Population
1970	3.6×10^9
2005	7.2×10^9
2040	14.4×10^9

energy use in the United States is due to population increase. However, the growth of energy use per capita is also increasing and, of course, this increase is independent of population growth.

9-5 World Growth

In Chapter 7 we noted that there is a large discrepancy between our energy consumption and that of many other countries in the world, including countries with large populations and high population growth rates. If these countries attempt to bring their per capita energy use to anything like that of the United States, there will be a very large increase in the world's energy consumption. Such effects are taking place as some of the underdeveloped countries try to stride into the technological age although the indications and predictions are still uncertain. For example, the U.S.S.R. increased its per capita energy consumption on the average by 14% each year from 1945–1965. Japan also has a growth rate larger than that of the United States. Presumably other countries like India, Brazil, and China will make similar spurts in their energy use.

9-6 A Cautionary Note

As has become clear from the discussion in this and previous chapters, we are on a dangerously increasing exponential growth curve of energy use. When and how we get off this growth curve are serious and difficult questions. We certainly will get off the curve at some stage due either to lack of resources or to some other fundamental limitation, as we will discuss in later chapters.

The predictions we make about the future may have large errors. Predicting the future has always been a difficult problem fraught with many uncertainties. However, to bury one's head blindly in the sand and hope that "somehow" someone will solve these problems with the touch of a magic wand is pure wishful thinking. We must try to make as accurate and realistic a prediction as possible, and then make decisions based on this prediction while there is still time to change the outcome. There is a French children's fable reported in *The Limits to Growth* by Meadows, Meadows, Randers, and Behrens [1] which makes this point very dramatically. A water lily in a pond grows to twice its size each day, so that in 30 days it covers the whole pond. If you wait till it covers half the pond before attempting to cut it back, you have only one day left. The water lily covers half the pond on the twenty-ninth day!

Science and technology have roles to play in terms of developing resources, but we should not become overconfident because of past successes. It has already proved easier to put a man on the moon than to produce an economic fission reactor. In fact in spite of about 30 years of intensive effort by the A.E.C., there are still only a few successfully operating nuclear reactors. We must face up to difficult decisions very soon.

Questions

1. Outline some of the factors that are likely to cause energy use to continue to increase over the next 30 years. Try to estimate quantitatively how much of an effect each factor might have.
2. "If population growth could be stopped, the energy problem would disappear." Defend or attack this statement.
3. Find as many predictions of total United States energy use in the year 2000 as you can (at least ten). Take the average of all the numbers. What average growth rate per year does this average represent from the 1970 value of about 71×10^{18} J?
4. Why is electrical energy use expected to increase faster than total energy use over the next 30 years? Can this discrepancy continue indefinitely?
5. Suppose world energy use continues to grow at 4% per year. How long would it be before the world energy use was 100 times the present value?

Bibliography

[1] D. Meadows, D. Meadows, J. Randers, and W. Behrens: *The Limits to Growth*. Universe Books, 1972.
[2] *Intertechnology Corporation Report C645*. National Science Foundation, November, 1971.
[3] *Briefings before the Task Force on Energy*. 92nd Congress, 1971.
[4] *The Economy, Energy and the Environment*. A Background Study prepared for the Joint Economic Committee, 91st Congress, September, 1970.
[5] *A Review and Comparison of Selected United States Energy Forecasts*. Battelle Memorial Institute, December, 1969.
[6] *Patterns of Energy Consumption in the United States*. Office of Science and Technology, January, 1972.

PART **THREE**

ENERGY RESOURCES

The Transient Resource: Fossil Fuels

10-1 Origins

Many millions of years ago the residues of primeval forests created vast deposits of coal. Likewise tiny organisms drifted to the bottom of ancient oceans and, under conditions of great pressure, produced the basins of oil that exist today. Since that time, these treasures have lain hidden until their use was discovered by man; then they were rapidly put into service. The consumption of all these fossil fuels is increasing each year, and it is necessary to ask how long these unique and irreplaceable substances will last. Once they are gone, burned in our automobile engines or to produce electricity, they cannot be replenished. Oil and coal are useful as sources of many synthetic materials, including nylon and many plastics, as well as being fuels. Do we have the right to continue to burn up these valuable substances, thus depriving future generations of their benefits?

There are three basic fossil fuel resources: oil, natural gas, and coal. In order to make comparisons between these fuels, an estimate of the energy content of a standard measure of each fossil fuel is given in Table 10-1. Let us look at each fuel in turn to see how much is available, how long the resource will last, and what are the advantages and disadvantages in its use.

Table 10-1
Energy Content of Fossil Fuels

Quantity	Energy Content (joules)
1 ton of coal	30.5×10^9
1 bbl (barrel) of oil	5.92×10^9
1 scf (standard cubic foot) of natural gas	1.09×10^6

10-2 Oil Resources

The use of oil as an energy source dates only from the beginning of this century, but in that time the world production of crude oil has shown a steady increase of about 6.9% per year. The growth of oil production in the United States is illustrated in Figure 10-1 together with the growth of the production of coal and natural gas. One of the main reasons for the rapid acceptance of oil is its versatility, and especially its use in both land and air transportation.

We must now consider two questions concerning this resource. First how much is available, and secondly, how long will this resource last under various assumptions of future use?

One estimate of the world's resources based on a 1967 study by Ryman of Standard Oil and quoted by M. K. Hubbert is shown in Figure 10-2. The total is about 2100×10^9 (billion) bbl* of oil. However the estimation of petroleum resources is very difficult. The oil usually occurs deep in the ground and in a somewhat random fashion. Perhaps the most extensively studied country is the United States, and

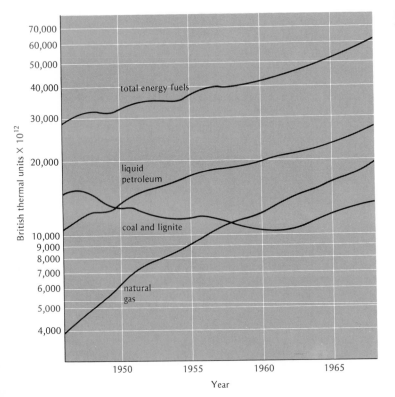

Figure 10-1
United States fossil fuel consumption from 1946 to 1968. Note the logarithmic vertical axis. [Information from U.S. Bureau of Mines.]

* 1 bbl (barrel) $\equiv$ 42 U.S. gal (gallons) $\equiv$ 0.159 M³ (meter³)

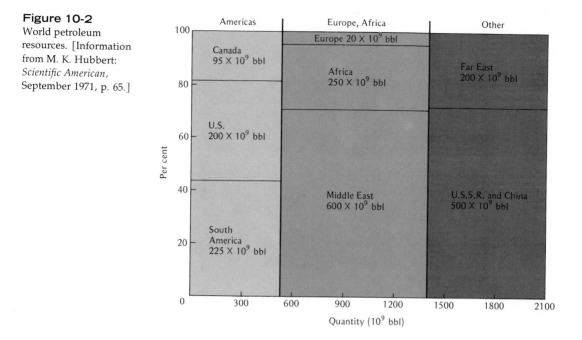

Figure 10-2
World petroleum
resources. [Information
from M. K. Hubbert:
Scientific American,
September 1971, p. 65.]

even there estimates have ranged from 145×10^9 bbl to about 600×10^9 bbl.

The high number was obtained by assuming that the oil produced per foot of exploratory well drilled will remain the same as it has averaged in the past (91 bbl/ft drilled). However production rates per foot drilled have decreased steadily from 1936, until now production stands at about 35 bbl/ft in spite of the increased sophistication of exploratory techniques. M. King Hubbert, taking account of the decreasing production per foot drilled, estimates the total producible crude oil to be 165×10^9 bbl. The proven reserves of the United States, which represent the amount of oil actually known to be available for recovery, have stayed fairly constant from 1963 (31.0×10^9 bbl) to 1967 (31.4×10^9 bbl).

One additional difficulty is that future production will likely come from less accessible regions, either the Arctic or offshore under the continental shelf. Exploration and especially production in these areas raise serious pollution questions. Similar problems are being experienced in the North Sea where 100 mph winds and 90 ft waves make recovery of oil and gas resources extremely difficult. The citizens of Aberdeen, Scotland, although benefiting economically from the oil discoveries, are also worried that oily tides may spoil their beaches and the fishing industry.

Another aspect of the resource problem is the efficiency of recovery. Without technical assistance, the amount of oil flowing from a well (primary recovery) varies widely, with the average being only about

20% of the total oil present. The flow depends on many factors including the pressure in the oil reservoir, the viscosity (resistance to flow or "stickiness") of the oil, and the nature of the surrounding rock. "Secondary recovery" has allowed up to 30% of the oil to be recovered, and this fraction is increasing as techniques improve. A method that is presently in the testing stage is to ignite the oil underground, thus heating the reservoir, increasing pressure and decreasing viscosity. Optimists hope that eventually 60% of the total oil may be recovered with improved recovery techniques. Even an increase to 40% from 30% recovered would increase the usable oil reserves by a large fraction. For example, the total estimate of 165×10^9 bbl could be increased to 220×10^9 bbl.

Given these large uncertainties in resources, we must next turn to the important question of how long our oil resources will last. The cycle of world production of oil is given in Figure 10-3 for two estimates of oil resources. Note that even for such a large difference in total amount of oil assumed, we only find a difference of less than 15 years when 90% of the oil will be gone.

The small difference in depletion time is because of the ever increasing use, the exponential increase law that we studied in Chapter 8. If we could hold consumption at the present rate of about 15×10^6 (million) bbl/day, or 5.5×10^9 bbl/year, and if we restricted our use to only domestic sources, then the total United States resource of oil (assuming an average number of 200×10^9 bbl) would be gone in only 36 years. In fact, the United States consumption rate has increased by

Figure 10-3

World oil production. The solid curve assumes total world resources of 2.1×10^{12} barrels; the dashed curve assumes 1.35×10^{12} barrels. [Information from M. K. Hubbert: *Scientific American,* September 1971, p. 69.]

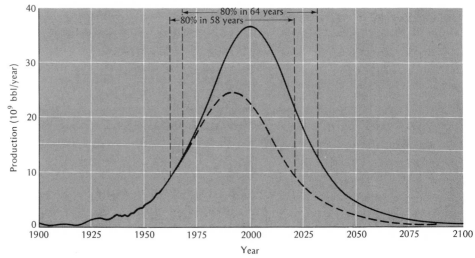

Figure 10-4
United States petroleum self-sufficiency 1954–1975. This chart shows that since mid-1967, the United States' spare oil producing capacity no longer exceeds foreign imports and the deficit is growing larger each year. [From *Briefings before the Task Force on Energy*, 92nd Congress, 1971.]

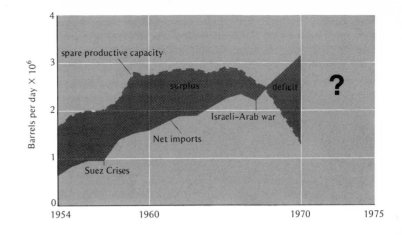

about 4% per year since 1950, and even faster since 1960, so that domestic resources would be used up in even less time. On the other hand, the United States has been able to import oil both from South America and the Middle East. At present these imports make up a growing part of the United States oil supply.

The situation up to 1970 is illustrated in Figure 10-4. Reliance on imports puts the United States in a vulnerable position politically, particularly if she is forced to rely on Middle East supplies to any great extent. Arab leaders may become increasingly eager to use their oil resources as a diplomatic tool in the already tense situation in that area of the world. Other major oil users, such as Japan and a number of European countries, are even more vulnerable to this kind of political pressure from Arab nations because oil imports make up a much larger fraction of their total oil use. Whether in the short term this becomes a political problem or not,* oil will almost certainly become an increasingly scarce commodity worldwide by the end of this century.

Much of the recent effort to find new sources of petroleum have involved drilling offshore on the continental shelf, and this effort will presumably continue and will include the eastern seaboard of the United States. Indeed, such assumptions are built into the estimates of oil resources discussed in the previous section. In this case the unfortunate consequences from "blowouts" from such production wells are much greater because the danger to the environment is so much greater at sea than on land, where a spill can be more easily contained.

In spite of increased precautions, we have witnessed two major examples of catastrophic oil spills in recent years. One was the Santa Barbara channel incident, which destroyed sea life and left stretches of beach covered with sticky black gum that was extremely hard to remove. A second example occurred in a drilling platform in the Gulf

---

* Since this was written, the oil embargo in 1973–74 has shown that Arab countries are prepared even now to use their oil supplies as a political weapon.

of Mexico near Louisiana, not far from shrimp and oyster beds worth $100 million. Gas ignited and burned for over a month before an attempt was made to snuff it out with dynamite—1000 bbl/day of oil were released.

In addition to dangers at production sites, pollution is common from oil tankers at sea either from accident or deliberate dumping. The coasts of both Florida and Alaska have been the recipients of this unwanted gift from the sea. The oil pollution of coastlines will undoubtedly increase as oil imports grow. Giant offshore ports are planned on the east coast even though these may result in unavoidable spillage problems which will threaten beaches and wildlife. The situation in Alaska is particularly severe because oil has a very slow rate of biodegradation in the cold Arctic conditions. A further worry discussed by two oceanographers, Campbell and Martin in *Science* [6] is that oil spills in the Arctic Ocean could alter the albedo of the pack ice, possibly causing it to melt and thus having widespread climatic effects.

Even on land, much of the oil production process is polluting not only from spillage but also from the unsightly derricks that march across the landscape. However, these problems are much less serious than those at sea, so that further exploration on land should be encouraged and greater controls with heavy penalties should be levied for mistakes in at-sea operations.

Oil can also be polluting in its normal use both in electrical production and, especially, in transportation. When oil with a high sulfur content is used in electric power plants, sulfur oxide emissions exceed allowable limits. Recent shortages of low sulfur oil have caused electrical companies to threaten that they will be forced to use high sulfur oil. But, by far the greatest air polluter in urban centers is the automobile. This is such a large problem that it is treated in detail in Chapter 17. Suffice to say here that the internal combustion engine, powering large vehicles that carry a single or few passengers, even with auto pollution controls, cannot be a long term solution to transportation needs. Antipollution controls, although important at present, also result in greater gasoline consumption, thus exacerbating the oil shortage.

10-3 Natural Gas Resources

Natural gas consists mainly of the gas methane, CH_4, mixed with heavier hydrocarbons and is usually found together with oil in the ratio (at present) of about 6500 ft^3 (cubic feet) of gas per barrel of oil. The first commercial application of natural gas was even more recent

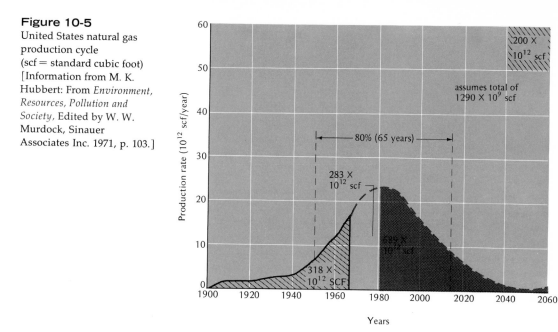

Figure 10-5
United States natural gas production cycle
(scf = standard cubic foot)
[Information from M. K. Hubbert: From *Environment, Resources, Pollution and Society,* Edited by W. W. Murdock, Sinauer Associates Inc. 1971, p. 103.]

than oil, but its use has grown very rapidly. In the early days of oil production, natural gas was simply burned at the well head. Since then its many advantages have led to much more extensive use. Natural gas is easy to handle, involves low capital investment in gas-fired facilities, has little waste disposal problems, and brings essentially no pollution. About 17% of the natural gas goes to generate electricity, about 35% into household and commercial applications, 50% for industrial applications, the remaining few per cent for transportation.

Natural gas consumption has been growing steadily (see Figure 10-5) and in 1969 totalled 21.2×10^{12} scf (standard cubic feet).* Estimates of the amount of United States natural gas range from 1050×10^{12} scf to 1290×10^{12} scf. A plot of its production cycle (Figure 10-5) implies that it will be 90% gone by before 2020 — less than 50 years away. The United States resources of natural gas have been falling steadily since 1966. The world production rate will generally follow that of oil so that natural gas will be in short supply early in the next century.

10-4 Helium

There is one component of natural gas that deserves special attention — helium. Helium occurs in natural gas in concentrations generally

* A standard cubic foot is measured at 1 atm (atmosphere) pressure and 15.6°C (60°F).

less than a few per cent but sometimes as high as about 8%. Helium is a very light gas (atomic mass = 4) so that the gravitational attraction of the earth on it is comparatively weak, and the helium is readily lost from the upper atmosphere. Helium plays an extremely important and probably unique role in a number of developing technologies, especially that of superconductive devices which we may need rather soon to transport massive amounts of electricity large distances without substantial losses. It may also be important in artificial atmospheres for space and ocean exploration and for fusion control.

Our present use is about 900×10^6 scf/year. It is vitally necessary that helium, an important and unique gas, be conserved. Research into recovery and reuse systems should be encouraged. Unfortunately the Department of Interior's purchase and storage program has been discontinued because of short term financial problems. As a result, helium is being vented to the atmosphere. Future generations may be forced to employ very energy intensive techniques of helium recovery because of the present lack of foresight. As Preston Cloud says, "Natural resources are the priceless heritage of all the people including those not yet born: their waste cannot be tolerated." This is especially true for helium.

10-5   Coal Resources

Coal is one of the earliest fossil fuels discovered by man. Its use dates from about the twelfth century when black rocks or "sea coals" found near the northeast coast of England were found to burn. As seen in Figure 10-1 the popularity of coal has decreased as that of oil and natural gas has increased, but this trend will be reversed as the amounts of oil and gas diminish towards the end of this century.

Coal resources are rather easier to estimate than are those of oil or natural gas so that we may expect better reliability from these. The world's resources estimated by M. King Hubbert are shown in Figure 10-6. The United States (1.5×10^{12} metric ton) and the U.S.S.R. (4.3×10^{12} metric ton) dominate the world's coal deposits, which total about 7.6×10^{12} metric ton. This estimate is based on a recent survey by Paul Averitt of the U.S. Geological Survey. A somewhat lower estimate based on actual mapping gives a world total of 4.3×10^{12} metric tons.

Since 1945, world coal production has increased by 3.5% per year. A production rate graph assuming three more doublings in the production rate implies a decrease beyond 2150. For the lower figure of 4.3×10^{12} metric tons for the total world resources and a fivefold

The Transient Resource:
Fossil Fuels

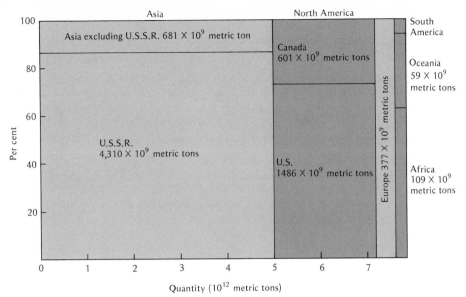

Figure 10-6

World coal reserves. [Information from M. K. Hubbert: *Scientific American*, September 1971, p. 64.]

increase in the present production rate, peak production would occur in 2100. If we allow the present rate of increase to continue for only 70 years, we would run out of coal in 110 years.

Similar statements could be made about the United States where the time scale ranges from 200 to 400 years. A table from a background study prepared for the Joint Economic Committee of Congress in September 1970 [4] shows a mapped total of 1.56×10^{12} tons and an estimated total of 3.21×10^{12} tons. About half of this latter total will probably be recoverable, in reasonable agreement with the estimates shown in Figure 10-6. However, at present only about 390×10^9 tons of coal can be considered as a proven, identified reserve. The United States production has stayed fairly constant at about 600×10^6 tons per year since 1950 of which about half is used to generate electricity. The cost of coal, which decreased through the first half of 1960s, has been rising again due to rising labor costs and to the cost of reducing some of the environmental damage from the production process.

10-6 Pollution Problems from Coal

Although coal is one of the more abundant of the fossil fuels, it is also one of the biggest sources of pollution. Coal gives rise to adverse environmental effects both when it is mined and as it is used as a fuel in industry or for electric generation.

There are two main techniques for producing coal from the ground, the traditional underground mining and the newer strip-mining. In this latter method, the scenery and soil (euphemistically termed the "overburden") is stripped away to leave the coal vein exposed for easy removal by gigantic machines. Because much of the low sulfur coal, particularly in the western states, can be mined by the stripping method, this technique will almost certainly increase in the years ahead as the demand for coal increases. Unfortunately, both mining methods have serious environmental problems. Underground mining has been plagued by accidents and by poor conditions for miners. Black lung disease and other respiratory problems are much more common among miners than among the general population. Miners' sons are increasingly and understandably reluctant to become miners so that labor shortages will undoubtedly increase in this field. Underground mining is often accompanied by ugly piles of mine tailings, by drainage of unwanted chemicals into streams and rivers, and by the collapse of land near old mines.

The more modern and less labor intensive strip-mining process seems certain to increase. The associated problems are readily visible. First there are the large piles of overburden, turning what may have

Figure 10-7
Strip-mining in Ohio. [Courtesy of BLACK STAR. Photo by Franklynn Peterson.]

been farmland into a moonscape (Figure 10-7). Even if the topsoil is put back, it is not known whether the land can be restored to its original use. Particularly in the west, with lack of abundant water, restoration appears a very difficult proposition. Cost estimates for reclaiming stripped land vary widely. The coal companies generally estimate that between $200 and $300 per acre is required. But recent estimates by the Appalachian Regional Commission of the cost of simply back filling and grading are about $1000 per acre. The total cost of reclamation, which agrees reasonably well with European experience, is likely to be between $1500 and $4000 per acre. Extensive legal battles are being fought and legislation is being proposed to limit or control strip-mining. Such legislation faces severe opposition from the powerful coal lobby who often find it difficult to understand the opposition. As an article by James Carraway [8] says, "The most common defense of strip-mining among those in industry is 'But there wasn't anything there before we started digging!'"

The production process, however, is only one part of the pollution picture. The air pollution produced by burning coal, especially by the power companies for the generation of electricity, has been extensively documented. One recent example is the large power complex at Four Corners near the point where New Mexico, Arizona, Utah, and Colorado join. What was formerly crystal clear desert air has now become murky smog, with smoke trailing continuously from the giant stacks. Under pressure from environmental groups and local residents, the Arizona Public Service Company has installed some controls, but these still allow more than *62 tons* of particle emissions from the plant per day. The whole story of power company reluctance to install control devices until pressed to the wall and the reluctance of Federal agencies to press the case is familiar in many United States cities today. Many cities now release air pollution warnings to their residents, and part of that pollution is due to coal burning. England has been forced to restrict coal burning greatly, but still many people over 40 suffer from respiratory disease.

Present legislation in many states is slowly beginning to attack this problem by placing restrictions on the allowed emissions. Such legislation forces the power companies to turn to coal with low emissions, for example to low sulfur coal, or to install control devices. However, not all the problems can be solved by legislation. Although technically feasible processes are available that can control the bulk of sulfur and large particle emissions, these methods are expensive. Power companies are reluctant to make large capital investments at present, hoping that better methods will be available in the future. The additional problem of small (micron) size particulate emissions is more severe because no satisfactory method is presently known to control emission of these particles.

10-7 Coal Gasification

An alternative technique, which holds a good deal of promise, is to convert the coal into gas, preferably near the mine. Natural gas consists mainly of methane, a simple compound of carbon and hydrogen. Methane has a high energy content, about 1000 Btu/scf, and it is important in converting the coal to gas to ensure that the final product contains a high quantity of methane. Without special precautions, a gas consisting mainly of hydrogen (H_2) and carbon monoxide (CO), with an energy content of only 450 Btu/scf, is produced, and this product is much less economical to transport.

The basic process is comparatively simple in principle. Carbon from the coal is combined with steam at high temperatures to produce methane. In practice, however, a number of combustion stages are required to ensure that both the carbon monoxide and hydrogen produced are efficiently converted to methane. Such techniques are not particularly new and a process, the Lurgi method, was developed in Europe more than 30 years ago. A number of United States companies are now planning to build plants using somewhat different and simpler techniques. It is hoped that some of these may be in operation by the end of this decade.

Engineering problems still remain, particularly in designing a continuous process combining the various subprocesses and operating at high temperatures (1500°C) and high pressures (20–70 atm). If high sulfur coal is used, the plant must also include filtering equipment to prevent release of sulfur dioxide. Large quantities of sulfuric acid would probably be produced and would have to be safely removed. Finally the coal ash itself would need to be disposed of in a non-damaging way, perhaps as land fill to help restore the land from which the coal was mined.

In spite of the difficulties, rapid development of this process is necessary if coal is to be used to back up our diminishing reserves of oil and natural gas. More research and engineering are still required and should be encouraged as rapidly as possible.

10-8 Tar Sands and Oil Shales

Not all our oil resources are in oil basins. A substantial amount of oil can also be recovered from other geological formations called tar sands and oil shales. Tar sands are a mixture of sand, water, and bituminous material, with the amount of bitumen ranging from about 13 to 60% of the total mass. By far the largest deposit of tar sands known is in Alberta, Canada. It is estimated that about 300 to 350×10^9 bbl of oil can be extracted from the Athabasca field, which is believed to be the world's major source. By contrast, United States deposits, centered mainly in Utah, probably have less than 8×10^9 bbl of oil recoverable. However, the tar sand technology is still not well developed, and numerous environmental problems, particularly with mine tailings, also remain. After a complex refining process, the tar sands produce a crude oil substitute called syncrude, which is competitive with natural crude oil.

Oil shale (oil impregnated rock) also contains much usable oil. A recent survey by Duncan and Swanson of the U.S. Geological Survey has indicated that a total of about 200×10^9 bbl of oil can be obtained from oil shale. The United States is well endowed in this regard, with about two thirds of the world's known resources. The estimated cost of extracting oil from shale is about $6 per barrel.

At present little use has been made of this resource in the United States, but it has been exploited in the U.S.S.R. Recently some large oil companies have begun to consider seriously the extraction of oil from shale. The greatest problem with exploiting shale oil is that a large amount of water is required for its treatment. The oil shale occurs in states (Colorado, Utah, and Wyoming) where water is a scarce commodity, and it is not clear that sufficient water can be diverted from other purposes for the treatment of shale. This problem becomes even more severe if one considers the restoration of the land after extraction of the shale.

Even for the highest grade shale deposits only one barrel of oil can be produced from every 1.5 tons of shale (compared to one barrel of syncrude from 0.5 tons of coal for example). Therefore a large oil shale plant producing say 50,000 bbls of oil/day would mean processing and disposing of nearly 30×10^6 tons of rock/year. Whether this can be done in an environmentally satisfactory manner with present techniques appears unlikely, especially considering the lack of water in the area.

10-9 Summary

A summary of the energy available from the world's fossil fuel resources (estimated by M. King Hubbert [1]) is given in Table 10-2.

As Hubbert emphasizes, the fossil fuels are indeed a transient resource on the scale of mankind's existence on the planet. They have proved to be a valuable tool for the rapid advance of technology and industrialization. It is important to carefully conserve these resources

Table 10-2

Fuel	Quantity	Total Energy Content (joules)
coal	7.6×10^{12} tons	232×10^{21}
petroleum liquids	2500×10^9 bbl	14.8×10^{21}
natural gas	12×10^{15} ft^3	13.1×10^{21}
tar sands	300×10^9	17.8×10^{20}
oil shale	190×10^9 bbl	11.2×10^{20}

to allow their unique properties to continue to be available to future generations. But in any case we will be forced to seek alternative sources of energy to meet our growing demands. We now turn to a discussion of some of these alternatives.

Questions

1. Will the world run out of either coal or oil by 2030? What about the United States? Make clear the assumptions implicit in your answer. Assume a variety of possible yet realistic growth rates.
2. The claim is often made that coal is a very long term energy resource for the United States. Discuss this claim.
3. "King Coal will make a comeback as the major fossil fuel in the United States within the next 30 years." Do you agree? Explain. Discuss some precautions which should be taken if this statement turns out to be true.
4. Order the following fossil fuels from least polluting to most polluting: coal, oil, natural gas, and oil shale. Justify your ordering.
5. Outline the advantages and disadvantages of strip-mining coal. What legislation would you propose to minimize the disadvantages?
6. Large quantities of oil shale are present in the western United States. Why has this source not been developed? Do you favor the rapid expansion of facilities to extract oil from shale? Justify your answer.
7. Suppose off shore exploration increases the estimate of natural gas available from 1200×10^{12} to 1800×10^{12} scf. Even if the use stays constant at 30×10^{12} scf/year, how much longer will these discoveries allow us to use natural gas?

Bibliography

[1] M. King Hubbert: Energy resources. In W. W. Murdoch (ed.): *Environment*. Sinauer Associates, 1971, p. 89.
[2] M. King Hubbert: The energy resources of the earth. *Scientific American*, September, 1971, p. 61.

[3] *Energy—the Ultimate Resource 68-184-0.* Study submitted to the Task Force on Energy, 92nd Congress, October, 1971.

[4] *The Economy, Energy and the Environment.* A background study for the Joint Economic Committee, U.S. Congress, September, 1970.

[5] *Briefings before the Task Force on Energy.* 92nd Congress, 1971.

[6] W. J. Campbell and S. Martin: Oil and ice in the Arctic Ocean: possible large-scale interactions. *Science,* July, 6, 1973, p. 56.

[7] The North Sea rush. *Time,* May 14, 1973, p. 94.

[8] James Carraway: The last of the West: hell, strip it. *The Atlantic,* September, 1973, p. 91.

[9] West Virginia: strip mining. *Science,* November, 1972, p. 485.

[10] A. Wolff: Showdown at Four Corners. *Saturday Review,* June 3, 1972.

[11] Gasification: a rediscovered source of clean fuel. *Science,* October, 1972, p. 4.

[12] William Metz: Helium conservation program: casting it to the winds. *Science,* January, 1974, p. 59.

[13] Edmund Nephew: The challenge and promise of coal. *Technology Review,* December, 1973, p. 21.

An Awkward Alternative: Fission

11-1 Nuclear Energy

In July, 1945, near Alamogordo in New Mexico, a blinding flash and awesome roar announced the birth of a brand new source of energy—energy from the nucleus. This new form of energy is often called **atomic** energy but more accurately the energy should be termed nuclear because it is released from the **nucleus** of the atom (see Chapter 2).

The breathtaking result of this explosion was described by an eye-witness [1].

The effects could well be called unprecedented, magnificent, beautiful, stupendous and terrifying. No man-made phenomenon of such tremendous power had ever occurred before. The lighting effects beggared description. The whole country was lighted by a searing light with the intensity many times that of the midday sun. It was golden, purple, violet, gray and blue. It lighted every peak, crevasse and ridge of the nearby mountain range with a clarity and beauty that cannot be described but must be seen to be imagined. It was that beauty the great poets dream about but describe most poorly and inadequately. Thirty seconds after the explosion came the air blast, pressing hard against the people and things, to be followed almost immediately by the strong sustained, awesome roar which warned of doomsday and made us feel that we puny things were blasphemous to dare tamper with forces heretofore reserved to the Almighty.

Although this new energy source, conceived in the extremities of war, was first used in a destructive manner, it also promised a whole new way of producing power in the future. As we have seen in Chapter 10, the growing use of fossil fuel resources has made us acutely aware of their finite lifetime. We are slowly realizing that a new source of energy is extremely important if we are to maintain our standard of living, based as it is on the use of large amounts of energy. What is this new source of energy? How can we obtain energy from the nucleus? Why was nuclear energy only discovered in the last 50 years?

The last question is the easiest to answer. The understanding of nuclear energy, and later its harnessing, depended on the growth of physics and its attendant technology. At the turn of the century, physicists were probing mysterious new effects in the atom with little or no concern for their utilitarian purpose. They were simply concerned with increasing their understanding of the atom. At the same time Albert Einstein was working in an even more esoteric area—the theory of relativity. This theory was expressed in a language so mathematical that very few people could hope to understand it. One of its consequences, however, was the famous concept that energy and mass are related by the equation

$$E = mc^2 \hspace{4cm} 11\text{-}1$$

In words this equation says that mass can be changed into energy and the multiplicative factor is the velocity of light squared—a very large number (approximately 9×10^{16} m/sec²). Rather than detail the historical steps that led to our understanding of nuclear energy, it is simpler to summarize the results from our present knowledge.

As we saw in Chapter 2, each element is defined by a particular number of protons (Z) in the nucleus, and nuclei with the same Z but different numbers of neutrons (n) are called **isotopes** of the same element. A number of extremely heavy nuclei with masses of about 240 amu (atomic mass units)* and Z of about 90, can undergo a process called fission. In this process, which can occur either spontaneously or when a neutron is absorbed, the nucleus splits (fissions) into two approximately equal parts, forming two new nuclei and releasing usually two or three more neutrons. A pictorial example of such a process is shown in Figure 11-1, where an isotope of uranium ($^{235}_{92}$U) absorbs a neutron, fissions into barium ($^{141}_{56}$Ba) and krypton ($^{92}_{36}$Kr), and releases three more neutrons.

If we now make a table of the masses involved before and after this reaction, see Table 11-1, we find that the sum of the masses after the reaction is less than the sum of the masses before the reaction. In other words, mass has been *lost*. This mass loss appears as energy, either kinetic energy of the nuclei or, perhaps, as electromagnetic radiation such as γ (gamma) rays. Although the amount of mass lost is quite small (about 0.2 amu or 0.33×10^{-27} kg), this mass is multiplied by a very large factor ($c^2 = 9 \times 10^{16}$ M²/sec²) to give the energy. Since,

* amu stands for atomic mass unit, a convenient unit of mass in describing nuclei; 1 amu = 1.66×10^{-27} kg.

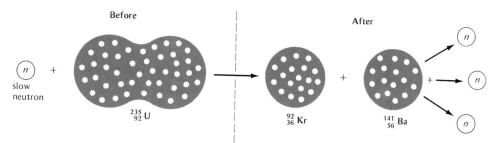

Figure 11-1

A schematic representation of the fission of the nucleus ^{235}U after it absorbs a slow moving neutron. The nucleus splits forming new nuclei krypton (^{92}K) and barium (^{141}Ba) and releases three neutrons. Because the products have less mass than the reactants, energy is released.

$E = mc^2$ the energy released $= 0.33 \times 10^{-27}$ kg $\times 9 \times 10^{16}$ m^2/sec^2

$$= 3 \times 10^{-11} J$$

(As always, if mks units are used throughout the calculation the answer will also be in mks units. In this case the energy is given in joules.)

Remember, too, that this quantity is just the energy produced from a single fission. But each kilogram of uranium contains about 2.5×10^{24} atoms. So, if even a small fraction, say 1%, of these atoms fissions at approximately the same time, then a very large amount of energy would be produced.

Total energy produced from the fission of 1% of a 1-kg mass of ^{235}U would be

total energy $=$ energy per fission $\times$ nuclei per kg $\times$ 1/100
$$= 3 \times 10^{-11} \times 2.5 \times 10^{24} \times 10^{-2}$$
$$= 7.5 \times 10^{11} J$$

In Chapter 10, we noted that the energy content of 1 ton of coal was about 3×10^{10} J. Thus, with the assumptions we have made, the energy content of 0.04 kg of ^{235}U (which has about the volume of a marble and could easily be held in the palm of your hand) would be

Table 11-1
Mass Loss in Fission

Before Fission		After Fission	
mass of ^{235}U	= 235.0439 amu	mass of ^{141}Ba	= 140.9139 amu
mass of n	= 1.0087 amu	mass of ^{92}Kr	= 91.8973 amu
		mass of 3 neutrons =	3.0261 amu
total mass before	236.0526 amu	total mass after	235.8373 amu

Products are 0.2153 amu lighter than the initial reactants

given by the product, (energy content/kg) × (mass of ^{235}U in kg) or

$$7.5 \times 10^{11} \text{ J/kg} \times 0.04 \text{ kg} = 3 \times 10^{10} \text{ J}.$$

That is, the energy content, even assuming only 1% fissions, is the same as that of 1 ton of coal.

This is the basis for producing energy from the nucleus. Mass is changed into energy, and very little mass is needed to produce a large amount of energy. However, before we can discuss the practical techniques for using this energy, it is necessary to understand another concept that explains why even a small fraction of the nuclei fission at one time. Perhaps a better question is why all the uranium in the world has not already fissioned with one enormous bang.

Natural uranium consists mainly of a mixture of two isotopes, 99.3% ^{238}U and only 0.7% ^{235}U. The rarer isotope, ^{235}U, readily undergoes fission with either fast or slow neutrons, although the process is most likely with very slow neutrons (called **thermal neutrons** because they move at speeds comparable to the thermal motions of molecules). The common isotope, ^{238}U, can only undergo fission under bombardment with fast neutrons, but even this process is rather unlikely. The ^{238}U is much more likely simply to capture the neutron, forming ^{239}U and emitting a γ ray.

Remember that in a single fission two or three neutrons are emitted as the nucleus splits up. Now, if these neutrons strike more ^{235}U nuclei, these will also fission and produce more neutrons, which can react with more ^{235}U nuclei, producing more fissions, producing more neutrons, and so on. This process is called a chain reaction. There is a Walt Disney film called "Our Friend the Atom" that illustrates this process. A very large table is closely covered with set mouse traps. Ping-pong balls sit on the mouse traps. A single ping-pong ball thrown onto the table sets off one mouse trap which releases another ping-pong ball, and so on. Soon ping-pong balls are flying everywhere as the mouse traps fire.

Of course if the neutrons do not strike a ^{235}U nucleus, the process will slow down. This is the reason that natural uranium does not undergo a chain reaction; neutrons from a ^{235}U fission are generally captured by a ^{238}U nucleus, which does not usually fission but instead generally emits a γ ray. In order to make a chain reaction self-sustaining, either in a nuclear reactor or in a bomb, it is necessary to separate ^{235}U from natural uranium so that a concentrated sample of fissionable material can be prepared. This is quite a difficult technical feat and was a significant accomplishment of the Manhattan project established to produce the first nuclear bomb during World War II.

Finally it should be mentioned that ^{235}U is not the only readily fissionable material. An isotope of a man-made element, plutonium ($^{239}_{94}$Pu), is also a suitable fuel and will be discussed in more detail in Section 11-7 on Breeder Reactors.

11-2   Fission Reactors

So far we have discussed the principles of energy production from the fission process. Most of these ideas were well understood by the middle of the 1940s. However, these concepts were not implemented in a commercial reactor to produce electricity until much later. Even now, nuclear energy is still a small, though growing, part of the United States energy economy.

The present type of nuclear reactor is generally called a **light water reactor (LWR)** where water is used both to slow down the neutrons in the fissioning core of the reactor and also to carry off the energy generated as heat. There are two main types of light water reactors, the pressurized water reactor (PWR) and the boiling water reactor (BWR).

A schematic diagram illustrating the principle components of a PWR is shown in Figure 11-2. The core of the reactor contains a matrix of fuel rods consisting of uranium dioxide enriched to about 3% ^{235}U. This enrichment is enough to ensure a self-sustaining, though controllable, chain reaction. The uranium dioxide is sealed in vacuum tight tubes of zirconium alloy which serve to contain the radioactive

Figure 11-2
A schematic diagram of a pressurized water reactor (PWR). The water acts as a coolant and as a moderator in this type of light water reactor.

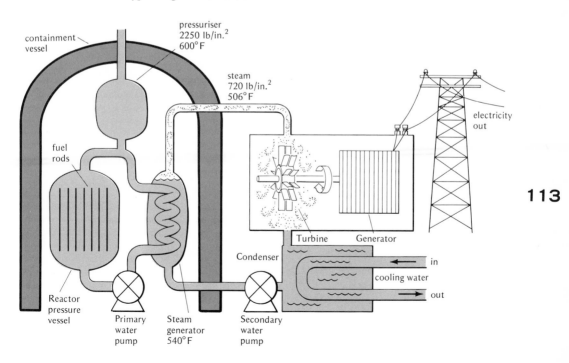

113

Figure 11-3
Partially assembled Big Rock
Point uranium fuel assembly.
[Courtesy of Consumers Power
Company.]

end products of the fission process (Figure 11-3). The core of the reactor is mounted in a steel pressure vessel, and hot pressurized water at 540°F and 2250 psi (pounds per square inch) pressure is forced through the matrix of fuel rods. The water serves two purposes. First, it slows (moderates) the neutrons in the core so that the fission of the ^{235}U is more likely, and thus helps maintain the chain reaction. Second, it transfers heat from the core and emerges at a higher temperature, around 600°F. This water flow is usually termed the primary water system.

The rate of the chain reaction is controlled by means of boron rods which very readily absorb slow neutrons. The rods can be raised from or lowered into the core of the reactor to speed up or slow down the reaction rate and, hence, control the rate of energy release. Usually boric acid dissolved in the primary water system acts as a further control element.

Heat is transferred from the primary water system at 600°F to the secondary water system, which operates at only 720 psi, in the steam generator and produces steam at 506°F. The steam passes through a turbine that runs an electric generator, producing electricity in a similar fashion to a regular fossil fuel powered plant. After passing

An Awkward
Alternative: Fission

through the turbine, the steam is condensed to water to complete the secondary water cycle. This condensation process requires cooling water drawn from a nearby river or lake. The water is then returned to its source, often as much as 20°F warmer. This is the effect referred to as thermal pollution by critics of the nuclear reactor.

Figure 11-4

A schematic diagram of a boiling water reactor (BWR).

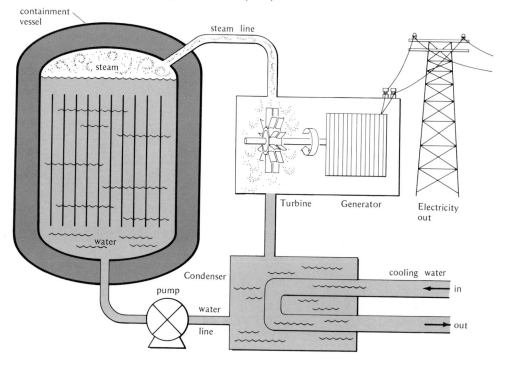

Such cooling techniques are also necessary for fossil fueled plants. However, fossil fueled plants have an important advantage because they typically operate at higher temperatures (near 1000°F) and are therefore more efficient. We will return to this point later in Section 11-4.

The other main type of nuclear reactor presently in use, the BWR, is outlined schematically in Figure 11-4. The main difference from the PWR is that, in the BWR, the primary water system is run at a much lower pressure (1000 psi) and the water then boils in the core of the reactor. The steam is used directly to turn a turbine-generator and produce electricity before condensation and recirculation. This system dispenses with the secondary water system. However, its thermal efficiency is similar to that of the PWR.

11-3 Advantages of Fission Reactors

Even apart from their value in helping to conserve valuable fossil fuel resources, nuclear power plants have a number of advantages relative to their fossil fueled counterparts.

If you have ever seen both a nuclear power plant and a coal fired plant in operation, one immediate advantage is apparent (Figure 11-5). The coal fired plant usually has a large chimney pouring smoke into the atmosphere. A 1000-Mw (megawatt) plant, for example, will typically add 10^7 tons of carbon dioxide, 10^5 tons of sulfur oxides and nitrous oxides, and about 10^5 tons of ash to the atmosphere each year. The nuclear plant, on the other hand, emits practically none of these

Figure 11-5
Big Rock Point nuclear power plant. [Courtesy Consumers Power Company.]

Table 11-2

Comparison of Cost of Electricity from Coal and Pressurized Water Reactor: Two 940,000 kw Generating Units Operational in 1974–75 Near Fredericksburg, Va.

	Coal	Nuclear
unit investment cost of plant ($/kw)	202[a]	255
kilowatt-hours generated per year per kilowatt capacity	5256[b]	5256[b]
cost of heat from fuel (¢/10^6 Btu)	45	18
cost of electricity (mills/kwh)		
plant investment	5.00	6.31
operation and maintenance	0.30	0.38
fuel	4.05	1.87
Total	9.35	8.56
Breakeven cost of heat from coal (¢/10^6 Btu)		36.2

[a] With no allowance for sulfur dioxide removal.

[b] In an actual system the coal plant would generate less electricity than the nuclear plant.

pollutants. In addition, because the nuclear plant does not use air for combustion, it can fairly readily be built partially or wholly underground to minimize its aesthetic impact on the environment.

Other advantages arise from the small amount of fuel required by the nuclear plant to produce the same total amount of energy. A 1000-Mw fossil fuel plant requires about 2×10^6 tons of fuel each year. This means constant traffic of fuel in and ash out. For a coal fired plant, large unsightly mounds of coal reserves have to be kept on-site, and handling these large amounts of coal is a noisy and cumbersome operation. A nuclear plant of similar capacity requires only about 35 tons of uranium dioxide fuel, which can be brought in with just one shipment a year. This also means that there are fewer problems with fuel interruptions because the plant can run for a year on the one "firing." It is also more economically feasible to transport this small load of fuel large distances so that plants need not be close to sources of fuel. In fact the cost of production of electricity is not too sensitive to the cost of fuel in the nuclear plant, whereas fuel costs are a very significant factor in a fossil fuel plant.

Perhaps the most important reason that nuclear reactors are now being built in large numbers is one of simple economics. In many parts of the country, they are simply cheaper than a new fossil fuel facility. This is illustrated in Table 11-2 where a comparison is made between a coal fired plant and a nuclear plant, each with a capacity of 0.94 Mw of electricity. Although the capital costs are greater for the nuclear plant, the fuel costs are so much lower that the overall cost is almost 10% less for the nuclear plant. This economic advantage is likely to increase as fossil fuel costs rise and as legislation requires more expensive antipollution devices on fossil fuel power plants.

11-4 The Problems with Nuclear Reactors: Thermal Pollution

Nuclear reactors have so many apparent advantages when compared with fossil fuel power plants that it may be difficult to see why there is so much controversy concerning their increasing use. Some of the opposition no doubt comes from a lack of understanding and possibly a general suspicion of the new and somewhat mysterious "atomic" energy. But this is by no means always the case. Many scientists and engineers are among the critics and have raised a number of important questions that must be faced by the nuclear industry and the Atomic Energy Commission. Dr. Laurant C. Cole, Professor of Ecology at Cornell University, expressed his opposition very strongly when he stated, "The rush to blanket the Northeast with nuclear power plants is one of the most dangerous and misguided steps ever taken by man." Although such an extreme view is not held even by most of the critics of nuclear plants, the concern is so widespread and the consequences so serious that it is important to consider now some of the problems with nuclear reactor power plants.

One of these problems has already been mentioned—the question of thermal pollution. Both fossil fuel and nuclear power plants produce waste heat, which is usually dissipated in the local region near the plant. However, limitations in the present LWR technology determine a highest operating temperature of around 506°F (263°C or 536°K, see Chapter 5), for these plants. In contrast, a typical fossil fuel plant can operate at around 1000°F (538°C or 811°K). This means that, even if both plants operated at maximum theoretical efficiency given by $[1-(T_2/T_1)]$ (See Chapter 5), where T_2 is the temperature of the outlet from the steam turbine and usually runs around 100°F (311°K), the fossil fuel plant would be about 60% efficient and the nuclear plant only 40% efficient. In practice the efficiencies of real plants are both lower because other conversion systems in the cycle are also less than 100% efficient, with a typical fossil fuel plant operating at around 40% efficiency and a nuclear plant at around 32%.

This means that a nuclear plant with the same capacity as a fossil fuel plant must dissipate more heat to the local surroundings. In addition some of the waste heat from a fossil fuel plant is directly vented to the atmosphere through the smoke stacks. For the nuclear plant on the other hand most of the waste heat is dissipated in the condenser cooling water. In practice this means that present nuclear power plants use about 50% more water than comparable fossil fueled plants.

Large amounts of water are involved in such operations. For example the Ginna Nuclear Power Station, a 490-Mw facility in Ontario uses 4×10^5 gal of water from Lake Ontario per minute and discharges it about 20°F above the ambient lake temperature. This warm water discharge is released at the surface of the lake and the "plume" is carried offshore in a narrow stream. About 500 yd out, the plume fans out on the surface and the heat is transferred fairly quickly to the atmosphere. However some heat differential can be detected over a region of about 85 acres.

Such "once-through" operations are fairly typical both for fossil fuel and nuclear power plants and are presenting an increasing burden on the availability of fresh water. It is estimated that by 1980, one sixth of all the fresh water available in the United States will be required for electric power production. Nuclear plants will add to this burden.

The ecological effects of such warm water discharges are still unclear. We do know, that virtually all the physical properties of water are influenced by temperature including density, viscosity, vapor pressure, surface tension, gas solubility, and diffusion. The biological implications of these changes become particularly critical when one considers dissolved oxygen. As the temperature of water increases, the amount of oxygen it can contain decreases. Higher or more desirable forms of fish may be replaced by noxious organisms more tolerant of the oxygen-deficient water. In addition, the ability of the lake or river to assimilate waste material may decline because less oxygen is available for decomposition. Warm water tends to produce a heavy growth of algae and other undesirable forms of vegetation. Otherwise "dormant" fungi and parasites may flourish, as has occurred near the Hanford plant in the State of Washington. Reactor thermal waste reactivated the disease bacteria Columnaris, which attacked salmon in the Columbia River.

Another notable effect of warmer water, is the acceleration of vital processes. A 10°F temperature rise will double the metabolic rate. Catfish in a discharge canal on the Connecticut River were noted to be in poorer condition than river fish in spite of the abundant food, both because of the higher metabolic rates and the extra energy required to fight the flow in the canal. In addition, migration and spawning behavior may be altered by warmer water leaving the young at the mercy of colder than normal conditions when they later encounter them, which could be extremely harmful to a species.

Although some of these effects remain in the realm of mere possibility, large fish kills have been reported directly related to thermal discharge. For example, the Con Edison Indian River nuclear plant at Buchanan, New York, reportedly killed 17,000 fish in 4 hr. Congressman Richard Ottinger charged Con Ed with 15 separate incidents killing millions of fish. Such effects, it should be stressed, are not limited to nuclear plants. For example, as reported in the *New York Times,* March 14, 1970,

The Department of Justice filed suit today to halt present and future thermal pollution of Biscayne Bay by the Florida Power and Light Company. In 1968, a year after the two (fossil fuel) plants went into fuel operation, the complaint stated, the thermal pollution had created a "barren area" of 300 acres. This had more than doubled by 1969. The removel of microlife will destroy the existing ecological cycle. The plankton and other small sea life that was cooked to death in passing through the plant would be discharged into Cara Sound as organic refuse.

Of course not all the effects of waste heat are bad. The turbulent action of warm discharge water may actually inhibit the growth of algae. At the Ginna Power Station referred to above, rotting masses of Clabophora were driven away from the plume, resulting in cleaner water, and the fish population was observed to increase. Similar effects were observed at Connecticut Yankee's Haddam Neck plant. The river bottom silt composition was altered by the mechanical action of the discharge water, resulting in a highly suitable habitat for both worms and insect larvae, probably leading to the increased fish catch observed near the mouth of the discharge canal.

The important point to realize is that great care must be taken before we indiscriminately disturb a complex ecological system that has built up over many thousands of years in a river or lake. Catastrophic damage can be done in the space of only a few years.

Many power companies are recognizing these problems and, under pressure from Federal agencies and environmental groups, are attempting to minimize the thermal disturbance to neighboring water supplies. A number of alternatives are available. Spray ponds, which lose heat to the atmosphere as the heated discharge is misted, or larger cooling ponds with no misting can both reduce the temperature of the discharge water considerably. The disadvantage is that these ponds occupy large areas of land and are therefore expensive. A similar technique, though somewhat less land intensive, is to have a long discharge canal so that the water is given time to cool before being vented to the parent river or lake.

Another alternative, which is enjoying more widespread acceptance, is the use of cooling towers. These can be classified as wet mechanical draft, wet natural draft, dry mechanical draft, or dry natural draft. A full discussion of these types is given in a report produced by Western Michigan University [9]. Their effect on power costs to the consumer, taken from this report, is shown in Table 11-3. Clearly the dry towers are more expensive, but these are also less likely to have a negative environmental impact. The wet natural draft tower is the next best choice, although some fogging may result that could present a problem, particularly if the towers were located near a busy highway or airport. Another problem of wet cooling towers is disposing of the "blowdown." Because of the evaporation, highly concentrated salt solutions, called **blowdown,** are produced that must be periodically removed from the towers. Disposal of the blowdown is usually carried out by dilution in a river or lake with possible environmental damage

Table 11-3
Effect of Cooling Towers on Power Generation Cost

Cooling System	Increase in Cost Above Once Through Cooling (%)
wet mechanical draft tower	$1\frac{1}{2}$
wet natural draft tower	3
dry mechanical draft tower	10
dry natural draft tower	9

due to the dissolved chemicals. Alternative disposal systems should be sought if wet cooling towers are used. Finally it should be noted that even dry cooling towers, which stand like huge thick chimneys, have a rather negative aesthetic appeal. Careful siting would be necessary to minimize this effect.

So far very few attempts have been made to make use of the heat discharged from power plants, probably because its low temperature differential with the surroundings makes it a rather inefficient source of energy. However, with some imagination, this large amount of energy may be valuable. For example, space heating, maintaining ice-free shipping lanes, ice-free roadways and footpaths, and aquatic crop production have all been proposed as possible uses of low temperature heat.

Recently, Samuel Beall of the Oak Ridge National Laboratory proposed the use of power plant waste heat in greenhouses, apartment buildings, and industrial complexes located nearby:

A hypothetical new city with a temperate climate was designed around a power plant capable of supplying electricity to about 390,000 people. Industrial consumers of low-temperature heat and 200 acres of greenhouses near the power plant would use condenser cooling water. Three-hundred degree turbine steam would be piped to residential and commercial areas for heating as far away as 12 miles. Two modes are possible: Use of relatively low-temperature plant condenser waters, or/and removal of partly exhausted high-temperature steam directly from turbines.

Consumers Power Company and Dow Chemical are presently attempting to construct a nuclear power facility in Midland, Michigan, that would provide the chemical company with large amounts of cheap raw steam to be used in various manufacturing processes. Such proposals would serve not only to minimize thermal pollution effects but also to help conserve energy for other useful purposes. It seems a tragedy that, with energy in short supply, we discard 60% to 70% of the energy used to produce electricity simply as waste heat.

Although in the short term venting waste heat to the atmosphere is comparatively harmless, as our energy use rises the problem of large scale thermal pollution will have to be considered. We will take up this point later, in Chapter 16.

In summary then, local thermal discharges to rivers or lakes can be harmful. These effects are significantly worse for nuclear plants because of their lower efficiency. Such harmful effects can be minimized, but at the expense of increased power costs to the consumer. More imaginative uses of the waste heat from power plants is clearly called for.

11-5 Biological Effects of Radiation

Although in particular cases, thermal pollution questions have plagued reactors at certain sites, the question most often raised about reactors is their potential release of radioactivity. Before discussing this question, it is helpful to have some understanding of the effect of radiation on the body. We have seen in Chapter 2 that natural radioactive isotopes emit different kinds of radiation, α particles, electrons (β particles), or γ rays. The same is true of artificially produced radioactive isotopes. The strength of the activity of such isotopes is measured in a unit called the curie. The **curie** refers to that amount of radioactive material which emits 3.7×10^{10} particles or γ rays per second. This is approximately the number of emissions from 1 g (gram) of pure radium. The curie is a very large unit and many sources are measured in millicurie (10^{-3} curie) or microcurie (10^{-6} curie).

The basic effect of radiation, of whatever kind, in biological material is a loss or deposit of energy from the particle in the material. This energy, deposited in tissue, can break chemical bonds and destroy cells. The energy loss will depend on the kind of radiation, and its biological effect will depend upon where the radiation falls on the body. Some areas of the body are more sensitive to radiation damage than others, but normally the smaller the area of the whole body exposed to a given radiation flux the better. Generally the more complex the system the more sensitive it is to radiation damage. The units of absorbed radiation are the roentgen (R) and the rad. (Table 11-4.) These are approximately equal (1 R = 0.9 rad) for γ radiation.

Because different kinds of radiation have different effects biologically, a dose equivalent or relative biological efficiency is defined with a unit called the **rem** (Table 11-4).

What then are the effects of different doses on the human body? Three stages are discussed by Lindrop and Rotblat [5]. First there is the effect of massive doses of radiation. From animal experiments and accidents to man, they conclude that a dose of 400 rads to the whole body is fatal in 50% of cases. Mortality rises to nearly 100% for doses above 650 rad. On the other hand, below 150 rads the mortality rate becomes very small, and longer term effects show up. These are

An Awkward
Alternative: Fission

Table 11-4
Definitions of Units of Absorbed Radiation

Unit	Definition
roentgen (R)	the amount of x or γ radiation that produces 1 esu of charge of either sign (i.e., 2.08×10^9 ion pairs) in 1.293×10^{-3} g[a] of dry air (1.293×10^{-3} g air occupies approximately 1 cm³)
rad	the amount of radiation of any kind that releases 100 ergs[b]/g in an absorber
rem	(roentgen equivalent man) the dose of any radiation that has the same biological effect as 1 R of x rays or γ rays

[a] 1 g (gram) = 10^{-3} kg (kilogram).
[b] An erg is also a unit of energy: 1 erg = 10^{-7} J (joule).

mainly different forms of cancer, eye cataracts, and a general acceleration of the overall aging process.

Because such disorders are produced by causes other than radiation, it is difficult to establish a definite correlation between incidence of cancer, say, and a particular dose, especially for doses below 50 rads. One study has shown that children whose mothers had abdominal x rays during pregnancy have about a 50% greater probability of dying of leukemia in their first 8 years than children whose mothers have not been x rayed, even though the doses involved may only be a few rad.

The problem of establishing definite correlations in human populations is even more acute when dealing with smaller doses which may perhaps produce genetic effects. Such effects are expected because the structure and position of genes on the chromosomes can be affected by ionizing radiation. In general such changes or mutations are expected to be harmful. We are forced to rely on information obtained from experiments on insects and mice. Even studies of genetic effects on the survivors of the atomic bomb dropped on Hiroshima are inconclusive.

An interesting study of about 8500 people who live on the Kerala coast in India is discussed by Morgan and Turner [19] in *Principles of Radiation Protection*. This is a region with exceptionally high background radioactivity from the mineral monozite. Of the group studied, 57 received doses greater than 2 R (roentgen)/year, 550 had doses greater than 1 R/year and about 2000 out of the 8000 studied received exposures greater than 0.5 R/year. The findings are given as follows:

Analysis of the demographic data indicated no statistically significant differences in fertility index, sex-ratio among offsprings, infant mortality rate, pregnancy terminations, multiple births and gross abnormalities between population groups receiving different levels of radiation exposure. However the lowest value of fertility and the highest value of infant mortality rate were recorded for a group of married couples who received radiation exposures greater than 20 times normal background levels; the total loss of offsprings in this group was significantly higher than in those receiving lower radiation exposures.

These results seem to confirm that there are some genetic effects, at least at high dose rates, but point up the unreliability in extrapolating to lower doses.

Although the effect of low level radiation are hard to evaluate, because we are dealing with such vital issues as life and death, or even the future history of man, we should be extremely cautious in our approach. This attitude has been reflected in the standards established by both the International Commission on Radiological Protection (I.C.R.P.) and by the U.S. Atomic Energy Commission (A.E.C.) and particularly for change of these standards with time. In 1924, the maximum permissable dose (MPD) for a radiation worker was set at 1.5 rad/week, but by 1956 the MPD had dropped to only 1 R/week. For the population as a whole, to minimize genetic effects, the I.C.R.P. recommends a dose limit of only one tenth of the MPD for radiation workers, that is, the dose received by the whole population should be less than 500 mR (milliroentgen)/year. The A.E.C. standard is 170 mrem (millirem)/year.

Another approach to standards is to compare radiation dose with the radiation received from other sources. Natural background radiation from cosmic rays, radioactive isotopes in the materials we use for example to build our houses, or even in our own bodies amount to 100 mrem/year, although this may vary widely from place to place. (For example, see the Kerala coast population discussed previously.) In addition we receive sizable radiation doses from medical and dental x rays, which also vary significantly from person to person.

One question that has been raised is whether there is a lower cutoff of radiation effects. Because some radiation damage to cells can be repaired through the body's normal recovery functions, it was believed that low enough doses had no biological effect. This assumption has been challenged by Gofman and Tamplin [20], who extrapolate the effects of large doses *linearly* down to lower doses and suggest that large numbers of people are being harmed by radiation and therefore argue for a lowering of emission standards from power plants. If these arguments are correct, of course, they imply that we should also be worrying about other sources of radiation, such as background from rocks or particularly medical x rays, more than we do.

Finally, to put the dangers from radiation in some perspective, it is useful to realize that we take risks in our lives all the time. In practice we weigh, sometimes subconsciously, the benefits from such risks. With nearly 700 deaths on the highways on a holiday weekend, driving may well be our most dangerous activity. Prof. B. L. Cohen, a physicist at the University of Pittsburgh, estimated that the life of a person receiving a steady 100 mrem/week from the time he is 18 until death (the MPD for radiation worker) would be shortened by an average of 1.3 years (0.5 years from cancer risk, 0.8 years from accelerated aging). By comparison, other occupations have the following life shortening

airplane crew (civilian)	2 years
fisherman	1.5 years
coal miner	1.5 years
construction worker	1.5 years

still other risks we take have the following effects on average life expectancy.

living in city (vicinity) decreases life expectancy	5 years
smoking one pack of cigarettes per day decreases life expectancy	8 years
being 10 lb overweight decreases life expectancy	1.5 years

Of course, the case Cohen chose was extreme even for radiation workers, and the risks of only 500 mrem/year are correspondingly less. Unfortunately this will be small consolation to you if *you* are the one to contract leukemia.

The final point to be made on this topic is that, although all of the risks mentioned above are voluntarily (more or less) accepted by the individual, this is not true of an increased radiation background. Perhaps, in such a case the risks should be required to be correspondingly smaller.

11-6 Radiation Dangers from Reactors

Because the basic principles of the nuclear reactor and a nuclear bomb both depend on the chain reaction, it might be thought that the danger of a nuclear explosion hangs over a reactor. *This is not the case!* Although there are problems associated with radiation and the nuclear industry, fortunately, the danger of an atomic explosion is *not* one of these, at least in the LWR's in present use. However there are four main areas that do present problems, and we shall look at them briefly. These are (a) an accident, (b) low level emissions, (c) transportation of radioactive material, and (d) long term storage of radioactive waste.

Because the effects of an accident in a nuclear power plant could be so catastrophic, extreme caution must be taken to ensure that such risks are minimized. In 1957 the A.E.C. published a study on the possibilities and consequences of major nuclear power plant accidents. For a 500-Mw reactor within 30 miles of a city, the report concludes that, if 50% of the fission products escape, as many as 3400 deaths and 43,000 injuries, between $0.5 million and $7 billion property damage, and an undetermined contaminated land radius could result. Presently conceived plants are now larger than the one cited in this study with, therefore, greater dangers.

Though the nuclear power industry is well aware of these dangers, it has little experience in using the extreme care in manufacturing that these new sophisticated power plants require. A single nuclear tragedy could set back the development of nuclear power many, many years. Fortunately the industry so far has been fairly safe, although the number of reactors in operation is still quite small. In spite of the safety claims made, the nuclear power industry is still dependent on the Price-Anderson Indemnity Act by which the U.S. Congress authorized the U.S. Treasury to pay up to $500 million to accident victims in the event of a plant failure. Private insurance companies are still reluctant to accept this risk.

If cooling water is removed from the core of a reactor by some accident (loss-of-cooling accident) in the primary liquid system, the core would quickly melt down. This could lead to an explosion which might breach the containment of the reactor releasing radioactive debris. The emergency core cooling system (ECCS) is designed to flood the core of the reactor with water in the event of an accident in the primary liquid system and thus prevent meltdown. Unfortunately no full scale experiments have been made on the ECCS, and recently questions have been raised regarding the validity of the assumptions that have gone into the computer models of the operation of the ECCS. The problem of ensuring that water penetrates through small passages to all parts of the core, as the core is heating and perhaps buckling and melting, is clearly severe. If the ECCS does not operate quickly and the temperature of the fuel rods rises too high, the zirconium cladding will react with the water, producing further heating. Unfortunately just at the time questions were raised about the ECCS, the response of the A.E.C. was to decrease rather than increase the research in this area. More recently however, the A.E.C. has ordered older plant systems upgraded and has limited the power output from four new plants. Further experiments on the ECCS are now in progress at Idaho Falls.

The debate over the ECCS has emphasized once again the ambiguous position of the U.S. Atomic Energy Commission. The A.E.C. has both the responsibility for developing nuclear power (along with the electricity producers) and for the regulation of the use of nuclear power. These two aspects are often in conflict, and it would make more sense to separate the two areas more clearly. A step was taken in this direction in 1967, but the regulation aspect is still often regarded as the poor sister within the A.E.C.

Even if great care prevents an unexpected accident from spreading large amounts of radioactive debris around a reactor site, there remains the problem of allowed emissions. These come from a number of sources and can exist as gases, liquids, or solids; they are usually vented either from the stack or in the cooling water runoff. As discussed in Section 11-5 the small emissions permitted by the A.E.C. regulations (1% of natural background radiation) appear to be an acceptable risk. The problem in this area is keeping a close check on such emissions. There have been a number of problems with the fuel rods leaking and causing increased contamination. It is expensive to close down the facility to replace such leaking rods so that the temptation is to run for some time with increased emissions. Great care must be exercised and close regulation imposed, to see that this does not happen.

A more serious problem of low level emissions is not from the power plants themselves but from the fuel treatment plants that process the spent fuel elements from a reactor. There is little or no regulation on emissions from such plants although they are at least as great a source of activity as the nuclear reactors themselves. Donald Geesaman writing in the *Bulletin of the Atomic Scientists* [7], pointed out that extensive plutonium contamination, following a fire at the Rocky Flats treatment plant near Denver, was caused not by the fire but from irresponsible waste disposal practices at the plant. This is clearly a case where legislation is needed to stop this source of contamination.

A third question, particularly with more widespread use of nuclear power, (see Figure 11-6) is the transportation of large quantities of highly radioactive material by our regular transportation facilities, either trains or trucks. It has been estimated that there will be between 20,000 and 50,000 shipments of spent fuel rods to reprocessing plants by the year 2000. Accidents do happen, and again the problem will be magnified by the radioactive nature of the material. Shipments have been misplaced. In fact there are cases on record of radioactive material that was supposed to be shipped to Michigan and instead sat in Boston for 3 months unnoticed. Radioactive material has even been shipped out of the country by accident.

When dangerous, yet potentially very valuable, material is shipped, there is always the danger of sabotage or theft. Some small nations that do not possess the technology to process material may be willing to pay for already separated, isotopically enriched ^{235}U. One can even imagine a criminal blackmailing New York City with a nuclear bomb, manufactured from stolen plutonium. Stranger things have happened.

All of this suggests to me that we should be seriously reconsidering the siting not only of reactors but also of the processing facilities to minimize such shipping problems. Perhaps large "nuclear parks," where processing is carried out on-site and only raw ore is shipped in is the answer. Certainly these could be carefully secured.

The final and perhaps most important question is that of waste disposal. If we do move to a nuclear energy economy, we will be pro-

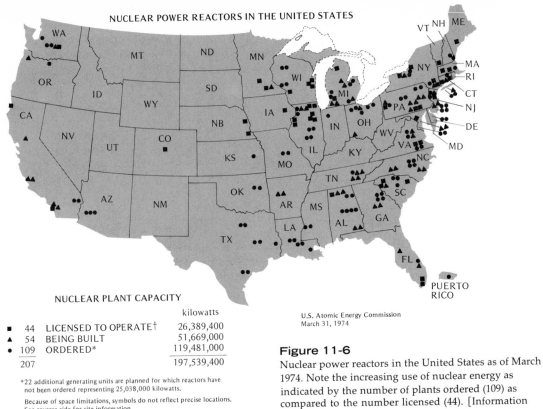

NUCLEAR POWER REACTORS IN THE UNITED STATES

U.S. Atomic Energy Commission
March 31, 1974

Figure 11-6

Nuclear power reactors in the United States as of March 1974. Note the increasing use of nuclear energy as indicated by the number of plants ordered (109) as compared to the number licensed (44). [Information from United States Atomic Energy Commission.]

ducing huge amounts of radioactive waste, with some of the isotopes having extremely long half-lives. For example ^{239}Pu has a half-life of 24,000 years. There have been a number of suggestions for disposing of, or rather storing, these wastes for long periods of time. One suggestion is to store the wastes in underground salt caverns. Salt deposits have a number of advantages as a storage medium. They are free of circulating ground water, they are usually located in stable geological regions, and there are a large number of such deposits available. Salt is also quite "plastic" under deformation and will "heal" any fissures or cracks relatively quickly. Unfortunately the site in Lyons, Kansas, where most extensive investigation has been carried out, does not appear to be suitable mainly because of uncertainty that ground water would be reliably excluded. However further investigation is proceeding with alternative sites.

Other suggestions for storage have included burying wastes in deep ocean trenches, letting them sink into the Arctic ice cap, or blasting underground storage caverns under processing plants with either nuclear or conventional explosives. All of these possibilities appear to have at least as many difficulties as salt deposit storage. In the case of the ocean trenches, the main difficulties appear to be in placing the wastes accurately and in the uncertainty that they would be permanently removed from the biosphere. Similar uncertainties exist for depositing wastes in the Arctic. Both of these storage areas also have the significant disadvantage that the wastes, once released, are probably unrecoverable if this proved necessary for any reason. In the case of underground caverns excavated by explosives, it is unclear that these would remain isolated, especially from ground water, for sufficiently long periods of time.

At present, radioactive wastes are kept in large storage tanks above ground. Of the 200 tanks in use over the last 30 years, 20 have developed leaks—emphasizing the urgent necessity of finding a more permanent solution to this important problem. Perhaps the most dangerous assumption in proposing a storage system that requires supervision over tens of thousands of years is that society will be stable over such a long time. Such a belief in the stability of society is a tremendous act of faith not at all justified by history. Perhaps we are already far along the path of reliance on the stability of society; our society is now extremely complex and interdependent. We rely heavily on other people even for basic necessities like food and energy. Any serious breakdown of this complex system would certainly be disastrous in terms of human life. Nevertheless, a large inventory of highly dangerous radioactive material does seem an unfortunate legacy to leave to future generations.

11-7 Breeder Reactors

Apart from the thermal and radioactivity problems with the LWR's, they have another basic limitation. They will not solve our long term energy problem because they use the rare isotope ^{235}U which is only 0.7% of natural uranium. This isotope is then lost in the fission process. With large scale use of LWR's our known uranium reserves will last only a few decades.

Fortunately there is an alternative type of reactor which has the seemingly miraculous property that it not only produces energy but also produces (breeds) more nuclear fuel as it operates. In addition these reactors make use of the abundant ^{238}U isotope, which enormously increases our effective fuel reserves. Precise estimates of such reserves vary but their lifetime is generally agreed to be at least 6000 years implying that fuel would not be a difficulty.

As mentioned in Section 11-1, ^{239}Pu is another fissionable isotope that emits neutrons. In a breeder reactor, the fuel consists of a mixture of ^{239}Pu and ^{238}U. Coolants are used that do not slow down (moderate) the neutrons. Some of the fast neutrons produce fission of ^{239}Pu, thus

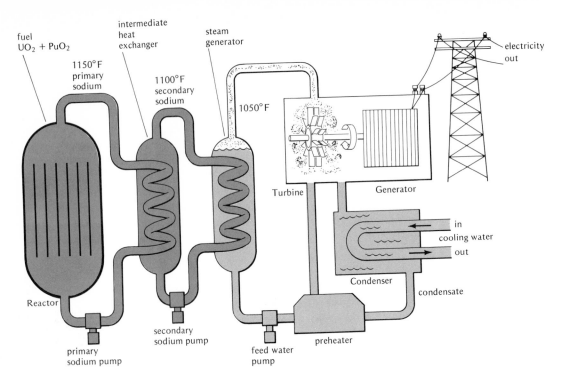

Figure 11-7
A schematic diagram of a liquid metal fast breeder reactor (LMFBR). The coolant in such a reactor is liquid sodium which becomes radioactive in the high flux of fast neutrons in the core. A secondary cooling loop must therefore be used to produce steam to turn a turbine.

maintaining the chain reaction. Others are absorbed by ^{238}U to form ^{239}U, a new isotope of uranium. The ^{239}U then emits successively two electrons, the longer half-life emission being only 2.4 days, and forms ^{239}Pu. Thus, energy is released as more ^{239}Pu is produced.

There are two main types of fast breeder reactors that have been suggested, differing mainly in the type of coolant used—the liquid metal fast breeder reactor (**LMFBR**) and the gas-cooled fast breeder reactor. A schematic diagram of a LMFBR is shown in Figure 11-7. The coolant used in the LMFBR is the metal sodium, which has excellent cooling characteristics. Thus the LMFBR will probably operate at higher temperatures (say around 1100°F) than current reactors and may permit the thermal efficiency to approach 40% instead of the 32% of the LWR.

However, sodium has a number of drawbacks as a coolant. It is opaque, so that refueling must be carried out blind. Sodium also becomes very radioactive in the presence of the high flux of neutrons, so that a secondary cooling loop has to be inserted as shown in the figure. (The radioactive sodium is contained in the primary loop and so

An Awkward
Alternative: Fission

is kept isolated from the remainder of the system.) Sodium is also extremely active chemically. It reacts rapidly with air, and will explode on contact with water so that extreme care must be taken to keep the sodium in an inert atmosphere.

The alternative coolant is helium gas. A high temperature gas-cooled, but not breeding, reactor has already been developed. The helium gas-cooled breeder could benefit from this technology. The reactor fuel and temperatures are similar to the LMFBR. Helium gas has the advantage that it is transparent so that the core assembly can be readily inspected. Helium gas does not become radioactive, even in the intense neutron flux in the reactor core, thus a secondary cooling system is not required. It therefore offers a number of advantages over the LMFBR. However, the helium has poorer heat removal characteristics than sodium metal so that most fast breeder development has taken place along the liquid metal direction.

The biggest problem with the fast breeder is that there are still no commercially feasible reactor designs available. Numerous test reactors have been built in the United States, in Europe, and in the U.S.S.R., but there still remain a number of technical problems, particularly with the behavior of materials in the presence of high neutron fluxes. A large test reactor is presently being built in the United States for the Tennessee Valley Authority, and it is hoped that this may lead to commercial reactors in the late 1970s or early 1980s.

11-8 Summary

Energy from the nucleus, if the problems of the breeder reactor technology can be solved, is a way of providing energy far into the future. The present LWR's, while offering some advantages vis-a-vis pollution compared to present coal fired plants, are profligate of the earth's ^{235}U reserves, which could become a real problem around the year 2000. Rapid development of the breeder program is therefore important.

Breeder nuclear reactors are a mixed blessing, however, particularly when we consider the large amounts of radioactive isotopes they produce. Even if great care in component testing and regulation is taken so that there are no accidents and low level emissions are kept to a small fraction of natural background, there still remains problems of handling and storage of enormous amounts of radioactive toxic materials.

The fission solution is by no means an ideal answer to the energy resource problem, and alternative methods with fewer drawbacks should be carefully investigated. We now turn to a discussion of some of the alternatives.

Questions

1. Nuclear power plants are often attacked because of their thermal effluents, as compared to fossil fuel plants. Are such attacks justified? Explain.
2. Ralph Nader has recently proposed closing 20 of the 30 nuclear power plants operating in the United States. Discuss briefly why you favor or reject this proposal.
3. Outline some of the alternative methods of disposal of radioactive wastes, listing their advantages and disadvantages.
4. How real are the dangers of radioactive pollution? Are present A.E.C. safety and licensing procedures adequate?
5. Should nuclear power plants be sited close to or far from consumers? Explain.
6. Why is the term breeder reactor used? How does this reactor type differ from the light water reactors currently in use?
7. The claim has been made that the United States will shortly have to rely on nuclear energy as a primary energy source. Discuss the likelihood of a 50% nuclear energy economy in the United States in the year 2000. Discuss the advantages and disadvantages of such a system.
8. Which statement is true when comparing fossil fuel to nuclear fission.
    (a) fossil fuels will last longer
    (b) fossil fuels pollute the air less
    (c) electric energy is produced more efficiently by fossil fuels
    (d) there are more radioactivity problems with fossil fuels.
    (e) in energy production, thermal effluents are increased when fossil fuels are used
9. Mark the *false* statement:
    (a) Fossil fuel plants are less capital intensive than nuclear plants.
    (b) A nuclear plant operating within A.E.C. regulations, may emit less radioactivity into the air than a coal fired plant of comparable electrical output.
    (c) Power companies prefer fission plants because they have cheaper fuel costs than fossil plants.
    (d) Light water reactors only need refuelling every 5 years which makes them very economical.
    (e) Most coal in the U.S. cannot be strip mined economically.
10. Outline methods of minimizing thermal pollution from nuclear power plants.

An Awkward
Alternative: Fission

Bibliography

The bibliography for nuclear fission is enormous and only a few of the many references can be noted.

[1] T. E. Farrel: Alamogordo: an eyewitness account. In R. Karplus (ed): *Physics and Man*. Benjamin, 1970, p. 302.
[2] A discussion of the fission process is given in W. B. Phillips: *Physics for Society*. Addison Wesley, 1971, Ch. 4 and 5.

[3] A more detailed discussion is given in Harold Enge: *Introduction to Nuclear Physics* by Addison Wesley, 1966, Ch. 14.

[4] An excellent description of power production by nuclear reactors is given in Manson Benedict: Electric power from nuclear fission. *Technology Review*, October/November 1971, p. 32; the *Bulletin of the Atomic Scientists*, September, 1971, p. 8. Radiation effects are discussed in a number of articles in the *Bulletin of the Atomic Scientists*, September, 1971 issue.

[5] Patricia J. Lindrop and J. Rotblat: Radiation pollution of the environment. *Bulletin of the Atomic Scientists*, September, 1971, p. 17.

[6] Arthur R. Tamplin: Issues in the radiation controversy. *Bulletin of the Atomic Scientists*, September, 1971, p. 35.

[7] D. P. Geesaman: Plutonium and the radiation controversy. *Bulletin of the Atomic Scientists*, September, 1971, p. 33.

[8] S. A. Hammond: Fission: the pro's and con's of nuclear power. *Science*, October 13, 1972, p. 147.

[9] D. G. Southwell: An evaluation of cooling towers for nuclear power plants. *Western Michigan Report*, April, 1972.

[10] R. D. Woodson: Cooling towers. *Scientific American*, October 1972, p. 70. There is an interesting series of articles by R. Gillette in *Science* discussing Nuclear Safety, the A.E.C.'s role and the ECCS.

[11] R. Gillette: Nuclear reactor safety: a new dilemma for the A.E.C., *Science*, July 9, 1971, p. 126; Nuclear reactor safety: at the A.E.C. the way of the dissenter is hard. *Science*, May 2, 1972, p. 492; Nuclear safety: the roots of dissent. *Science*, September 1, 1972, p. 771; Nuclear safety (III): critics charge conflict of interest. *Science*, September 15, 1972, p. 970; Reactor safety: A.E.C. concedes some points to its critics. *Science*, November 3, 1972, p. 482; Nuclear safety: A.E.C. report makes the best of it. *Science* January 26, 1973, p. 360.

[12] The A.E.C. and the loss of coolant accident. *Nature*, **241:** 312 (1973).

Some classic pro fission articles are the following:

[13] W. H. Jordan: Nuclear energy: benefits versus risks. *Physics Today*, May, 1970, p. 32.

[14] A. M. Weinberg: Social institutions and nuclear energy. *Science*, July 7, 1972, p. 27.

Breeder reactors are discussed in the following articles.

[15] A. Hammond: Breeder reactors: power for the future. *Science*, November, 19, 1971, p. 807.

[16] F. L. Culler and W. O. Harms: Energy from breeder reactors. *Physics Today*, May, 1972.

[17] An excellent survey of nuclear energy is given in a book by David Inglis: *Nuclear Energy: Its Physics and Its Social Challenge*. Addison-Wesley, 1973.

[18] J. O. Blomeke, J. P. Nichols, and W. C. McClain: Managing radioactive wastes. *Physics Today*, August, 1973, p. 36.

[19] Morgan and Turner: *Principles of Radiation Protection*, John Wiley & Sons, 1967.

[20] J. W. Gofman and A. R. Tamplin: *The Case Against Nuclear Power Plants*, Rodale Press, 1971.

[21] *Nuclear Power and the Public*, H. Foreman Editor. Univ. of Minnesota Press, 1970.

133

Bibliography

CHAPTER 12

One Hope for the Future: Fusion

12-1 Energy Release from Fusion

We have seen in the previous chapters that energy can be obtained from the nucleus of the atom. In the fission process, energy is released when a heavy nucleus splits up into two roughly equal mass nuclei plus a few neutrons. The total mass of the products is less than the original mass, and the mass lost is converted into other forms of energy—mainly heat. Energy can also be obtained by building up nuclei from lighter ones. This process is called **fusion.** As in fission the mass of the products is less than the mass of the initial nuclei, and the mass lost is converted to energy with a multiplying factor of the square of the velocity of light (9×10^{16} m²/sec²).

Some examples that illustrate this principle are shown in Table 12-1 where we refer back to Chapter 2 for the notation. Figure 12-1 illustrates one of these processes.

Because the amount of energy released in reaction 3, the deuterium-tritium (D-T) process, is nearly 3 times larger than in the deuterium-deuterium (D-D) process, the D-T reaction is the most likely candidate for the first fusion reactors. (Although reaction 4, also releases approximately the same amount of energy as the D-T process, it has a very significant disadvantage that we will discuss shortly.) In all the processes listed in Table 12-1, two products are formed, and the total energy released is shared between these nuclei inversely as their mass. The lighter products carry off the most kinetic energy. Thus, for the most promising reaction (the D-T process) much of the energy released is carried off by a neutron that has no charge. This has some disadvantages, because charged particles are easier to stop; thus, their energy

135

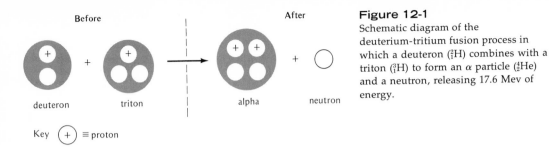

Before ... **After**

deuteron + triton → alpha + neutron

Figure 12-1
Schematic diagram of the deuterium-tritium fusion process in which a deuteron ($^2_1$H) combines with a triton ($^3_1$H) to form an α particle ($^4_2$He) and a neutron, releasing 17.6 Mev of energy.

Key $+$ ≡ proton

 ○ ≡ neutron

Table 12-1
Examples of Fusion Reactions

	Initial Nuclei*	Final Nuclei	Total Mass of Initial Nuclei (amu)†	Total Mass of Products (amu)	Mass Lost (amu)	Energy Release for each Fusion Reaction (Mev)‡
1.	$^2_1$H + $^2_1$H	$^3_2$He + ^1_0n	4.02820	4.024695	0.003505	3.3
2.	$^2_1$H + $^2_1$H	$^3_1$H + $^1_1$H	4.02820	4.023875	0.004325	4.0
3.	$^2_1$H + $^3_1$H	$^4_2$He + ^1_0n	5.03050	5.011265	0.018885	17.6
4.	$^2_1$H + $^3_2$He	$^4_2$He + $^1_1$H	5.03013	5.010425	0.019705	18.4

* Note that $^2_1$H and $^3_1$H are the heavy isotopes of hydrogen and the atoms are called by the special names **deuterium** and **tritium** (and are sometimes written **D** and **T** respectively) although in chemical reactions they behave exactly like normal hydrogen. Thus, reaction 3 could be written

$$D + T \longrightarrow {}^4_2He + n$$

and is usually called therefore the D-T process. Similarly reactions 1 and 2 are examples of the D-D process.

† The amu (atomic mass unit) is a unit of mass: 1 amu = 1.66×10^{-27} kg.

‡ The Mev (million electron volt) is a unit of energy; 1 Mev = 1.6×10^{-13} J. Thus the energy released in the D-T process per fusion = 28.2×10^{-13} J.

can be released as heat in a more localized region. The neutrons travel further through any material than charged particles, such as protons, so that thicker shielding walls are required to stop the neutrons and to collect their energy. There is also the possibility that rapidly moving charged particles can be used directly to generate electricity by passing them through a magnetic field.

12-2 Plasma Physics

These arguments seem to suggest that reaction 4 (D-^{3}He), which releases a large amount of energy and has charged particles only as products, would be favored over the D-T process. However, one important criterion has been left out of our discussion so far. In all cases, the incident nuclei are both positively charged and, before they can get close enough to interact through the strong but short range nuclear force, they must overcome the repulsive coulomb (charge) forces that tend to keep them apart. Saying this another way, the particles must have sufficient kinetic energy to penetrate or tunnel through the "coulomb barrier." High kinetic energy means high speed or high temperature. Thus, a gas consisting of deuterium and tritium must be heated to a high temperature to make the fusion process go. At these high temperatures, atoms become completely dissociated into electrons and bare nuclei. This mixture of negatively charged electrons and positively charged nuclei is called a **plasma,** and it has proved necessary to study the properties of this exotic state of matter to try to make the fusion process workable.

Although the temperature of the plasma must be very high, the total amount of heat is not very great because the total number of atoms involved is comparatively small. If the plasma reached the wall of a containing vessel however, it would be quickly cooled. In the case that the plasma density were high enough, the extremely hot plasma would quickly melt through any containing wall. It is therefore necessary to prevent the plasma from reaching the containing walls.

Every fusion reaction produces the energy listed in Table 12-1, but a large number of such reactions must occur each second in order to generate more total energy than is required to produce, maintain, and heat the plasma in the first place. This is called **breakeven.** It means that there must be a large number of atoms per unit volume (large density) and they must be contained long enough to interact. The condition necessary for breakeven may be expressed

$$\frac{\text{number of atoms} \times \text{time}}{\text{unit volume}} = 10^{14} \text{ atoms sec/cm}^3*$$

This condition is called the **Lawson criterion** and is a goal at which physicists and engineers have been aiming to prove the scientific feasibility of fusion.

In a sense we know that fusion works because the sun is really a large fusion reactor where protons are combining to form helium. The sun is so massive, however, that gravitational forces keep the proton and electron plasma in a comparatively stable mode (as the familiar gigantic sphere in the sky). Our problem is to produce a similar situation on a much smaller scale on earth.

At present there are two main directions being pursued in the attempt at controlled fusion. One is containment of the plasma by a magnetic field, which will act as a nonmaterial container and so will not lower the temperature of the plasma. The other method uses a very intense laser beam to heat a solid pellet of deuterium and tritium very

---

* Note: 1 cm (centimeter) $= 10^{-2}$ m (meter); therefore, 1 cm^3 $= 10^{-6}$ m^3.

quickly, producing the fusion reaction as a controlled explosion. We now consider each of these methods in detail.

12-3 Magnetic Containment

There have been at least three main approaches to devising a magnetic bottle to contain a D-T plasma long enough to exceed the Lawson criterion. The one with most promise, the Tokamak, shown in Figure 12-2 was developed by Artsimovich of the Kurchatov Institute, U.S.S.R., and was first reported in 1968. The Tokamak (T3) is an example of a toroidal confinement system. In this scheme, current windings around a donut shaped ring produce a field within the donut. The interaction of the plasma with the field produces a complicated magnetic field. In the Tokamak system, an externally generated induced current within the loop produces stability and can also heat the plasma. A similar toroidal scheme, called the stellarator, uses a somewhat different field shape to contain the plasma. Although re-

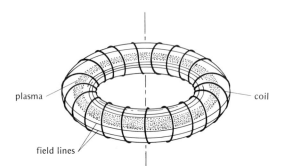

plasma

coil

field lines

Closed System—Simple Torus

Figure 12-2
Simplified diagram of the Tokamak configuration. The plasma is contained within the donut shaped torus and confined by a helical shaped magnetic field. The coils around the donut produce an azimuthal (ϕ direction) magnetic field (B^ϕ). Current induced in the plasma produces a θ direction field B_θ. The sum of the fields should give confinement. [Information from D. J. Rose, *Science* Vol 172, p. 798 (1971).]

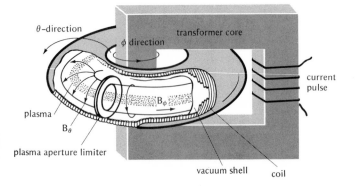

θ–direction

ϕ direction

transformer core

current pulse

plasma

B_ϕ

B_θ

plasma aperture limiter

vacuum shell   coil

Figure 12-3

An open ended "magnetic mirror." Plasma ions approaching the pinched end of the field of axis are reflected back. Such devices are inherently leaky for particles on the axis.

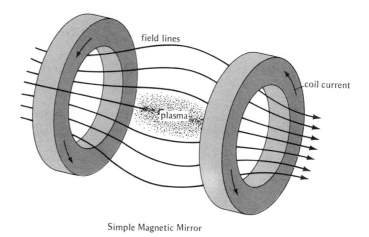

field lines

coil current

plasma

Simple Magnetic Mirror

lated to, and in fact preceding, the Tokamak, the stellarator has not performed as well as the Tokamak. In both of these devices, in theory, the plasma gets trapped by the magnetic field lines and only slowly diffuses to the walls of the containing chamber. In practice, however, instabilities arise that cause the plasma to escape more rapidly.

One other problem in the toroidal system is to devise a technique for heating the plasma. The resistive heating produced by the induced current is not sufficient. A recent test on a small stellarator at the Princeton Plasma Physics Laboratory, where the temperature of a plasma was raised by shrinking it to a smaller volume, seems to have proved that heating of the plasma by compression works well and may solve the heating problem for the larger Tokamaks.

A second device for magnetic containment is based on the principle that the charged particles in a plasma will be reflected at regions of very strong magnetic field. Such a device is called a **magnetic mirror,** and a simple view of the required field is shown in Figure 12-3. Unfortunately, the plasma near the central weak field region of such a magnetic bottle is unstable and will quickly drift to the containing walls. The field must therefore be twisted in the center to remove this instability. Such devices, for example the X2, are being pursued at the Lawrence Radiation Laboratory, Livermore, California.

One basic difficulty with mirror devices is that, even with negligible instabilities, particles that are parallel to the field lines will stream out the ends. There will always be collisions that produce particles in these directions so that this is a fundamental difficulty. Suggestions for making the device longer, for rapidly replenishing the plasma, or for using the ions streaming from the ends for direct electrical generation would have to be implemented before this device could be feasible as a power source. Nevertheless, although mirror machines may never be used as power sources, they are useful devices for studying rather high density and especially high temperature plasmas.

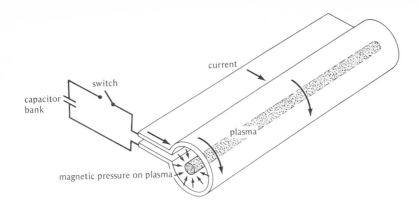

Figure 12-4
Simple schematic diagram of the theta pinch device. The plasma is compressed and heated by a rapidly rising magnetic field that exerts a radial force on the plasma. Confinement time is short because ions squirt out the ends as the plasma is compressed.

A third method of magnetic containment is the **theta pinch** device, such as the Scylla machines at Los Alamos Scientific Laboratory, New Mexico. This device starts with a low density, low temperature plasma and then compresses it by a rapidly increasing magnetic field. The current that produces this field is obtained by discharging a large capacitor bank (Figure 12-4). In Scylla IV, a current of 8.6×10^6 amp (ampere) produces a maximum magnetic field of 150 kgauss (kilogauss) in only 3.7×10^{-6} sec. This produces a very dense plasma (5×10^{16} ions/cm³) at high temperature [3.2 kev (thousand electron volts)]. However, the plasma lifetime is very short. As the field compresses the plasma, it tends to squirt out the ends of the containment region. The present aim is to close the ends of the device to prevent this loss and increase the containment time. This will then take one into the toroidal containment problems but, because of the increased density, smaller confinement times are required. At present a device that covers one third of a totally closed loop (120°) is being built at Los Alamos to test this principle.

Although a theta pinch device in this form might well demonstrate scientific feasibility, it seems unlikely that this kind of device can be used as a power source because of the very long cycle time. It takes a few seconds to pump away impurities and charge up the capacitors for each firing. This is far too long to make a usable device. However, such machines may continue to be useful as a means of studying high density plasmas to increase our understanding of this exotic state of matter, which could in turn lead to improvements in other containment techniques.

The present status of the attempts to demonstrate scientific feasibility is shown in Table 12-2.

An examination of this table shows that, although there is a good deal of optimism that scientific feasibility will be demonstrated shortly, all the present devices still fall at least a factor of 100 short of the needed density-containment time product. The Tokamak or stellarator concept is probably the most promising at this stage. The mirror machines would need to behave very close to their theoretical limit to be practical, and some technique for much faster recycling would be required in the pinch device.

The large question with the Tokamak is whether any new instabilities will arise when the present devices are scaled up to larger size (at much greater cost). In many previous cases such instabilities have arisen. However the fairly long lifetime (30×10^{-3} sec) of the plasma in the present machine suggests that the plasma is fairly quiescent and that its decay is caused mainly by diffusion (drifting and colliding). If this is the case, then making the devices bigger will slow down this process and increase the lifetime sufficiently to reach the breakeven region. The other question, of how to heat the plasma to ignition temperature, has been at least partially answered recently by the success of the compression experiment with the Adiabatic Toroidal Compressor at Princeton University. Compression tripled the plasma temperature and should be a technique that is applicable to other machines.

Present plans call for completing the Princeton Large Torus (PLT) by 1975. This device will be twice as large as the present largest United States machine and will test the scaling principle. If the PLT performs up to its ultimate limit, it may even demonstrate scientific feasibility.

Although optimism has always been the watchword of the fusion enthusiasts, the present feeling does seem at last to have some substance. As Professor Lawrence Lidsky writes in *Technology Review* of January, 1972 [1], "The distance remaining to the goal of fusion is relatively small, so the unexpected has a small domain in which to lurk." The director of the A.E.C. Division of Controlled Thermonuclear Research, Robert L. Hirsh, is also optimistic, and stated in *Physics Today*, February, 1973, that the A.E.C. has "formally adopted the immediate goal of establishing the feasibility of fusion by 1980 to 1982. . . . While ultimate success cannot be guaranteed, the probability is much higher now than it has ever been before."

Table 12-2

	Tokamak T3	Mirror X2	Theta Pinch	Breakeven Requirements, Lawson Criterion
n (ions/cm³)	3×10^{13}	5×10^{13}	5×10^{16}	
τ(sec)	30×10^{-3}	4×10^{-4}	10^{-5}	
$n \times \tau$(ions sec/cm³)	9×10^{11}	2×10^{10}	5×10^{11}	10^{14}
max. temp.*	0.6 kev	8 kev	3.2 kev	10 kev

Note: Temperature is related to the speed of particle motion and therefore to kinetic energy. Temperature is sometimes expressed in terms of energy as in this table where 10 kev is equivalent to about 8×10^7 K, that is 80 million Kelvin. The temperature of the sun's surface is only about 5×10^3 K and the maximum temperature of the core of the sun is estimated to be about 1.57×10^7 K.

12-4 Laser Induced Fusion

While the magnetic containment devices are steadily progressing towards the scientific feasibility goal, a radically different approach is now being pursued in parallel. Instead of containing a plasma of deuterium and tritium within a magnetic "bottle" of some kind, a solid pellet of these materials is heated very rapidly with a very high powered laser* beam. At first, calculation showed that an exceedingly powerful laser would be required, but a further idea of simultaneous bombardment of the pellet from all sides (Figure 12-5) reduced the laser requirements by about a factor of 1000. This is primarily because the bombardment from all directions is expected to compress the D-T pellet to a superdense state where fusion will readily take place.

The occurrence of laser induced fusion was first demonstrated in 1968 by Nikolai Basov at the Lebedev Institute in Moscow. Since then a number of other countries including France, Germany, and Japan have all begun laser induced fusion studies. A large and growing program is in existence in the United States, primarily in government laboratories like the Lawrence Laboratory, Livermore, California, and Los Alamos Scientific Laboratory, New Mexico. However, the promise is so great that even some small private companies such as KMS-Fusion, Ann Arbor, Michigan have going programs, mainly theoretical.

It has been estimated by Nuckolls and Wood that, in spite of the large advantages of simultaneous bombardment, lasers of 10^5 to 10^6 J will be required for a practical power plant. The more immediate goal of a breakeven condition, where more energy is generated than is contained in the laser beam, should be achieved with a laser of about 1000 J if the energy is delivered in less than 10^{-9} sec [1 nsec (nanosec)]. At present Basov has a nine-beam laser that delivers 600 J in 2 nsec, and he hopes to reduce this time by a factor of 4. In addition, the U.S.S.R. has begun construction of a 27-beam laser. In the United States there are plans to build a 1000-J laser that can deliver a pulse in about 10^{-10} sec, although the largest known laser we have is a 215-J laser at the Naval Research Laboratory. Further research on tailormaking the pulses so that they first create a sheet of plasma on the outside, which will help the compression process is also being pursued, for example at KMS-Fusion.

The laser that lends itself most to high power and short pulses is a "neodymium doped" glass laser, which is made from a special glass to which the rare earth element neodymium has been added. Although

* Note: The term **laser** stands for light amplification by the stimulated emission of radiation. This is a device for producing a very high energy density, parallel beam of electromagnetic radiation. The wavelength of the radiation depends on the type of laser producing it, but the radiation is often in the visible range so that we can *see* it as a beam of light.

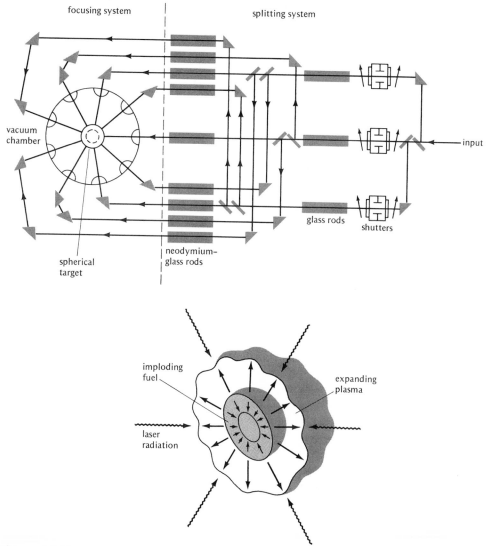

Figure 12-5
Upper: Nine-path laser at Lebedev Institute produces 1300 J in 16×10^{-9} sec and 600 J in 2×10^{-9} sec. The beam is split into three parts, each of which is then amplified by a rod. Then each beam is again divided into three, and each is again amplified. The nine beams then converge onto a single solid pellet of deuterium-tritium. [Information from *Physics Today*, August, 1972, p. 17.] **Lower:** Fuel is compressed to high density by the reaction and thermal pressure of hot plasma generated by the absorption of laser light.

these advantages make it very useful for studying laser-plasma interactions, the neodymium laser has a number of disadvantages which probably make it impossible to use as the basis of a power producer. First the energy output of the laser is only one thousandth of the input energy, that is, its efficiency is only 0.1%. The neodymium laser is also a very slow pulse rate device. For example, the 215-J laser at the Naval Research Laboratory requires about 4 min between pulses, whereas for power production a pulse rate of about one per second is required. Finally these systems are expensive (about $1000 per joule) to build and are probably not durable enough to be practical.

Another possibility is the carbon dioxide laser, which has a much higher efficiency than the neodymium laser (perhaps as high as 20%) and is also less expensive to build ($100 per joule). Although the present carbon dioxide lasers are small, Keith Boyer of Los Alamos is planning a 1000-J unit that will produce pulses in the 10^{-9} range and possibly shorter. He has hopes for lasers in the 2000 to 5000 J range. There is one serious difficulty with the carbon dioxide laser, namely the wavelength of the radiation produced. Calculations suggest that shorter wavelength radiation may be more efficient in penetrating the pellet and depositing more energy to produce compression. The neodymium glass laser emits radiation with a wavelength of 1.06×10^{-6} m, whereas the carbon dioxide laser radiation has a longer wavelength, 10.6×10^{-6} m. Laser technology, however, is an extremely rapidly growing field, and the required laser may now be waiting in the wings. For example a high pressure xenon gas laser, which emits 0.17×10^{-6} m radiation and which could be up to 90% efficient, has recently been demonstrated at Livermore.

Because the whole field of laser induced fusion is so new, little thought has yet been given to the design of an actual power plant. There is the hope that these could be built on a smaller scale than the magnetic confinement system, which would therefore make the laser fusion reactors more versatile. Small local power stations would eliminate the need for transmission lines and could help avoid large scale power failures. Laser induced fusion may also lend itself to direct conversion programs, without the need for steam turbines, with the payoff of much more efficient production of electricity.

The A.E.C. and also the Defense Department are very interested in pursuing this field with the Federal research and development support growing from $13 million in 1972 to $23 million in 1973. With a strong effort, there appears to be the possibility that scientific feasibility could be demonstrated either in the United States or in the U.S.S.R. within the next few years.

12-5   Engineering Difficulties

While the scientific feasibility studies with magnetic confinement and laser induced fusion are being pursued, it is worth giving some

Figure 12-6

Schematic of a fusion reactor. The central core contains the hot reacting plasma at around 100×10^6 K. In a magnetic confinement device, the magnetic coils would probably be superconducting and therefore kept near liquid helium temperature (4 K). They would have to be shielded from neutrons and radiant heat from the remainder of the reactor.

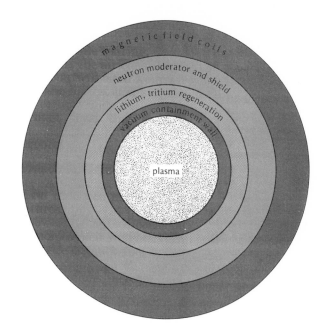

thought to the construction of a reactor. Many of the details cannot be worked out until it is clearer which of the many techniques discussed in the last few sections is most promising as a method of producing power. However there are some general problems that are largely independent of the specific device employed which should be considered.

A simple schematic diagram is shown in Figure 12-6 which illustrates some of the features required in a working fusion reactor. The plasma itself is at the core, and because this will not be perfectly contained, it must be continually replaced. The plasma is also heated by the fusion process, once triggered, particularly by the charged particles emitted. Fusing or "burning" a larger fraction of the plasma lets the reactor operate at higher temperatures and higher power levels. This can bring attendant difficulties, as we shall see. The vacuum wall surrounding the plasma and separating it from the tritium regeneration region and neutron shield must be thin to pass neutrons readily but strong enough to withstand high temperatures. The heat comes not only from radiation from the hot plasma (neglecting actual plasma losses) but also from energy deposited by neutrons as they pass through and from heat from the tritium generating blanket behind. Metals like niobium and molybdenum, which retain their strength at high temperatures, seem likely choices for these thin walls.

In a D-T fusion reactor, the tritium for continued operation must be produced by the operating reactor, similar to the breeding of ^{239}Pu in a fission breeder reactor. The most likely technique for breeding tritium is to use the reaction of both the fast neutrons and also slowed down neutrons with lithium isotopes. Both reactions produce tritium.* The lithium could be present either as metal or as a lithium salt. Neglecting possible direct electrical generation devices, heat would normally be drawn from this region to produce power along similar lines to a fission reactor. The fusion reactor is a very efficient breeder of tritium and could probably double its inventory almost every year.

Large numbers of neutrons are produced in D-T fusion and, unlike the slow moving neutrons from a fission reactor, these neutrons have fairly high energy. This makes them harder to stop and also increases the damage each neutron will cause in any material. It is extremely important to prevent these neutrons from reaching the magnet coils, both to reduce radiation damage to the coils and also to minimize the heating of the coils under neutron bombardment. A shield layer or moderator for the neutrons must be introduced. Water makes an effective neutron shield, but lithium reacts violently with water so that graphite (a form of carbon) is a more likely choice. The graphite could be mixed into the lithium region and the energy released by the neutron reactions with the graphite could also be extracted as heat.

The magnet coils on the outside must be able to produce very high magnetic fields (assuming a containment device) probably about 150 kilogauss. The most likely technique for producing such fields would be superconducting magnets, which operate close to a temperature of absolute zero. Thus the temperature gradient across the reactor is enormous. Such low temperature coils could not be operated with any significant thermal load from heat within the reactor or from neutrons so that the thermal and neutron shielding must be very effective.

All of these requirements imply that a fusion reactor, unless of the laser induced variety, will probably have to be a rather large size device to operate economically. Numbers as high as 10,000 Mw may be needed with the implication of a more centralized power producing system.

12-6   Advantages of a Fusion Reactor

In spite of the problems discussed, the fusion reactor has a number of tremendous advantages when compared to other sources of energy. The first of these is the ready and cheap availability of fuel. Deuterium, the primary fuel, is a stable isotope of hydrogen containing one neutron as well as one proton in the nucleus. It occurs naturally

* Specifically
$$^7Li + n \rightarrow T + {}^4He + n; \text{ energy absorbed} = 2.5 \text{ Mev.}$$
$$^6Li + n \rightarrow T + {}^4He; \text{ energy released} = 4.8 \text{ Mev.}$$

with an abundance of 0.015%. This may not seem like very much at first glance, but there are large quantities of hydrogen available, primarily in the sea, where two hydrogen atoms link with one oxygen molecule to form water. One out of 6500 of these hydrogen atoms is a deuterium atom, and the water so formed is sometimes called "heavy" water. It is relatively simple, because the mass difference between hydrogen and deuterium is so large, to separate these heavy water molecules from ordinary water. The estimated cost is only about 3×10^{-4}¢/kwh, much less for example than coal or uranium costs.

The energy content of 1 m³ of water from its deuteron content is 6×10^9 J. In other words, 1 m³ of sea water has the same energy content as 2000 bbl of crude oil. As we know, there is plenty of water in the oceans (actually about 1.5×10^{18} m³ of water) so that the energy content of the ocean represents a virtually unlimited energy source.

The other reactant in a D-T fusion device, tritium, is an even heavier isotope of hydrogen with two neutrons as well as a proton in the nucleus of the atom. Tritium, however, is unstable and decays to ³He with a half-life of 12.3 years, emitting a low energy electron (the maximum energy of the electron is 18.6 kev; the average energy is about 9 kev). Therefore tritium must be bred in the reactor, as discussed in Section 12-5. This presents no great difficulty but does require the use of lithium metal, which is of comparable abundance with uranium. Further development of the D-D fusion process would eventually eliminate the need for lithium as a breeding agent.

Apart from the abundance of fuel, the fusion reactor would present fewer environmental hazards than the fission reactors. The end products of the fusion process are helium and hydrogen isotopes. No long lived heavy element isotopes are produced, and there is no production or handling of the biologically dangerous and radioactive plutonium. There is no need to transport radioactive fuel elements, and all processing would be done on site. Because the fusion process readily shuts itself off, there is probably less danger of an accident, and in any case this would be less biologically damaging.

The two main sources of radioactive hazard that do exist come from the release of tritium and from the activity in the structural materials produced by the neutrons emitted in the fusion process. This latter effect is estimated to be similar to the effect produced in a fission reactor. The tritium release is the more serious question. Tritium is a light gas and under the conditions of high temperature in the reactor can readily pass through most materials. Fraas and Postond estimate that, of the total inventory of 10^8 curies of tritium, about 60 curies/day would normally be emitted. Roughly one quarter of this would be emitted in the water output. Biologically, tritium gas is rather inactive, much less so than the comparable quantity of ^{131}I that would be emitted from a fission reactor. The water release is more dangerous because water containing tritium is more readily absorbed into the body than tritium gas. However with some care, such as housing the reactor in a vacuum, which would not be too difficult, the tritium emission could readily be reduced to 1 curie/day.

Finally, the thermal pollution from a fusion reactor, even neglecting the possibility of direct electrical conversion, should be significantly better than alternative energy sources. Estimates suggest an efficiency of 50 to 60% for a fusion reactor compared to around 40% for a modern fossil fuel plant and only about 32% for the present generation of fission reactors.

12-7 Summary

We have seen that the promise of the fusion reactor is high — unlimited resources with a small environmental impact. However, we are still far from achieving a working reactor. There does seem hope of demonstrating breakeven fusion or scientific feasibility within the next decade but the way to a working reactor will still be long and difficult. Scientific feasibility was demonstrated for the breeder reactor almost 30 years ago and we still do not have a reactor commercially available, in spite of large investments of research and development funds. There is probably no reason to hope that the path to a fusion reactor will be any easier.

Because fusion is a more long term hope, it is reasonable to expect the government to play a large role in this development. Perhaps now is the time to start transferring funds from the fission program, leaving that to the power industry which can see more immediate returns from such an investment. Certainly other countries, especially the U.S.S.R., are mounting large scale fusion programs, while the United States still spends less than 10% of the total Federal research and development energy expenditure on fusion research.

David Rose writing in *Science,* May, 1971 [3], on the status of fusion states, "My own guess is that fusion power will be available in appreciable quantity by 2000 . . . A few optimists propose 1990: pessimists propose never." The situation has not changed substantially since then, but the promise is so great that we must pursue the fusion possibility as hard as we are able.

Questions

1. Critically discuss the statement: "Nuclear fusion will solve all the United States energy problems by the year 2020."

2. How can the fusion process be used as an energy source on earth, when it requires temperatures higher than at the center of the sun?

3. Laser induced fusion is a recent hope for controlled thermonuclear fusion. What are the main difficulties with the current technology?

4. Explain how energy can be produced from both the fission and the fusion processes, when one involves breaking up a heavy nucleus and the other consists of building up a heavier nucleus from lighter pieces.

5. Why is the D-T process more likely to be used to demonstrate fusion than the D-^{3}He process?

6. Explain why such high temperatures are required to make the fusion process go in a fusion reactor.

7. Which statement is true about energy production using a fusion reaction?
   (a) cheap and available fuel.
   (b) increased radioactive hazards compared to fission.
   (c) lower operating efficiency than fossil fuel.
   (d) a heavy nucleus breaks into two lighter nuclei.
   (e) a laboratory reactor has already worked.

8. Discuss some of the main problems of magnetic confinement fusion reactors.

Bibliography

[1] L. M. Lidsky: The quest for fusion power. *Technology Review,* January, 1972.

[2] R. F. Post: Fusion power, the uncertain certainty. *Bulletin of the Atomic Scientists,* October, 1971, p. 42.

[3] D. J. Rose: Controlled nuclear fusion: status and outlook. *Science,* May 21, 1971.

[4] Magnetic containment fusion: what are the prospects. *Science,* October 20, 1972.

[5] Laser fusion: a new approach to thermonuclear power. *Science,* September 29, 1972.

[6] A.E.C. opens up an laser fusion implosion concept. *Physics Today,* August, 1972.

[7] Princeton Tokamak exceeds supposed density limit. *Physics Today,* January, 1973.

[8] Walter Sullivan: Laser technique is tested in search for clean power. *New York Times,* October 22, 1972.

[9] K. Boyer: Laser-initiated fusion—key experiments looming. *Astronautics and Aeronautics,* January, 1973.

[10] America's fusion director. *New Scientist,* April, 1973, p. 86.

[11] M. J. Lubin and A. P. Fraas: Fusion by laser. *Scientific American,* June, 1971, p. 21.

An Ultimate Answer? Solar Energy

13-1 Introduction

The sun is indeed profligate in the production of energy, and life on earth depends very much on its abundance. This fact was realized by primitive peoples who worshipped the sun almost since man first walked the earth. While we use the sun's energy in many ways, primarily in agriculture, our main energy resource remains solar energy stored over millions of years in fossil fuels. Direct use of the sun's energy to meet our needs has been the poor sister in energy resource utilization, and very little effort has been put into the development of this technology.

For many years solar energy was felt to be a resource for more primitive and technologically underdeveloped countries that could not afford the advanced technology of nuclear reactors or were short of fossil fuels and could not afford to buy them. However, both balance of payments problems (in 1972 the United States spent $4 billion in energy imports) and environmental issues have combined to make solar energy increasingly attractive as an energy source for technically advanced countries as well.

Solar energy is attractive on two main grounds. First, it is a renewable resource that can be tapped for billions of years, longer than anyone cares to project the future of the human race. Second, it has few adverse environmental impacts compared to either fossil fuels or nuclear energy.

151

13-2 Reappraisal of Solar Energy

As was discussed in Chapter 6, the energy emitted by the sun reaches the radius of the earth's orbit with an intensity of about 1400 w/m² (watt per square meter). Of course not all of this radiation reaches the surface of the earth. We noted also in Chapter 6 that on the average about 36% of the incident radiation was reflected back into space. The amount falling on a square meter on the earth's surface also depends upon location particularly the latitude. The effective area at a latitude θ is equal to (area $\times$ cos θ) (see Figure 13-1). For example, East Lansing, Michigan, is at a latitude of approximately 43° north. Therefore the effective area of a 1 m² for accepting solar radiation is

$$1 \text{ m}^2 \times \cos 43° = 0.73 \text{ m}^2$$

Thus the amount of radiation falling on a *1 m² area* in East Lansing, even assuming no reflection in the atmosphere is

$$1400 \times 0.73 \text{ J/sec} = 1.02 \times 10^3 \text{ w}$$

Only at the equator (latitude 0°) is the effective area equal to the actual area on the ground.

The situation is slightly more complicated because of the tilt of the earth, which gives rise to summer and winter variations of the energy deposited, but since these tend to average out this effect will be neglected. The other big factor, which obviously plays a role in the variation of the amount of solar energy falling on a given spot on the earth's surface, is the rotation of the earth, giving rise to night and day. For these reasons, much less energy than 1400 w/m² is effectively available on most of the earth's surface. A recent NSF/NASA (National Science Foundation/National Aeronautics and Space Administration) report gives a value of about 180 w/m² for the United States averaged over 24 hr. In certain areas, such as the southwestern deserts of Ari-

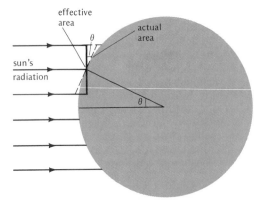

effective area

actual area

sun's radiation

Figure 13-1
The latitude determines the effective area on the earth's surface on which sunlight will fall.

effective area = actual area $\times$ cos θ where θ is the latitude.

152

An Ultimate Answer?
Solar Energy

zona and New Mexico, the value could be considerably larger. A report prepared by the University of Minnesota and Honeywell [7] shows measurements of the total solar energy falling on an area in Arizona in December. The value obtained is about 350 w/m² averaged over the 24-hr period—almost twice as high as the average quoted previously.

Assuming the average (24-hr) value of 180 w/m² it is interesting to calculate the magnitude of the total energy falling on a square mile (mi²) of land. Since 1 mi² = 2.59 × 10⁶ m², the total energy falling on 1 mi² in 24 hr (1 day) is given by,

$$\text{energy/mi}^2 = (180 \times 24)(2.59 \times 10^6) \text{ wh (watt hours)}$$
$$= 1.12 \times 10^{10} \text{ wh}$$
$$= 1.12 \times 10^7 \text{ kwh (kilowatt-hours)}.$$

The United States has a total area of about 3.68×10^6 mi² so that the total energy falling on the United States in 1 year is calculated as,

$$\text{energy/year} = (1.12 \times 10^7)(3.68 \times 10^6)(365) \text{ kwh}$$
$$= 1.50 \times 10^{16} \text{ kwh}.$$

We saw in Chapter 7 that the total United States consumption of energy in 1970 was 70×10^{15} btu or about 20×10^{12} kwh. In other words 750 times more solar energy falls on the United States than was used in 1970. Thomas Paine, former NASA director, has emphasized the abundance of solar energy by stating that more energy has fallen on power plants than they have produced.

Solar energy is a sizable resource. It is free for the taking and is not depleted by use. In addition it is comparatively nonpolluting, especially when compared to either fossil fuel plants or to nuclear reactors. Depending upon the efficiency of energy conversion, there may be some local thermal problems but overall thermal problems are minimal for most solar energy utilization schemes.

However, there are difficulties in utilizing the sun's radiation. Although the total magnitude of the energy available is very large, it is spread very widely. It is a very diffuse resource. Therefore fairly large areas of land are required to generate substantial amounts of power. We saw that 750 times the amount of energy used in 1970 falls on the United States each year. But, if we assume say a 10% conversion efficiency ratio, then 1.3%, that is about 50,000 mi² of land would be needed to produce the energy used in 1970. If we take the projected use in the year 2000 to be about 3 times that of 1970, then 4% of the land area of the United States (about 150,000 mi²) would be needed, which is approximately 70% of the area of New Mexico and Arizona combined.

The other major difficulty associated with almost all solar energy applications is the question of reliability. When I was about to demonstrate a solar cell to a class, I remember being unable to do this for a number of class periods because of the lack of sunlight. Even in more compatible regions of the country where the sun does shine as many as 330 days in a year, there remains the fact that night inevitably follows day. Therefore solar energy schemes require some device for storing energy during those periods when the sun is not shining. Some imaginative proposals have been suggested for such storage, including the production of hydrogen, and this will be discussed in a later chapter.

The remaining questions of cost and technical feasibility must be discussed for each separate proposal. Before turning to detailed discussion of the various proposed applications of solar energy, it will be useful to review some of the physical principles involved.

13-3 Absorption, Reflection, and Emission of Radiation

We saw in Section 6-4 that the temperature of an object will remain constant only if the amount of energy emitted is equal to the energy absorbed. If more energy were absorbed than was emitted, the body would get hotter, and vice versa. This principle may be used to produce a high temperature from solar absorption.

The absorption, reflection, and reemission properties of a body are all related. Bodies that are very good absorbers of radiation are also good emitters of radiation but very poor reflectors. A perfect absorber (or emitter) is often given the name **black body** because black objects tend to be poor reflectors but excellent absorbers of radiation. Conversely, white or particularly shiny objects are good reflectors but poor absorbers or emitters of radiation. We often make use of such properties in our clothing. In summer we use light colored clothing which tends to reflect sunlight. We know that darker clothing is much hotter because it is a better absorber of radiation.

The absorption and reflection properties thus depend upon the nature of the surface. These properties can also depend upon the wavelength of the radiation considered so that it is possible to produce surfaces that are good absorbers at one wavelength but good reflectors (and therefore poor absorbers or poor emitters) at a different wavelength. This can be accomplished, for example, by a series of thin layers of materials that produce interference effects on the incident or emitted radiation.

We saw that the solar spectrum has a peak in the visible region and contains most of the energy at fairly short wavelengths (Figure 6-2). The predominant wavelength emitted depends on the temperature of the body. Bodies at lower temperature tend to emit longer wavelength radiation. Therefore by using a body whose surface absorbs strongly at the shorter wavelengths dominant in the sun's spectrum but which is a good reflector (and therefore a poor emitter) at longer wavelengths, the temperature of the body can be raised significantly. Specific examples will be discussed later in Section 13-7.

13-4 Photovoltaic Cells

A different approach to tapping the sun's energy is the use of a photovoltaic device or solar cell. We are all familiar with these devices, both on a small scale where they can provide a power pack for a transistor radio or in the space program where solar cells provide a good deal of the electrical power for space capsules. One of the early problems of the first manned orbiting laboratory was the fact that one of its banks of solar cells did not open, requiring the vehicle to operate on greatly reduced power.

A solar cell consists of a slice of a special type of material called a semiconductor, so called because it behaves partly like a conductor and partly like an insulator (most plastics and wood are examples of insulators). We are familiar with semiconductors, such as silicon or germanium, when they are used to make transistors which serve as the active elements in many of our radio and TV receivers. These materials when properly purified and "doped" with minute quantities of particular elements, such as boron or arsenic, have the property that electrons are freed within the material when electromagnetic radiation is incident upon it. A small voltage is established across the slab which can then produce electrical current if connected through a circuit. The device then directly converts sunlight into electrical energy.

The most common material used for solar cells is the element silicon, although cadmium sulfide and gallium arsenide have also been used. Silicon is an abundant material that can be fairly readily produced with reasonably high purity. However, to produce silicon solar cells, a single crystal of ultra high purity is required. These pure crystals are very difficult to manufacture and are therefore not easily mass produced. One of the difficulties is that molten silicon from which the single crystal is produced is a very reactive material and typically will dissolve part of the die that determines the shape of the final crystal. The dissolved impurities then destroy the high purity and degrade the performance of the silicon. If less soluble die materials could be produced, substantial improvement of the process might be obtained and lead to the lower cost which comes with mass production. An alternative technique, which awaits the development of space stations, would be to purify and grow pure silicon crystals in a weightless environment in orbit around the earth, thus dispensing with the need for a container.

Silicon cells typically operate at about 13% efficiency for converting electromagnetic radiation into electricity although it is hoped that this efficiency can be raised to around 20%. Small gallium arsenide solar cells with efficiencies as high as 18% have been produced. The efficiency of cadium sulfide cells is only around 6%, although these are much easier to produce since large single crystals are not required.

What then are some of the practical applications of the use of solar energy and how soon could they play a significant role in total energy use?

13-5   The Solar Home

A recent NSF/NASA report on solar energy estimated that, by the year 2020, 35% of the energy used for heating and cooling buildings could come from solar energy. Already in many countries, including

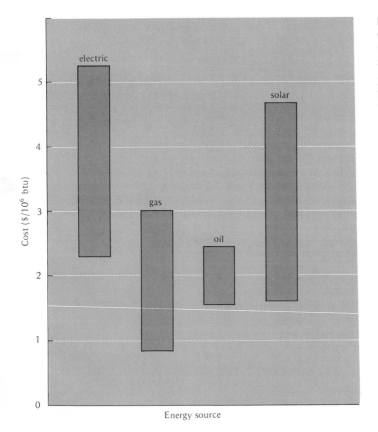

Figure 13-2
Costs of space heating. The length of the vertical bars give the range of costs in various parts of the United States for the different methods of space heating. [From NSF/NASA Solar Energy Panel Report.]

Australia and Israel, solar water heaters are commercially available and are growing in popularity. Solar space heating is also competitive with electrical heating in many parts of this country and even with gas and oil heat in other areas (Figure 13-2). There is a growing number of people who are attempting to build solar heating into their homes. A recent report in the *Los Angeles Times* told of a solar powered house built by Bob Reines in New Mexico which was able to survive cold winter nights down to 30°F below zero.

For water or space heating, the solar collector is usually a simple blackened metal sheet, which readily absorbs sunlight, covered by a sheet of glass which does not transmit the longer (infrared) wave-

Figure 13-3
Schematic diagram of a solar heating and cooling system for a house. In winter solar radiation absorbed by a collector on the roof of the house warms water which is then directly circulated through an air heating system. In summer, the hot water is used to run an absorption cooling refrigeration unit which cools the air. The summer operation requires higher temperature water but this is easier to produce in summer because of the greater amount of energy available from the sun in the summer. [From NSF/NASA Solar Energy Panel Report.]

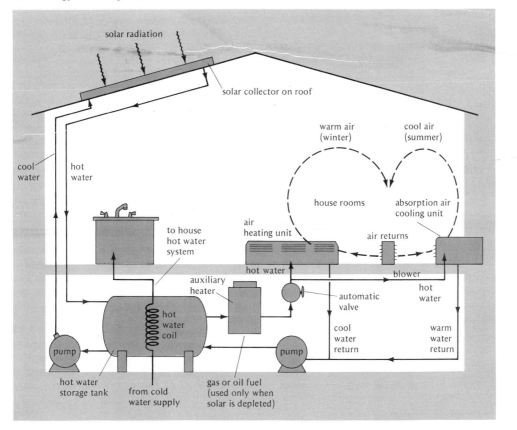

lengths emitted by the hot metal. Water pipes bonded to the metal collector transfer the heat to a storage tank.

For cooling a house, a more elaborate system is required, involving either absorption or evaporation of a coolant liquid. For these systems to operate satisfactorily, higher temperatures, near 120°C, are required. This may involve more complex collectors with evaporated coatings, as discussed in Section 13-7. A schematic of such a home is shown in Figure 13-3.

A more ambitious proposal is to develop a solar house supplying both electricity and heating. Dr. Karl Boer at the University of Delaware is developing such a prototype. He proposes to use a cadmium sulfide solar array on the roof to provide electricity, with conventional batteries as storage devices. Thermal heating of the panels would also provide heating and cooling for the house.

Perhaps the unique feature of this proposal is the suggestion of connecting the house also to the main electricity grid by a two-way system. When the sun is shining, excess energy can be tapped by the power company to help meet its peak load which often comes during daylight hours. At other times the power company could supply electricity to the house as needed. Dr. Boer feels that perhaps the power companies would gain up to 20% increased capacity through the use of such small scale solar collectors.

13-6   Agriculture for Energy

At present 500,000 mi² of land in the United States (about 15% of the total area) is used for farming. As an energy producer this is generally rather inefficient; the efficiency is probably less than 0.1%. However it may be possible to raise this efficiency to around 3% and to use dried solid material, with an average heat content of 16×10^6 btu/ton, as a source of fuel at competitive costs. Trees, grasses, algae, and water plants have all been proposed as possible sources of fuel.

The farming is already carried out so that little additional technology would be required, except that the aim would now be to optimize the total mass produced per acre including branches and roots. Grasses are claimed to produce up to 15 tons/acre each year and algae up to 30 tons/acre per year of dry material. Many water plants, such as water hyacinth have a very rapid growth rate and are normally regarded as pests. With proper conditions up to 85 tons/acre per year of dry product may be produced.

The economics of such processes do not appear to be very far out of line with current fuel costs. For example, wood chips cost about $20 per ton and, including transportation, would be about $1.50 to $2.00

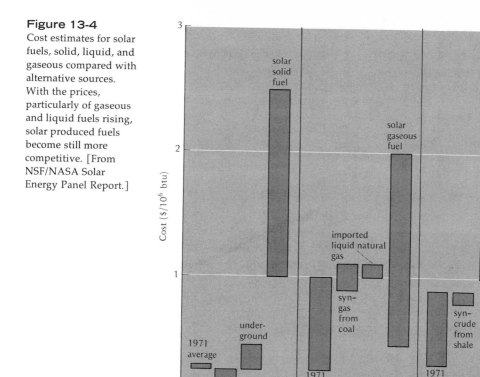

Figure 13-4
Cost estimates for solar fuels, solid, liquid, and gaseous compared with alternative sources. With the prices, particularly of gaseous and liquid fuels rising, solar produced fuels become still more competitive. [From NSF/NASA Solar Energy Panel Report.]

per 10^6 btu. These costs are comparable to, although somewhat higher than, present fossil fuel costs (Figure 13-4). Estimates of costs for the other materials are more difficult because very little experience is available in mass harvesting of such materials. More research would be required to improve such estimates.

Although the environmental impact of growing plants appears to be much less than mining coal, there are still problems of air pollution in burning organic materials. Sulfur dioxide and particulate removal would still be required, and the problem of microscopic particulate emission would still remain as a major difficulty. Whether these problems would be easier to solve with the burning of organic material than with coal is not yet clear.

An alternative approach to the use of organic materials is to produce liquid and gaseous fuels. This can be done by chemical reduction, by pyrolysis, or by fermentation (remember alcohol has a fairly high energy content). Table 13-1 taken from the NSF/NASA Solar Energy Panel Report gives a comparison of these three techniques. Pyrolysis basically consists of burning the materials in a closed vessel without

159

13-6 Agriculture for Energy

Table 13-1
Comparison of Methods of Conversion of Solid Wastes to Clean Fuel Data taken from NSF/NASA Solar Energy Panel [1].

Process Requirements	Chemical Reduction	Pyrolysis	Fermentation
Form of feed	aqueous slurry (15% solids)	dried waste	aqueous slurry (3–20% solids)
temperature	320–350° C	500–900° C	20–50° C
pressure	2000–5000 psi	atmospheric	atmospheric
agitation	vigorous agitation	none	slight
other	uses carbon monoxide	none	none
Form of product	oil	oil and char	gas
yield (percent of original material)	23%	40% oil; 20% char	20–26% (maximum)
heating value	15,000 btu/lb	12,000 btu/lb oil* 9000 btu/lb char*	23,800 btu/lb
percent of original heat content recovered in product (assume 8000 btu/lb dry waste)	37% (corrected for carbon monoxide use) 65% anticipated	82% (60% if char not included)	60% (77% maximum)

* All of gas and one third of char used to supply heat.

Figure 13-5
Schematic diagram of solid waste pyrolysis plant to produce gas and oil. [From NSF/NASA Solar Energy Panel Report.]

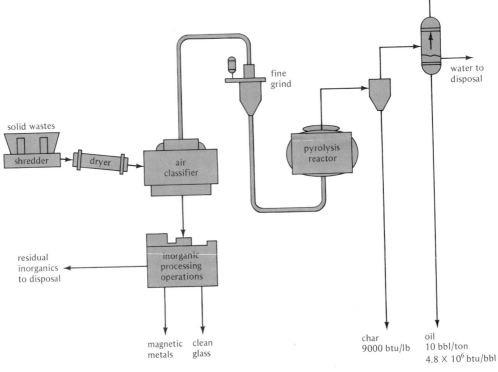

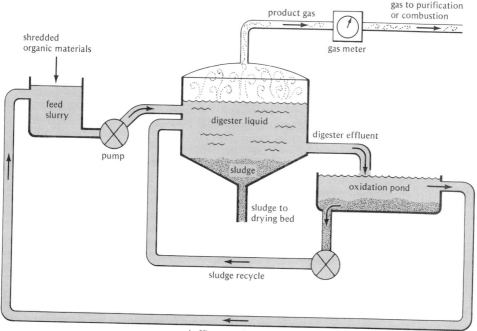

Figure 13-6

Schematic diagram of a fermentation plant to produce combustible gas (mainly methane) from organic materials. [From NSF/NASA Solar Energy Panel Report.]

oxygen. A schematic of such a pyrolysis plant is shown in Figure 13-5. At higher temperatures gaseous products with a high methane content can be produced. Note also that a pyrolysis plant could handle solid wastes from urban centers as an additional source of raw materials.

Fermentation to produce methane gas is also a possibility (such processes occur naturally in marshes). A schematic of a fermentation plant is shown in Figure 13-6. As noted in Table 13-1, 60% of the heat content of the original organic material could be recovered by such a fermentation process.

All of these processes need further investigation before they can be assessed accurately for cost compared to fossil fuel costs, but they do appear to serve as attractive alternatives.

13-7 Solar-Thermal Electric Energy Production

While it is possible that applications of solar energy in the home may be the first to have an impact on our energy economy, there has been revived interest in much larger scale applications to produce electricity. At least two groups have considered this question in detail and have put forward proposals to test their schemes with pilot plants.

Professor Aden Meinel and his wife Marjorie at the University of Arizona are investigating a system that they call a solar farm. The basic idea of their proposal is to set out a large array of very carefully constructed collectors in a suitable desert area. These collectors will be made by evaporating a series of thin films over a stainless steel surface. Various detailed designs are possible, the idea being to maximize absorption of the solar spectrum and to minimize emission of longer wavelengths. They expect to have ratios of absorption to emission at 500°C of better than 10. A schematic of a complete collecting element is shown in Figure 13-7. The sunlight is collected over a large surface by a simple lens (Fresnel type) and then concentrated on a stainless steel pipe which is coated with the special selective layers. The pipe is suspended in an evacuated glass pipe to minimize heat losses by convection and conduction. Some heat transfer fluid, probably liquid sodium, is passed through the stainless steel pipe to collect the heat.

The Meinels propose to store the heat in a thermal storage subsystem consisting of a salt solution which can then be tapped to operate a standard high pressure steam turbine and generator (Figure 13-8). Large quantities of salt are required (3×10^5 metric tons/day of reserve for a 1000-Mw power plant) but the costs are apparently not large. This storage system would also serve to operate the plant on cloudy days.

With a high quality surface and concentration of sunlight, the hope

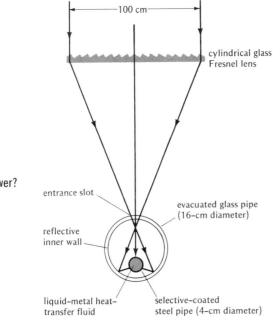

Figure 13-7
Meinel's solar energy collector. Incident radiation is focussed and absorbed by a coated pipe through which flows a transfer fluid, such as liquid sodium. The Meinels hope to operate at temperatures as high as 500°C. [Information from *Physics Today*, February, 1972, p. 49.]

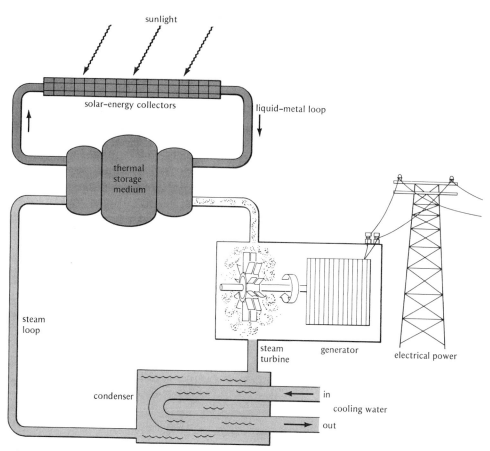

Figure 13-8

Thermal conversion system. In this basic schematic model note the three subsystems—an energy-gathering subsystem at the top, a thermal-storage subsystem in the middle, and the "using" subsystem in the bottom loop. The turbine draws energy from thermal storage according to the demand, and the use rate is therefore uncoupled from the solar input rate.

is to run the system at a temperature as high as 500°C. Even including the various transfer cycles, this could lead to an overall efficiency as high as 30% which is comparable with the present nuclear power plants. Such efficiencies will require large volumes of cooling water but, by using sea water and combining the system with a desalination plant, the waste heat could also be used to help supply fresh water to the southwest where it is most needed.

Nevertheless there are some difficulties that remain. One is to find a cheap way of manufacturing the high quality selective coatings required. Another problem is how long the coatings will last under field conditions. Will they tarnish or buckle when operated at high temperatures and how will they stand repeated washings? The concentrator lens is also a difficulty. For optimum operation this will

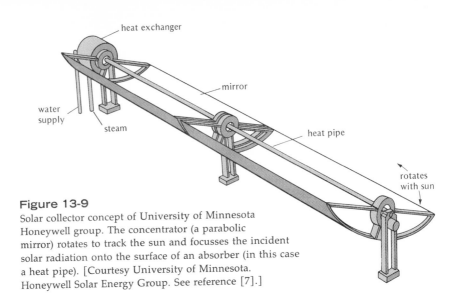

Figure 13-9
Solar collector concept of University of Minnesota
Honeywell group. The concentrator (a parabolic
mirror) rotates to track the sun and focusses the incident
solar radiation onto the surface of an absorber (in this case
a heat pipe). [Courtesy University of Minnesota.
Honeywell Solar Energy Group. See reference [7].]

need to "track" the sun's motion, thus adding expensive steering
devices. Nor will such lenses operate well on hazy days when the
sunlight is more diffuse.

Another major effort in solar-thermal energy production is being
pursued at Minneapolis jointly by the University of Minnesota and
Honeywell [7]. Although the overall concept of a "solar farm" consisting of a large array of collectors is common to this scheme and the
Meinels' scheme, there are detailed differences in particular components.

In the Minnesota/Honeywell scheme the collectors consist of trough
shaped parabolic mirrors (Figure 13-9) mounted to follow the sun's
motion. The reflected sunlight is concentrated on a pipe placed at the
focal line of the parabolic mirror. Like the collector used by the
Meinels, this pipe is also covered with a selective coating to maximize
absorption and is contained in a larger diameter evacuated pipe. However, instead of pumping a transfer fluid like liquid sodium through
the collector, the pipe consists of a heat pipe that uses gravity to return
the working fluid.

Heat exchangers are located at the end of each collector rather than
having one large common heat exchanger. The heat is transferred to a
working fluid, such as steam, which is then used in a conventional
power system. Again it is hoped to operate this system in the temperature range of 300 to 500°C.

It should be stressed that both of these schemes, although promising, require further work in research and development before even
accurate cost figures are available. However the promise of comparatively pollution-free electric power generation suggests that further
support for such investigations is very worthwhile.

13-8 Solar Space Satellite Power Station

A dramatically different approach to the generation of electricity from solar energy has been proposed by Dr. Peter Glaser, of A. D. Little Inc. He has suggested orbiting a satellite in such an orbit that its period matches the period of the earth's rotation (1 day). Such a satellite is said to be in synchronous orbit and it will appear to stay stationary in the sky above a particular point on the earth. A synchronous orbit satellite will be at a distance of approximately 22,000 miles above the earth's surface.

The satellite will consist of large arrays of photovoltaic cells to convert sunlight directly into electricity (Figure 13-10). To generate 10,000 Mw of power in the satellite two symmetric arrays, each 4 km (kilometer) on a side are needed. Mirror arms on the side will help to direct even more sunlight onto the solar cell array.

The electricity would then be beamed to earth as electromagnetic radiation with a frequency of about 3×10^9 Hz (cycles per second). Radiation of this frequency is called microwaves and can readily penetrate the earth's atmosphere even on cloudy or rainy days with very little loss of intensity. The microwave beam can be collected quite efficiently on earth by a large (7-km diameter) receiving antenna. Glaser

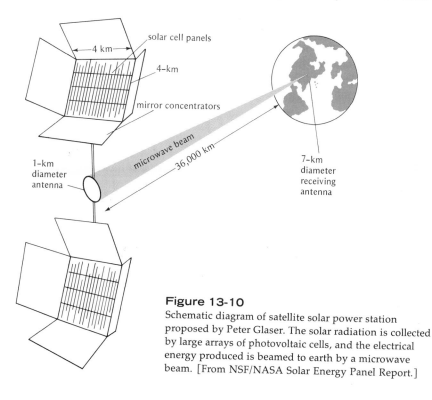

solar cell panels

4 km

4–km

mirror concentrators

microwave beam

36,000 km

1–km diameter antenna

7–km diameter receiving antenna

Figure 13-10

Schematic diagram of satellite solar power station proposed by Peter Glaser. The solar radiation is collected by large arrays of photovoltaic cells, and the electrical energy produced is beamed to earth by a microwave beam. [From NSF/NASA Solar Energy Panel Report.]

expects a transmission efficiency of between 55% and 75% for transmission from the satellite to earth.

The main advantages of this system are that in a synchronous orbit the sun is virtually shining all the time at full intensity. There are no cloudy days and only about an hour of darkness, so that the power collected for a given size solar cell is probably 6 to 10 times greater than for a similar cell on earth. Continuously available sunlight also eliminates the need for any large storage device because power can be beamed down virtually at all times.

But it is clear that many questions remain to be answered before such a scheme is even attempted. The first problem is cost. Present prices for solar arrays used in space range from $1000 to $8000 per ft^2 or at least $10,000 ($10^4$) per m^2. Because the solar arrays in the 10,000-Mw station considered had an area of about 32×10^6 m^2, the total cost of the cells alone would be $320 billion. Thus a very substantial reduction in solar cell cost is needed. As discussed in Section 13-4, continuous batch processing for producing ultra pure single crystals of silicon is under investigation, but there are still technical difficulties to overcome.

Another basic problem is the difficulty of assembling, operating, and maintaining such a device in the alien environment of space. A cheap delivery system such as a space shuttle is required. Such a scheme is on the drawing boards but is some distance from reality.

Another question that requires study is the safety of the microwave beams to people, both those who might fly through the beam or who might reside near the receiving antenna. The United States and the U.S.S.R. have standards for microwave exposure that differ by a factor of 1000, the U.S.S.R. having much stricter standards. This question would also need further investigation. The microwave beam will also heat up the atmosphere as it passes through, and this phenomenon needs further study.

Although the solar satellite power station has many technical and economic difficulties, it has comparatively few adverse environmental effects. It also represents the imaginative thinking that may be required to come to grips with the energy problem some decades hence.

13-9 Solar Sea Power

A very different concept for using solar energy to produce electricity makes use of the temperature differences of the tropical oceans. This concept, basically a simple heat engine, was first suggested in 1881 by the French physicist Jacque D'Arsonval. Small operating plants based

Figure 13-11

Typical temperature profile in the tropical ocean. The black dots are readings at 3°22′N 27°27′W and the solid curve is a continuous recording at 8°24′N 27°27′W. [From F. C. Fuglester, quoted in *Physics Today*, January 1973, p. 52.]

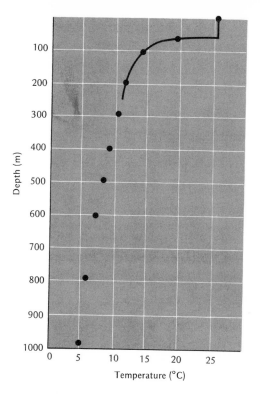

on this principle have been built in Cuba in 1929 and off the Ivory Coast in 1956.

Near the equator much of the earth's surface is water, the surface layer of which is kept heated by the tropical sun to a temperature always above 25°C. A temperature profile of the ocean is shown in Figure 13-11. At a depth of 1000 m, the temperature has fallen to only 5°C. This temperature profile is maintained by solar energy; the sun directly heats the surface layer, and the cold water in the depths is replenished by runoff from melting snow which slides to the bottom.

A simple calculation shows that, if we had a heat engine operating between 5°C and 25°C, the maximum thermodynamic efficiency would be

$$\text{Eff}_{\max} = \frac{T_{\text{hot}} - T_{\text{cold}}}{T_{\text{hot}}} = \frac{20}{298} = 0.067$$

$$\approx 7\%.$$

A practical efficiency of about 3% or 4% might reasonably be expected. At these low efficiencies very large quantities of water would have to be processed to generate significant amounts of energy. However, very large quantities of water are available so that economic factors are the prime limitation.

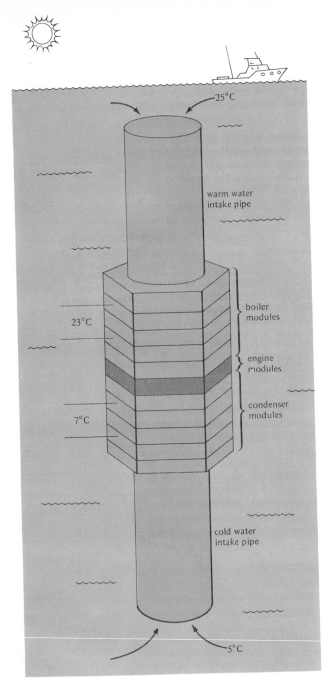

25°C

warm water
intake pipe

boiler
modules

23°C

engine
modules

condenser
modules

7°C

cold water
intake pipe

5°C

Figure 13-12
Artist's impression of a projected solar sea
power plant, operating between ocean levels at
25°C and 5°C. The entire plant is neutrally
buoyant at a depth of about 200 ft. [From
Physics Today, January 1973, p. 49.]

A schematic diagram of such a solar sea power plant is shown in
Figure 13-12. It consists of a long vertically floating tower with hot and
cold water intakes at the top and bottom respectively. The operation

would in principle resemble a conventional turbine generator with heater and condenser sections. The working fluid would need to have a high vapor pressure at the low temperatures of operation so that the turbine could be kept to a reasonable size. Ammonia, propane, or the refrigeration fluid freon—a fluorocarbon—have all been suggested as possible working fluids.

Although the boiler and condenser need to be very large to handle large quantities of water, they would operate at low temperature and with practically no pressure difference. Thus the walls can be made very thin and consequently less expensively. An important consideration is the heat transfer across a surface linking the warm water to the working fluid. Recent advances in such surfaces have decreased the thermal impedance, making possible much more efficient heat transfer.

The overall economics look quite promising. In 1966, two engineers, father and son named Anderson, estimated that the capital costs of such a power plant would be comparable to that of a conventional fossil fuel plant. Since fuel costs make up about half the cost of operating a fossil fuel plant, this implied that electricity from a solar sea plant may be only half as expensive. However, more detailed testing and costing would now be required.

One other problem with solar sea plants far from land would be the transportation of energy from the site to the users on land. Large scale electrical transmission across the ocean is probably impractical and certainly uneconomic. One suggestion to overcome this problem is the production of hydrogen from the electrolysis of sea water using electricity produced by the solar sea power plant. This process could be carried out deep under the ocean surface, giving an automatic pressurization of the hydrogen. The hydrogen could be towed underwater to the coast for transmission along normal natural gas pipelines. Further discussion of the use of hydrogen will be given later in Chapter 15.

The environmental impact of such plants is probably very small. They would involve no land use and no emissions of pollutants. The main effect of such plants would be to cool slightly the surface of the tropical oceans. Professor Zener estimated that to supply power to a world population of 6 billion people at the same rate as was used by the United States in 1970 would involve a temperature drop of 1°C in the surface ocean temperature. He also points out that this is merely a redistribution of heat from surface to the depths, and that decreased evaporation and radiation would involve a net increase in heat input from the sun. This would tend to be dissipated worldwide causing a slight rise in temperature of the temperate regions. Many people in cooler climates might welcome a slight warming trend. However the large scale environmental impact of these temperature changes would need to be investigated.

In summary, an alternative use of solar energy could be to tap the temperature difference of the tropical oceans. This appears to need comparatively few technological innovations and to be reasonably competitive economically. It certainly seems like a worthwhile proposal to pursue.

13-10 Summary and Conclusions

We have seen that solar energy is a real possibility as a large, clean, renewable energy resource. The first applications will probably be to hot water heating, space heating, and later to space cooling. But the real impact will come when larger scale uses can be realized either by large, carefully optimized agricultural plants, which could supply liquid or gaseous fuels, or in large solar power plants to produce electricity.

The three principle proposals for such large electrical generating plants, the solar thermal farm, the satellite solar power station, or the solar sea power plant all have promise but still have a number of difficulties. Many of these difficulties are technical, such as the production of efficient long lived selective films to increase the efficiency and therefore the operating temperature of solar collectors. Or there is the problem of the design of effective heat transfer surfaces for transferring heat energy from the sea to the working fluid in the ocean power plant. The satellite power station requires the development of a reusable space shuttle.

However for both the solar thermal farm and the solar sea power concepts, no very large technical breakthroughs seem to be required. One might well argue that many more technical questions remain unanswered for a working fusion reactor. In fact, the same statement is probably still true of the fission breeder program in spite of the large amounts of federal research and development funds the breeder has received. The large and important question remaining is one of economics. Can these plants be built at a cost competitive with nuclear and fossil fuel plants in the near future? The proponents of each type of plant are of course optimistic and feel that solar energy is competitive economically. The case appears sufficiently strong, especially for solar sea plants, that more detailed cost studies and development work is called for.

The satellite concept is further in the future. The cost of photovoltaic cells is still prohibitive and awaits the development of mass production techniques. Dr. Glaser is optimistic that large scale production will cut the cost substantially, but whether the factor of 100 to 1000, which is required, will be gained is an open question.

Solar energy has been the poor cousin of other forms of energy, particularly fission, in the federal research and development budget. In 1971, less than 1% of Federal research and development money went into solar research. Following reports like the NSF/NASA Solar Energy Panel Report [1] and that of Senator Jackson's committee, the situation may improve somewhat. The NSF/NASA report called for a total research and development expenditure of $4 billion for solar research, leading to savings of as much as hundreds of billions of dollars in later years due to decreased dependence on fossil fuels. There has been a small absolute (but large percentage) increase in Federal funding in the last few years and, hopefully, this will continue.

Perhaps one cannot expect the power companies to extend themselves in this direction. They have a short term commitment of profits to their stockholders and it may require more imagination than they are capable of to invest in solar power plants at present. The Federal government on the other hand, should be willing to pass on some of the fission work responsibility to the electrical power industry and instead fund research that may have longer term payoffs. This seems to be especially true of solar energy where the benefits compared to fission seem so large.

Questions

1. "Solar energy is too diffuse a source ever to make a significant impact on world energy needs." Support or criticize this statement.
2. How realistic is the proposal to meet 30% of the total United States energy needs in the year 2000 by solar energy?
3. Discuss some of the indirect methods of using solar energy. Give some examples of past and present applications of solar energy.
4. Assume that 180 w/m² of solar energy falls on the United States averaged over 24 hours. If the total energy use of the United States is 20×10^{12} kwh/year, what area of land is required to provide this total energy, assuming a conversion efficiency of solar energy into other forms of 20%?
5. Which applications of solar energy are likely to be used earliest in the United States? Why?
6. Mark the *false* statement concerning solar energy:
   (a) it is diffuse.
   (b) it poses few environmental problems when compared to fossil or nuclear energy.
   (c) it is non-renewable.
   (d) it is not yet economically competitive with either fossil fuels or nuclear energy.
   (e) it is not available 24 hours a day.

Bibliography

[1] *Solar Energy as a National Energy Resource.* NSF/NASA Solar Energy Panel, December, 1972.

[2] *Energy Research and Development.* Report of the Task Force on Energy, 92nd Congress Second Session, December, 1972.

[3] Solar energy: the largest resource. *Science,* September 22, 1972.

[4] Photovoltaic cells: direct conversion of solar energy. *Science,* November 17, 1972.

[5] Solar energy: proposal for a major research program. *Science,* March 23, 1973, p. 1116.

[6] A. B. Meinel and Marjorie Meinel: Physics looks at solar energy. *Physics Today,* February, 1972.

[7] *Research Applied to Solar-Thermal Power Systems, NSF/RANN/SE/91-34871/PR/72/4.* December, 1972. Prepared by University of Minnesota and Honeywell.

[8] Peter E. Glaser: Solar power via satellite. *IEEE Intercon,* 1973. Reprinted by Arthur D. Little Inc. Cambridge Mass.

[9] Clarence Zener: Solar sea power. *Physics Today,* January, 1973.

[10] W. D. Metz: Ocean temperature gradients: solar power from the sea. *Science,* June 22, 1973, p. 1266.

[11] G. C. Szego: The US energy problem. *Intertechnology Corporation Report C645,* National Science Foundation, November, 1971.

[12] B. J. Brinkworth: *Solar Energy for Man.* John Wiley & Sons, New York, 1972.

[13] F. Daniels: *Direct Use of the Sun's Energy.* Ballantine Books, 1974.

CHAPTER **14**

The Possibilities Remaining

14-1 Introduction

Thus far we have examined the major energy resources being used at present plus some sources that appear likely to supply a major fraction of the energy needs in the future. None of these energy sources has been without problems. Either the resource has a comparatively finite lifetime, or it is extremely polluting or has associated health hazards, or there are significant technical problems that remain to be solved before the resource is really usable. For some of the resources, for example the exploitation of fission energy by means of the breeder reactor, more than one of these difficulties must be overcome.

Let us now ask the question—what are the other possibilities? Are there other energy resources that we could tap which might supply a significant fraction of our energy needs? In this chapter we will briefly discuss these remaining possibilities and see whether any of them could be a significant component of the future energy economy.

173

14-2 Geothermal Energy

One form of energy that has been known and used for some time is heat from the earth itself—geothermal energy. In 1904, this source was being used in Larderello, Italy. This geothermal field now has a generating capacity of about 400 Mw. Another field, in Wairakei on the North Island of New Zealand, already has a capacity of nearly 200 Mw.

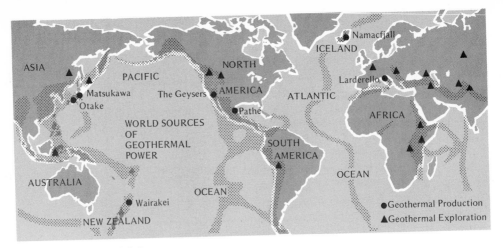

Figure 14-1
The dotted regions indicate geothermal activity.

In the United States, the only operating geothermal plant is the Geysers, north of San Francisco, with a capacity of about 82 Mw, although expansion to almost 500 Mw is planned.

Where does this energy come from and what is its potential for future expansion? The crust of the earth is only 20 to 35 mi thick, much thinner than the layer beneath, called the mantle, which stretches down about 1800 mi to the hot molten core. The mantle provides the source of molten hot rock and gases called magma that erupts in a volcanic explosion. The heat comes from the radioactive decay of materials within the core. This heat is so intense that it can melt rock in the mantle. The hot rock may produce pockets of heat near the surface which can interact with water to form steam or hot water. Because the system is usually confined, these fluids are often found to be at a high pressure and at temperatures above the boiling point of water. For example, at the Geyers field the steam is emitted at a pressure of 100 psi* (pounds per square inch) and 205°C.

These geothermal features usually occur in the volcanic regions at the boundaries of the earth's crustal plates. Figure 14-1 shows that these regions occur on nearly all continents. The western states appear to be the major promising areas for further exploration in the United States.

There are three main types of field from which geothermal power may in principle be extracted. The first and most useful is dry steam, such as is available in the three geothermal fields mentioned above. This source can be used directly to turn a turbine and generate electricity at substantial savings over fossil fuel or nuclear plants.

* Note 1 psi = 6.89×10^3 N/m² (newton per square meter); atmospheric pressure ≈ 15 psi.

Although more dry steam regions may be found following further exploration, this is unlikely to be a major resource.

A more common source of geothermal energy gives wet steam mixed with hot water at generally lower temperatures (150–200°F) than the dry steam areas. Although this provides a larger resource, it is also more difficult to use and has not enjoyed any commercial exploitation to date. One suggestion for using the lower temperature fluids is to use these to heat a secondary fluid, such as isobutane, which has a higher vapor pressure than water. This is a similar technique to that suggested for the solar sea power plants, but higher operating temperatures could be used. New turbines would need to be designed to operate efficiently at lower temperatures, but if this could be done it would open up much larger reserves of geothermal energy. There is an additional advantage in this method in that it would not expose the turbine to the corrosive materials usually contained in the hot primary fluid.

In particular locations, hot water and steam have been used as local heat sources. For example, the city of Reykjavik, the capital of Iceland, uses geothermal hot water to heat houses and buildings, swimming pools, and greenhouses. The stone covered hot water pipes even serve as year around bicycle paths (Figure 14-2). Similar use, although on a smaller scale, is made of geothermal hot water in the United States both in Oregon and in Idaho.

Figure 14-2
Hot water pipes in Reykjavik, Iceland, make snow-free bicycle paths even in winter. [Courtesy of United Nations.]

The largest geothermal source near the surface is probably hot rock, but this may also be the most difficult to exploit. Exploration by a group at the Los Alamos Scientific Laboratory (LASL) has uncovered rock with a temperature around 300°C at a depth of 2300 m. A different field in Montana is estimated by the discoverer Dr. Blackwell to have temperatures of 500 to 700°C within 1000 to 2000 m of the surface. The cost of drilling through hard rock is sizable and techniques have still to be tested for extracting the heat from the dry hot rock.

One such process, called hydrofracturing, consists of creating large cracks in the hard rock and then making water flow down one well and up another to extract the heat. This process would probably also involve the use of a secondary fluid as the working fluid for a turbine to generate electricity. Much testing of such schemes and further exploration for convenient fields are required before this can be considered a significant source. If suitable methods can be found, hot rock fields would be the main hope of geothermal energy as a substantial resource.

Geothermal energy is not without its problems. First, the power plant must be located at the source of steam to optimize the efficiency by operating at the highest possible temperature. However such locations will probably not be near to the use points so that the electricity produced will have to be transported, thus adding to the total cost. In locations nearer to centers of population, problems of land subsidence as water is extracted from the field can also be severe. This problem may be partially solved by pumping water back into the ground after the heat has been extracted. Seismic effects of drilling into rock and especially the fracturing of hard rock can also be dangerous.

Returning the water deep underground may also be advantageous in preventing the release of very saline solutions into the ground water system. Much of the hot water has a very high salt content which, as was mentioned previously, can be a problem in corroding turbine parts as well as possibly polluting streams of rivers. For example in Salton Sea in California, the salt content of the ground water is 20% compared to only 3.3% in the oceans.

Nor is a geothermal energy plant free of air pollution problems. Even in the dry steam plants, the steam usually comes mixed with some amount of hydrogen sulfide which has the smell of rotten eggs (and is extremely toxic). Depending on the site, the amount of sulfur released may be comparable to that from a coal burning plant. Controls on sulfur emission would also need to be imposed in many cases. Another form of pollution, which is particularly characteristic of geothermal plants, is noise pollution. The noise of escaping steam is ear-piercing and, although silencers are usually employed, noise can be a particular nuisance.

Finally, because geothermal plants work with low temperature steam when compared to fossil fuel plants, they are intrinsically less efficient. The Geysers plant, for example, has an efficiency of only about 22% compared to about 40% for a modern fossil fuel plant. Therefore geothermal plants have a correspondingly larger thermal effluent. However much of the heat energy is vented directly to the atmosphere. Nevertheless, the output of hot water is another reason for returning the flow-through water into the ground again.

In summary, geothermal energy is a useful supplement to present energy sources, particularly in certain locations. However, it is not without its environmental impact, although most of the problems do not seem to be extremely difficult to overcome. The most serious weakness of geothermal energy appears to be its rather limited availability. Unless the technology of energy release from hot rock at great depths is developed or dramatic new drilling techniques are found, then energy from the earth will prove to be only a limited, albeit useful, resource.

14-3 Hydroelectric Power

Hydroelectric power is very widely used throughout the world supplying almost one third of the world's electricity. Norway, which has the highest electrical production per capita in the world, uses hydroelectric power almost exclusively. In the United States about one sixth of the electric power is generated by water (hydro) power turning large water turbines.

Hydroelectric energy is really a form of solar energy because the sun's energy evaporates water causing streams and rivers to flow as the water falls again to the earth as rain. Large dams stop the flowing rivers and produce large stored quantities of water. The stored water possesses potential energy. The height of the water in the dam gives rise to a high pressure at the base. Water released near the bottom of the dam spouts out with a high velocity and spins special water turbines to produce electricity.

The technology of hydroelectric power generation is well developed, and very large plants have been built both in the United States and in other countries. The largest project in the world is the 4500-Mw Bratsk Dam plant in the U.S.S.R (Figure 14-3). Two other Russian power plants have capacities around 2500 Mw. The largest United States plant, of about 2000 Mw, is associated with the Grand Coulee dam, and a new plant of 3600 Mw has been authorized for this same site.

Hydroelectric power is one of the cheapest and cleanest ways of producing electricity, which explains its high degree of implementation in many countries. This is also a renewable resource in that the dams are kept filled by rainfall year after year. There is the probability

Figure 14-3
Hydroelectric energy: the Bratsk Dam in the U.S.S.R. supplies 4,500 Mw of power.
[Novosti Press Agency Photo.]

that a particular dam will silt up over the years and become less useful, but this process seems to be extremely slow for most dams.

The main difficulty of this energy source is the lack of suitable sites for more plants. The Report of the Task Force on Energy of the 92nd Congress, in discussing the future of hydroelectric power generation in the United States stated,

If hydropower expansions occur as planned, about 60 percent of the potential hydroelectric energy in the United States will be harnessed by 1985. The remaining undeveloped potential will be found in widely scattered, small sites in the range of 50 to 150 megawatts that may never be developed for economic reasons.

One might also question whether these sites should be developed for ecological reasons. It would be a great pity if all our wild rivers were tamed to produce power. Some intrinsic values, although hard to quantify, are present in wilderness, and we should be hesitant to destroy what little remains.

In any case, with hydropower supplying about 4% of the present United States energy needs and with the percentage almost certainly decreasing as our total energy use increases, hydropower is definitely not a possible answer to the overall resource problem.

14-4   Magnetohydrodynamics

This long word, usually abbreviated **MHD,** describes a system that in principle is very simple and would allow more efficient use of fossil fuel resources. The basic idea is to replace the copper current windings in a conventional generator with a stream of ionized gas (Figure 14-4). The ionized gas is produced in a combustion chamber that could burn a number of fuels. Coal and natural gas have both been suggested, and in the United States the MHD process is thought to be an advantageous way of using large coal resources. Small amounts of an alkali metal, such as sodium or potassium, are added to increase the conductivity of the flowing gas. The ionized gas serves as a moving conductor and generates a dc current which flows off through electrodes in the wall of the chamber. Because essentially no moving parts are required, very high temperatures can be used (2400°C) which would normally melt the turbine blades of a conventional generator.

The high operating temperature means that the efficiency of an MHD plant will be greater than that of a conventional generating plant, thus saving fossil fuels. At present, most modern fossil fuel plants are only 40% efficient, which means that 60% of the energy in the fuel is simply expelled as heated water to pollute the surroundings

Figure 14-4
A schematic of an MHD generator. Powdered coal burns fiercely in a combustion chamber (1). Squirting through a nozzle (2) at supersonic speed, combustion gases stream between magnets (3), yielding an electric current taken off by electrodes (4).

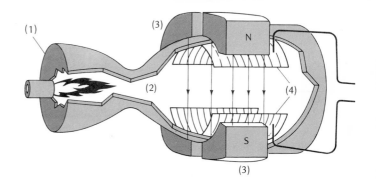

thermally. Because electric power plants use about 25% of the total United States energy budget, a 40% efficiency means that 15% of the total United States energy use is simply discarded. With the MHD process combined with a regular steam generator, efficiencies as high as 50% are expected, and with larger MHD plants the efficiencies could run as high as 60%. Even at 50% efficiency, a saving of 20% in fuel supply is realized to produce the same electrical output. This increase in efficiency also leads to less thermal pollution by such power plants. Once again basic physics tells us that the higher the temperature, the greater the efficiency, and the less waste heat.

The MHD generators also appear to have the additional advantage of decreased pollution from emission of gaseous nitrogen oxides or sulfur compounds. At first it was thought that these products would pose more serious emission control problems at the higher temperatures involved. It turns out, however, that the sulfur reacts readily with the alkali seed material to form alkali sulfates that are easily precipitated. The nitrogen oxides appear also to be fairly easily controlled by burning a fuel rich mixture and adding extra air downstream. This means that MHD plants could burn higher sulfur content coal without seriously damaging the environment.

Although the United States was one of the early proponents of MHD, research in this country has not been pursued as rapidly as in other countries. Japan, West Germany, and the U.S.S.R. are all probably ahead of the United States at the present. For example, a 70-kw generator using natural gas as a fuel has been operated in the U.S.S.R., and designs for much larger plants up to 1500-Mw are under way. The compact design of the MHD generator lends itself to large scale plants, which is in keeping with the general trend of modern power plants and will probably also tend to increase their efficiency.

MHD work in the United States is still on a small scale, with Dr. Kantrowitz of Avco Cooporation, an early pioneer in MHD, working on development of a pilot plant. The United States effort is funding the development of a coal fired MHD plant and is therefore involved in a rather more difficult problem than the other countries which are using cleaner fuels.

Some of the difficulties that are worrysome in such a scheme are the buildup of coal ash or alkali compounds on the walls of the flow-through tube as well as the uncertainty about the lifetime of the generator at the high temperatures involved. Another problem is that high magnetic fields are required. These are best supplied by superconducting magnets. Fortunately large superconducting magnets have been developed for studying short lived particles in high energy physics so that a good deal of the basic technology exists. Detailed designs and cost estimates are now required.

In summary, MHD could extend the lifetime of fossil fuels, especially coal by 20 to 40% because of the increased operating efficiency. This technique may also permit burning high sulfur coal with less pollution. MHD is being developed in other countries and should be pursued more vigorously in this country. A Massachusetts Institute of Technology study proposed a 10-year research effort culminating in the design of a 1500-Mw MHD power plant.

14-5 Energy from Solid Wastes

One of the products of our consumer society is an ever increasing amount of solid waste—garbage, which must be disposed of. Each day, on the average, 5 lb of garbage are produced for every person in the United States. An even greater amount of agricultural wastes are produced so that the total amount of solid waste produced every year is about 3×10^9 tons.

The question arises whether this supply of fuel, much of it organic, can be used as a source of energy. The city of St. Louis already burns shredded trash mixed with coal and saves half a ton of coal for every ton of garbage burned. There are economic advantages because the trash must be collected and disposed of in any case at a cost of around $10 per ton.

However there are a number of obvious disadvantages. Although the total amount of solid waste is quite large, about half of it is water and only about 15% is readily collectable (see Table 14-1). At best this would supply about 3% of the 1971 consumption of oil and 6% of the consumption of natural gas. Therefore, unless improved collection

Table 14-1
Amounts (10^6 tons) of Dry, Ash-Free Organic Solid Wastes Produced in the United States in 1971

	Wastes Generated	Readily Collectable
manure	200	26.0
urban refuse	129	71.0
logging and wood manufacturing residues	55	5.0
agricultural crops and food wastes	390	22.6
industrial wastes	44	5.2
municipal sewage solids	12	1.5
miscellaneous	50	5.0
Total	880	136.3
Net oil potential (10^6 bbl)	1098	170
Net methane potential (10^9 ft^3)	8.8	1.36

SOURCE: L. L. Anderson, Bureau of Mines Information Circular 8549, (1972), p. 131. See also [3].

processes are developed, solid waste will not have a major impact on our total energy requirements.

The main processes for handling these solid wastes to produce energy have already been discussed in Section 13-6 when we dealt with the production of oil and gas from specially cultivated agricultural products. These are hydrogenation—a chemical reduction of the organics producing oil at a net return of about 1.25 bbl/ton of dry waste; pyrolysis, which involves burning the dry waste, producing solids (char), oil, and a low quality gas; and bioconversion through treatment with bacteria. This latter process has been used to treat sewage for some time and has promise of producing a high quality gas containing a large proportion of methane.

As mentioned before the main questions to be answered in these areas are economic, and these can probably only be decided by building pilot plants as test runs. In any case, although any of these methods of treatment may be an attractive method of waste disposal it does not appear that they will have a major impact on the energy economy.

14-6   Tidal Energy

Standing on an ocean beach, especially after a storm, one cannot help but be impressed by the energy contained in surging waves. Although it is impractical to tap the energy of a breaking wave, there have been attempts to harness the gravitational energy of tidal motion of the ocean. The technique is to build a low dam that traps the high-tide water. The water can then be released to run a water turbine and produce electricity in a similar way to hydroelectric generation.

The only working tidal power plant is in the Rance River Estuary in France (Figure 14-5) where a 240-Mw generator has been in operation since 1967. A few other sites, which either have narrow entrances to a bay or have extremely high tides, look promising. The Bay of Fundy on the Atlantic Ocean between Maine, New Brunswick, and Nova Scotia has possibly the highest tides in the world—53 ft. A site in northeastern Australia, Collier Bay, has tides up to 40 ft and, in addition, has a very narrow inlet channel. The tidal velocity is extremely high.

The main difficulty in exploiting this resource is the high capital cost of building the large dam usually required. There appear to be few pollution problems associated with the use of tidal energy so that its viability may increase as the cost of pollution control equipment drives up the cost of other energy sources. This is also a renewable resource that we do not deplete with use.

Figure 14-5
Looking upstream at the Rance River Estuary Power Plant—the first in the world to generate electricity from tidal energy. [Courtesy of Electricité de France.]

However, at best, tidal energy will provide a local energy source because the number of suitable sites is not nearly enough to make any significant impact on the total energy picture.

14-7 Energy from the Wind

Wind power is another energy resource that man harnessed many years ago. Sailing ships used wind power to transport men and cargo around the world. The sight of a modern sailboat with full sails on sunlit water can still expand one's spirit. On a more mundane level, windmills have been used to pump water and generate electricity for many years. As recently as 1950, there were still about 50,000 kw of wind-driven generators in the midwest. In Denmark before World War II, 100 Mw of electricity was generated using wind energy. Perhaps the largest windmill in the world (175 ft in diameter) was used for about 4 years on Grandpa Knob in Vermont to power a 1.25-Mw generator. This produced a total of 3.6×10^5 kwh of electricity before a blade broke in 1945.

With electricity readily available from large central power stations, the use of wind power has decreased over the years. Recently because of its minimal environmental impact, wind power has enjoyed somewhat of a revival of interest. Bob Reines, who built the home in Arizona discussed in the chapter on solar energy, used a windmill to generate electricity. Windmills can be found advertised in books like the last *Whole Earth Catalogue* [8]. In some cases wind power can still be advantageous on a small scale, for example, in remote areas where the installation of power lines would be expensive.

Wind is really a form of solar energy because the winds are generated by differential heating of air by the sun or by sun warmed land or sea. It is therefore a renewable, long term resource.

On the other hand, wind power is notoriously unreliable and intermittent, so that it must be coupled to a storage system to be useful. On a small scale, wind generators are usually used to charge batteries,

Table 14-2
Maximum Electrical Energy Production From Wind Power*

Site	Annual Power Production (kwh)	Maximum Possible by Year
(1) Offshore, New England	159×10^9	1990
(2) Offshore, New England	318×10^9	2000
(3) Offshore, eastern seaboard, along the 100-m contour, Ambrose shipping channel south to Charleston, S.C.	283×10^9	2000
(4) Along the east-west axis, Lake Superior (320 m)	35×10^9	2000
(5) Along the north-south axis, Lake Michigan (220 m)	29×10^9	2000
(6) Along the north-south axis, Lake Huron (160 m)	23×10^9	2000
(7) Along the west-east axis, Lake Erie (200 m)	23×10^9	2000
(8) Along the west-east axis, Lake Ontario (160 m)	23×10^9	2000
(9) Through the Great Plains from Dallas, Texas, north in a path 300 mi wide west-east, and 1300 mi long, south to north. Wind stations to be clustered in groups of 165, at least 60 mi between groups (sparse coverage)	210×10^9	2000
(10) Offshore the Texas Gulf Coast, along a length of 400 mi from the Mexican border, eastward, along the 100-m contour	190×10^9	2000
(11) Along the Aleutian Chain, 1260 mi, on transects each 35 mi long, spaced at 60-mi intervals, between 100-m contours. Hydrogen is to be liquefied and transported to California by tanker	402×10^9	2000
(Estimated total production possible: 1.536×10^{12} kwh by year 2000)		

* Data taken from "Solar Energy as a National Energy Resource" NSF/NASA Solar Energy Panel, Dec. 1972.

although on a larger scale alternative storage systems such as hydrogen storage are possible.

Professor Heronemus of the University of Massachusetts argues that large scale wind production is technically and economically feasible, using suitable sites, such as off the East Coast, in the Great Plains, and especially on the Aleutian Island chain in the North Pacific. Table 14-2, taken from the NSF/NASA study on solar energy lists possible likely sites and the maximum electrical energy that could be produced by the year 2000. The total is about 1.5×10^{12} kwh/year, generated either by 200-ft, 2-Mw or 60-ft 100-kw wind turbines.

This can be compared with the total United States energy use in 1970 of 20×10^{12} kwh or the expected total of 55×10^{12} kwh by 2000. Thus, the maximum impact of wind power would be rather small (less than 3%) on this scale, or about 12% of the expected electric capacity. Although small this quantity of pollution-free energy is not negligible, and a large scale test plant should be tried. This same report lists a number of research and development tasks that still need funding, such as more modern windmill and generator designs and studies of the effects of large scale extraction of kinetic energy from the atmosphere.

14-8 Summary and Conclusions

We have looked in detail at some of the alternative sources of energy that might possibly have relieved our resource problem. All have a role to play, either by increasing the efficiency of our use of fossil fuels (MHD) or as useful supplementary energy sources. Many of these sources, such as tidal or geothermal power, may have significant local impact. Others, for example wind power, will require the development of better storage systems, such as hydrogen storage. The renewable nature of most of these resources as well as their general nonpolluting nature are significant advantages. Unfortunately, none of these resources appear likely to supply sufficient total quantity of energy to meet the growing demand.

Questions

1. What fraction of the United States demand for energy in the year 2000 is likely to be met by geothermal energy?
2. In what ways does the production of electricity from geothermal energy differ from more conventional electrical production?

3. Name two technological advances that would substantially increase the utility of geothermal energy. Explain the reasons for your choice.
4. Why is hydroelectric power not seen as having a significant impact on United States energy needs?
5. "Apart from fossil, fission, fusion, or direct solar energy, no other source can meet more than 10% of the energy needs of the United States by the year 2000." Defend or attack this statement.
6. Name 10 sources of energy and outline the main advantages and disadvantages of each of them.
7. Why is wind energy regarded as a form of solar energy?
8. What are the main problems with the widespread use of wind energy?

Bibliography

[1] Geothermal energy: an emerging major resource. *Science*, September 15, 1972.
[2] Magnetohydrodynamic power: more efficient use of coal. *Science*, October 27, 1972.
[3] Fuel from wastes: a minor energy resource. *Science*, November 10, 1972.
[4] R. G. Brown and E. A. Groh: Geothermal—earth's primordial energy. *Technology Review*, October/November, 1971.
[5] *Energy Research and Development*. Report of the Task Force on Energy, 92nd Congress, December, 1972.
[6] K. F. Weaver and E. Kinstof: The search for tomorrow's power. *National Geographic*, November, 1972.
[7] The promise of unconventional energy source. *Batelle Research Outlook*, Vol. 4, No. 1, 1972.
[8] *The Last Whole Earth Catalogue*. Random House, updated August, 1972, p. 69.
[9] E. W. Golding: *The Generation of Electricity by Wind Power*. Philosophical Library, New York, 1955.
[10] P. C. Putnam: *Power from the Wind*, D. Van Nostrand Co., 1948.

PART **FOUR**

OTHER PROBLEMS

Energy Transportation and Storage

15-1 Introduction

In the last five chapters we have examined many possible energy resources both those presently used and others proposed for the future. We have seen that oil and gas resources are extremely short lived and that coal is also a finite though longer lived resource. The use of coal as a major energy resource is also accompanied by the environmental problems of air pollution and land despoilation. The major available alternative — energy from fission — also has serious environmental questions associated with its use, including safety, monitoring emissions, and the storage of long lived radioactive wastes.

We also noted in Chapter 14 that a number of exotic alternative resources will almost certainly not meet a substantial fraction of our growing energy demand, although they may be useful local supplements. This left as the only two viable alternatives for comparatively nonpolluting major energy resources — fusion and solar energy. Neither of these alternatives are technically or economically available at this stage and they both still suffer at present from lack of sufficient research and development support and emphasis. Considerable effort, therefore, still needs to be devoted to the development of energy resources, particularly long term resources.

Even if we were able to solve our resource problem, there would still be other difficulties associated with our rapid increase in energy consumption. One of these problems, which poses a fundamental limitation to our energy use, is global thermal pollution which will be discussed in the next chapter.

189

15-2 The Power Problem

Another problem which is seen most clearly for electric energy is the problem of fluctuating demand. This could possibly be characterized not so much as an energy problem but rather as a power problem. (Power, remember, is the time rate of energy use.) The demand for electricity changes with the time of day and with the temperature outdoors as well as with long term seasonal variations. Electric utilities must prepare for these variations by increasing their maximum operating capacity to meet peak loads, although this means that a particular power plant is often operating at only 50% of its peak capacity. Such variations are also seen in other energy demands although usually less noticeably than for electricity.

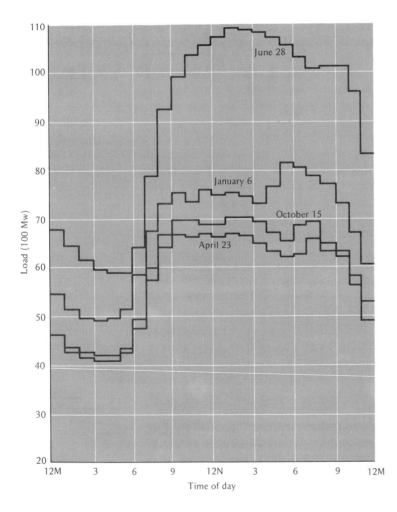

Figure 15-1
Daily load profiles of Commonwealth Edison, which serves the metropolitan Chicago area, for four days in 1971. The peak load for the system, 10,953 Mw, occurred between 1 and 2 P.M. on June 28. The maximum temperature, 101°F, equaled the all-time record for that date. During June 28 the power required from Commonwealth Edison varied from a low of 5987 Mw between 4 and 5 A.M. to the 10,953 Mw peak, a near doubling of required generating capacity on stream. The winter peak, 8349 Mw, occurred between 5 and 6 P.M. on January 6, 1971, when the temperature ranged from −5 to +7°F. Between 3 and 4 A.M. on that day 4938 Mw of power were demanded. These two days represent the peak summer and winter load demands of Commonwealth Edison. The April 23 and October 15 profiles are typical of spring and fall days for that utility. [Courtesy of Commonwealth Edison.]

Figure 15-2

This shows a load duration curve used by electric utilities in system analysis. The variation in power demands results in about 30% of the peak capacity being required at *all* times. (Commonwealth Edison, for example, had a minimum 1971 demand of 3002 Mw, 27% of the 10,953 Mw peak.) This power is produced by "base-load plants"; in fact, up to 45% of the peak power often comes from base-load units. These are the newer, more efficient fossil fuel and nuclear plants that are kept in almost constant service (except for required maintenance) to take advantage of their low delivered energy cost, and, because they are "on" most of the time, they provide 70% of the energy.

The top 20% of the maximum capacity is required for only about 15% of the year and produces, at high unit cost, only a few per cent of the total energy output of the system. The units used to provide this power are commonly referred to as peaking units. Between the base-load plants and the peaking units are the intermediate cycling plants, which are routinely cycled on and off load. These units are often operated during the peak daily hours from early morning to evening and are taken out of service overnight. [Information from Argonne National Laboratory Report ANL–7958 March, 1973.]

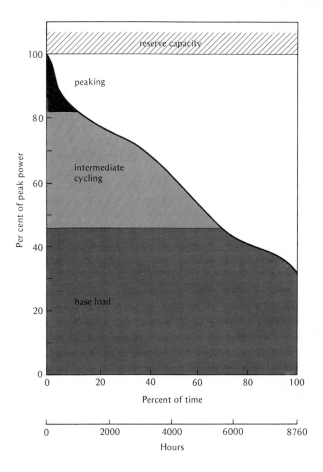

As fossil fuel supplies have tightened we have become more aware of the fuel oil shortage in winter and a gasoline shortage in the summer months as people drive more. New car introductions and seasonal shopping also introduce fluctuations into the manufacturing and commercial sectors of the energy picture. However the problem is particularly acute for the electric utilities. In addition, the indication from our energy consumption patterns is that we are going to become increasingly dependent upon electricity. This makes the power problem even more important.

Both daily and seasonal fluctuations are clearly seen in the electric load profiles of Commonwealth Edison (which serves metropolitan Chicago) shown in Figure 15-1. Note that there is usually about twice the demand in the middle of the day as there is around 4 A.M. The figure also clearly shows the extremely high demand during the summer months (for air conditioning) and the less noticeable peak in January due to increased heating and lighting demands.

The electric utilities divide their generating capacity into three main kinds to help meet the fluctuating demand. These are called base load, intermediate cycling, and peaking. The use of these different capacities is shown in Figure 15-2. The base-load plant, which is generally the cheapest producer of electricity, runs most of the time (except for maintenance) and provides between 30 and 50% of the peak power demand. Peaking power, often provided by gas turbines, is generally much more expensive and provides only a few per cent of the total demand. Intermediate cycling is usually used to take account of regular daily fluctuation. Substantial cost savings would result if more of the total demand could be provided by the base-load facility. In addition, because base-load facilities are usually more modern, either fossil fuel or nuclear, they are generally less polluting than the intermediate cycling or peaking units.

Some imaginative proposals have been developed for smoothing out some of these fluctuations, including suggestions for improved storage of energy or the transportation of energy less wastefully. Many of these suggestions also involve more dispersed energy use systems, which are generally less vulnerable to either accident or deliberate attack. The great blackouts we have seen, including the one that darkened New York City and much of the northeast seaboard in 1965, would be much less likely if energy systems were more dispersed. We now turn to a discussion of some of these proposals.

15-3 Hydro Storage

The advantage of using spare electric capacity during off-peak hours to store energy in a large water reservoir has been realized for some time. However it is only since 1971 that substantial pump storage systems have been used. The largest pumped hydro storage facility in the world has recently been completed at Ludington, Michigan, on the shores of Lake Michigan. Six reversible water turbines pump water into a huge reservoir (Figure 15-3). As demand requires, the water can be released to turn the same turbines and generate electricity. The capacity of this giant facility is almost 2000 Mw.

The main advantage of this system is that it requires a smaller capital cost to provide a peak load capability than the provision of additional generating facilities. The base-load facility can be used at off-peak times to fill the reservoir, thus allowing it to run at a more constant rate, and therefore cutting costs and increasing its lifetime. Hydro storage, like hydroelectric generation from a normal dam, is also a rather clean, nonpolluting source of power, if one neglects the effects of generating the electricity to pump the water.

On the negative side, the fact that the water rises and falls so much means that, at best, the lake formed is unusable for recreation and at

Figure 15-3

This pumped-storage hydroelectric facility built at Ludington, Michigan, is the largest of its kind in the world. During off-peak hours, such as late at night and on weekends when demand for electricity is low, water from Lake Michigan is pumped by six reverse hydraulic turbines up the hill and into a 27×10^9 gal man-made reservoir. There it is stored until the power need is at its peak during the day and early evening. Then the water is released to fall through the facility's pump-turbines, generating electricity on its way back to the lake. Each of the six pump-turbine motor-generator units will be able to produce 312,000 kw of electricity. When all six are operating, the generating capacity will be about 1.9×10^6 kw. By 1980, when Michigan's residents are expected to be using twice as much electric energy as they do today, a substantial portion of that tremendous amount of electric power will come from this vast storage facility. [Courtesy of Consumers Power Company.]

worst may be a eyesore as the water retreats. Care will also be needed to ensure that erosion of the surroundings is not accelerated by the large volume of water that is regularly emitted at high velocity from the plant. The Storm King project in Cornwall, N. Y., has been delayed since 1965 by questions raised concerning the environmental impact of the plant.

Another disadvantage is that through the cycle of pumping and regeneration of electricity, there are significant losses of efficiency. A pumped-storage plant probably runs at only about a 60 to 70% efficiency which, coupled to the 30 to 40% initial generating efficiency, means that substantial amounts of fuel are being used to provide the peak load.

Perhaps the biggest handicap to the growth of pumped-storage systems is the lack of suitable sites. A high site overlooking a large body of water, preferably near a large consumer area is required, and there are just not very many such sites available.

15-4 Compressed Air Storage

A similar concept, but one that seems to suffer from fewer disadvantages, is the proposal to use compressed air as a means of storing energy. Instead of pumping water at off-peak times, the base-load facility could be used to compress air in a large underground reservoir.

Because gas turbines use a substantial fraction of the power developed to compress air injected into the combustion chamber, a source of compressed air would mean substantial savings in fuel costs. Such gas turbines can work at much higher efficiencies, particularly if waste heat is added to the stored gas as it is released, so that this system is much less wasteful of primary energy resources. The underground reservoirs could be man-made with explosives and would not be extremely constrained by siting requirements. Alternatively, natural caverns could also be used after suitable leak-proofing. Even if small leaks did develop, these would probably not be serious because only air would be released.

Further detailed studies are required on both gas turbine modifications and geological surveys to find and test suitable sites. Environmental impacts (which appear small) and comparison of the economics, especially compared with hydro storage, would also be required before some pilot plants are tried. Nevertheless, this does seem a promising and fairly simple storage system that should be pursued.

15-5 Storage Batteries

Chemical storage batteries may be the most familiar energy storage system. Every automobile has a lead/acid battery permanently installed. Small dry cells are used to energize flashlights, operate transistor radios, and power numerous other small appliances. In both of these systems, the basic principle is that chemical energy is transformed into electric energy. The big advantage of the lead/acid automobile battery is that the process is reversible so that the battery is recharged as the engine turns over. The property of rechargeability is very important for any realistic long term storage system.

The use of batteries as a means of storing energy for peak load use by utilities has many advantages. The main one probably is that the batteries can be readily distributed near the point of use so that transportation facilities do not need to be scaled to peak power use, thus reducing cost. Widely used but polluting supplies of peak power, such as gas turbines, could also be eliminated. In addition, batteries come in modular units so that a system can be readily enlarged as the peak demand increases.

As well as serving as peak load suppliers of electricity, batteries could also be used in a number of emergency applications by police, fire stations, hospitals, computer centers, or research installations where temporary loss of power may be extremely damaging to people or sensitive materials. All-electric automobiles, especially if used in cities, would relieve the drastic air pollution problems caused by the internal combustion engine. Both Great Britain and Germany are investigating battery powered public transportation systems.

Unfortunately no suitable battery system is yet available, although recent and continuing research on lithium/sulfur and soldium/sulfur cells looks promising. To compete economically with alternative forms of energy storage, batteries must cost about $12 to $15 per kwh of energy stored and have lifetimes of 5 years in which they may be cycled up to 1500 times. The total energy storage per unit mass should also be high, to allow continual use for a significant time without excessive mass. The power deliverable per unit mass should be as large as possible because this would imply rapid recharging. This feature is probably even more important for automobile use than for storage batteries, although cost and lifetime sacrifices could perhaps be tolerated even for automobile batteries.

Table 15-1 taken from the Intertechnology Report to the NSF lists some characteristics of current battery systems. While most of the batteries listed have better characteristics than the lead/acid automobile battery, the costs are prohibitive for widespread use because of the fairly expensive materials involved.

Recent work has focussed on higher temperature batteries that operate at 300 to 600°C. Two of the main types that are being investigated are lithium/sulfur (Li/S) and sodium/sulfur (Na/S) systems. The Argonne National Laboratory has done much of the work in the Li/S system and a number of large private companies including Ford, General Electric, and Dow Chemical all have active programs on the development of a Na/S battery.

Present cells are in the 400 w range, but larger batteries up to 30 kw are planned. The overall goals of the program are to produce cells with energy storage capacity of 200 wh/kg that will operate for thousands of cycles at a cost of about $15 per kwh. Although the prognosis

Table 15-1
Characteristics of Current Battery Systems

	Energy Content (wh/kg)	Maximum Number of Cycles	Cost ($/kwh)
lead/acid	22	1000	55
nickel/cadmium	33–44	2000	320
silver/cadmium	55	200	415
silver/zinc	110–145	100	470

from the Argonne Group is promising, they admit that it will be at least 5 years before a suitable prototype cell is completed.

15-6 The Hydrogen Economy

A recent imaginative proposal for both the storage and transportation of energy is to produce hydrogen. Many of the energy producing systems discussed in the past few chapters, especially solar energy and large scale electrical generation from the winds, depend upon hydrogen production as an important element in the overall design.

Hydrogen normally occurs as a light gas (the mass of one molecule = 2 amu approximately), but it can also be liquified at −253°C (or 20 K). The heat content of 1 scf (standard cubic foot) of hydrogen is 325 btu compared with about 1000 btu/scf for natural gas (mainly methane, CH_4). However, because of its low molecular weight, the energy content per unit mass of liquified hydrogen is 2.75 times that of natural gas. This property has made it an ideal fuel for rockets and makes it an attractive alternative for other types of transportation.

In addition, the most attractive property of hydrogen as a fuel is that the product of its combustion with oxygen is simply water. When hydrogen is burned in air, small amounts of nitrogen oxides are also produced, but these are fairly easily controlled. Hydrogen is therefore a clean fuel, *par excellance*.

Hydrogen gas could be fairly readily transported over the well developed network of natural gas pipelines (Figure 15-4). Although the energy content per unit volume is smaller than natural gas, hydrogen can be pumped more easily so that a given pipe will carry about the same amount of energy of either gas. Hydrogen could be used as a replacement for natural gas in many household and commercial uses with only small modifications to existing systems.

Because of the excellent distribution facilities already existing for natural gas, transportation of hydrogen is probably easier than electric

MAJOR NATURAL GAS PIPELINES
AS OF JUNE 30, 1973

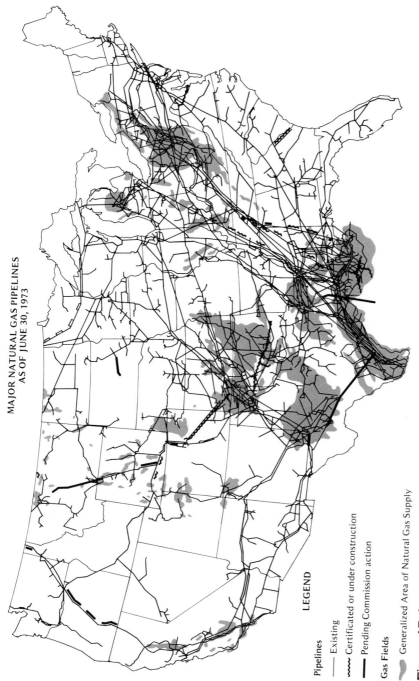

LEGEND

Pipelines
—— Existing
～～ Certificated or under construction
━━ Pending Commission action

Gas Fields
▨ Generalized Area of Natural Gas Supply

Figure 15-4

Trunk pipelines extending for 252,000 miles (black lines) already exist in the United States for transmission of natural gas from areas where the gas is produced (gray) to areas where it is consumed. The system, which is constructed almost entirely of welded steel pipe, carries approximately 61.4×10^9 ft^3 (or 1.5×10^6 tons) of natural gas per day. Similar networks of underground hydrogen gas pipelines would enable the giant nuclear (or solar) power stations of the future to be located far from the load centers. [Courtesy of American Gas Association and Federal Power Commission.]

power transmission, at least over long distances. In addition much of the ultimate use of electricity is in a heating application which could be met more directly by burning hydrogen. Using hydrogen directly for heating may reduce the need for electric production, depending on the technique used for producing the hydrogen. However it seems likely that in its initial applications at least hydrogen will be used as a means of decreasing peak demand on electrical power plants.

Because hydrogen is so light, it diffuses rapidly so that there has been some question as to whether it could be stored in large underground caverns like natural gas. The answer seems probably yes, because a gas consisting of 50% hydrogen has been stored in caverns in France with no difficulty. An attractive alternative is to liquify the gas and store it in the liquid form at low temperatures (called cryogenic storage). The technology for such a storage system has been developed both in the space program and in high energy physics where liquid hydrogen is used in large bubble chambers to detect short-lived particles. An extremely large storage tank at Cape Kennedy (Figure 15-5) has a capacity of 9×10^5 gal of liquid hydrogen with an energy content of about 11×10^6 kwh. This is almost three quarters of the energy capacity of the Ludington pumped hydro storage facility discussed in Section 15-3.

Another method of storage relies on the fact that hydrogen diffuses readily into certain metals, such as titanium. The hydrogen molecule is so small, it can squeeze between the metal atoms in the crystal. Surprisingly large amounts of hydrogen can be stored this way by simply exposing the metal to pressurized hydrogen. The concentration of hydrogen absorbed in a metal can be greater than that of liquid hydrogen. The hydrogen can then be easily released by heating the metal. Unfortunately most of the metals that readily absorb hydrogen, namely, titanium, vanadium, and niobium, are also expensive; less expensive metals that serve the same purpose will need to be found to make this technique economically competitive.

At present, hydrogen is commercially produced from fossil fuels, but as these supplies run low new methods of producing hydrogen will be needed. Water (H_2O) is in principle an abundant source of hydrogen, if suitable methods of decomposing the water can be found. A number of methods have been used or are proposed for the production of hydrogen from water. The first of these, electrolysis of water, has already been used commercially in areas where cheap electricity is available.

Electrolysis is a process in which a voltage is applied across a solution. Current is carried through the solution by ions. (An ion is simply an atom or molecule with one or more electrons added or subtracted; it is a *charged* entity unlike atoms or molecules which are electrically neutral.) The ions give up or gain electrons at the electrodes from neutral atoms.

Figure 15-5
Energy storage in the form of liquefied hydrogen is already a routine practice in the space industry. This vacuum-insulated cryogenic tank at the John F. Kennedy Space Center, for example, contains 9×10^5 gal of liquid hydrogen for fueling Apollo rockets. It is the largest facility of its kind in existence. In terms of energy its contents are equivalent to 37.7×10^9 btu of heat or 11×10^6 kwh of electricity. [Courtesy of Chicago Bridge and Iron Company.]

In the electrolysis of water, hydrogen gas is given up at the anode (negative electrode) and oxygen at the cathode (positive electrode). Commercially this process is about 60 to 70% efficient although test cells at high pressures have had efficiencies as high as 85%. In principle efficiencies near 100% should be possible. Electrolysis does seem therefore a reasonably efficient means of storing and transporting electrical energy especially over large distances.

An alternative proposal that does not require the prior generation of electricity, with its typical 30 to 40% efficiency factor, is the direct decomposition of water at high temperatures. Unfortunately the temperature required is around 2500°C, far above that available in a nuclear reactor for example. However, by a multistep process involving mercury and bromine, water can be decomposed at only 730°C with an efficiency of around 50%. So far this process has only been tested in the laboratory, but its proposer Dr. de Beni, hopes shortly to build a pilot plant. If this works then such direct decomposition could probably be done in a nuclear reactor without the need to generate electricity.

A more exotic suggestion by Bernard Eastland of the U.S. Atomic Energy Commission is to generate hydrogen by direct decomposition of water in a fusion reactor—when these are available. He points out that, if aluminum were added to the plasma, radiation would be produced of such a wavelength that it would dissociate water readily into hydrogen and oxygen. The experimental test of this suggestion awaits the development of the fusion reactor (Chapter 12).

Perhaps one of the biggest problems in the widespread use of hydrogen is the "Hindenburg syndrome." In other words there is the concern over the danger of explosion and fire with this dangerous substance. This concern does have some substance not only because hydrogen forms an explosive mixture with air over a wide range of mixtures but more importantly because its ignition energy is only 2×10^{-5} J. For comparison the ignition energy of natural gas is approximately 30×10^{-5} J, 15 times greater. Although this low ignition energy has advantages in combustion processes, it does mean that extreme care in handling hydrogen is required because even small static electrical sparks can cause ignition. However large amounts of hydrogen are widely used in industry and as a rocket fuel and, with proper precautions, few problems have been found. Nevertheless the risks remain as witnessed a few years ago when the hydrogen bubble chamber at the Cambridge Electron Accelerator exploded. It has been argued that because of its rapid diffusion, which clears the hydrogen from an area very quickly it is less dangerous than either natural gas or gasoline, both of which we live with comparatively comfortably.

There still remains the question of cost. At present commercial hydrogen, produced from natural gas, costs about $0.77 per 10^6 btu.

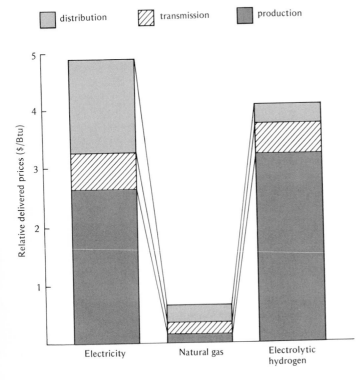

Figure 15-6

Relative delivered prices of various forms of energy are broken down in this bar chart into the shares represented by production (dark shading), transmission (cross hatch), and distribution (light shading). The comparison reveals that, at present, it is much cheaper to buy energy in the form of natural gas than in the form of electricity. Moreover, the breakdown shows that, although the cost of hydrogen produced from electricity must always be higher than the cost of the electricity, the lower transmission and distribution costs of hydrogen already make it possible to sell hydrogen energy to the gas user at a delivered price lower than what he now pays for electricity. It is expected that natural gas prices, together with all fossil fuel prices, will increase rapidly in the future. [From D. Gregory: The hydrogen economy. *Scientific American*, January, 1973.]

Gregory has estimated the production cost of electrolytic hydrogen from water to be around $3.00 per 10^6 btu. However, when one adds transportation and distribution costs, hydrogen comes out ahead of electricity, although both of these are far more expensive than natural gas (Figure 15-6). Natural gas prices will undoubtedly rise due to the increasing shortage so that, at some point, hydrogen will be competitive. In any case, for transporting and storing certain forms of energy such as solar, wind, and probably nuclear, which initially produce electricity, this seems like a reasonable direction in which to proceed.

15-7 Transportation of Fossil Fuels

The hydrogen economy discussed in the last section involves both storage and transportation issues. Let us now turn to more conventional techniques for transporting energy both as fossil fuels and electricity. The technology of fossil fuel transportation has changed little in recent years, although some techniques presently in use, particularly pipeline transportation, are already quite sophisticated.

The widespread use of natural gas stemmed from the development of a nationwide network of pipelines for transporting gas from production site to user. At present in the United States there is about 2.3×10^5 miles of high pressure transmission line, and 5.5×10^5 miles of lower pressure distribution lines carry gas to the consumer. Recent changes have been in the direction of liquifying the gas either domestically as liquid petroleum gas (LPG) or as liquid natural gas (LNG) from overseas. Large cryogenic tankers for transporting the LNG are now in operation and are proving even cheaper per mile than pipeline delivery. Additional costs are involved in liquifaction and storage, but LNG from Algeria is proving a useful supplement to diminishing domestic supplies.

Petroleum liquids are also transported principally either by tanker or by pipeline. With the closing of the Suez Canal in 1966, tanker size has grown tremendously; giant tankers of 3×10^5 tons are in operation and some almost twice as large are on order. Although substantial economies of manpower and fuel are realized with such large tankers, the dangers of substantial spills increase when such huge amounts of oil are carried on one ship. Tankers have an extremely bad reputation, well deserved in most cases, of causing pollution on the open sea. In an attempt to eliminate the worst of these excesses, such as using seawater as ballast and then flushing the oily water back into the sea, a number of new regulations have been drawn up. What impact these will have remains to be seen. In spite of such precautions, there seem to be enough accidents involving tankers to make oil spills an almost inevitable price for transporting oil from one country to another.

Pipeline transportation is generally less hazardous to the environment, although the recent proposal to run a pipeline from the Alaskan Northslope across the arctic tundra has raised serious ecological questions. There are two possibilities: One is to carry the oil through a 48-in. pipeline from Prudhoe Bay to Valdez, Alaska—a distance of 800 miles. The alternative proposal is to take the pipeline through Canada. Although the first alternative involves a shorter distance and is therefore cheaper and is favored by the oil companies, the route is through an earthquake region of Alaska. If the pipe is fractured, considerable damage may be done to the delicate tundra. The other proposal is less subject to damage from earthquakes, but both pipes will have to be laid on permafrost. The heat from the pipe will slowly melt the permafrost and the pipe will sink and possibly break. The second alternative seems preferable (particularly as it will avoid the further ecological dangers of tanker shipment), but much testing remains to develop a suitable pipeline. One suggestion might be to have a mixed pipeline carrying gas and oil with the gas on the outside.

The other fossil fuel, coal, is generally moved by train, which is one of the most expensive means of transportation. Some savings are derived by the use of unit trains, which travel more directly from coal face to consumer without being uncoupled. In some areas, such as the Ohio river, coal barges have also been used. Although this is a cheap technique, it does not provide much flexibility. Unless the consumer can be reached directly by barge, unloading and reloading costs are prohibitive.

A recent approach to coal transportation which is still in the development stage is slurry pipelines for intermediate distances. The coal is finely divided and mixed with water before being pumped through a pipe. A new pipe in Arizona is about 275 miles long and will carry 5×10^6 tons of coal each year. Further development of even longer pipelines is expected.

15-8 Electric Power Transmission

Most projections of United States energy use suggest a rapid growth of electric use, with electricity supplying a growing fraction of the total energy budget. The transmission of electric energy will therefore be of major concern in the years ahead. There have been steady changes in the technology of electricity transmission, mainly in the direction of increasing the voltage of overhead transmission lines. However, a number of possible technical breakthroughs that could dramatically change the carrying capacity of underground lines are in the wings. An efficient, and comparatively cheap, transmission system could also relieve peak load problems in the United States because these occur at different times across the country. With easy transmission, electric power could be pumped across one or more time zones to match the peak load.

There are a number of requirements for a satisfactory transmission line. First let us consider the power transmitted. Power, measured in watts or kilowatts, is the product of the voltage V at which the electricity is transmitted (measured in volts) times the current I flowing in the wire (measured in amperes).

$$power = V \times I$$

Also the power dissipated in the transmission line, which therefore represents a net loss, is proportional to I^2R, where R is the electric resistance of the conductor. These two simple relationships indicate the basic directions in which we must move to minimize losses.

For constant power transmitted, if V is increased then I can be smaller. But the losses are dependent upon I^2. The smaller I is, the smaller will be the losses. Therefore it pays to operate at as high a voltage as possible. At present the highest voltage transmission lines used are 765 kv (kilovolt), that is 7.65×10^5 v (volt). Present plans call for voltages of 1000 to 1500 kv. However, other problems arise as the voltage increases. Breakdown near the wires, or corona, also causes losses at higher voltages. Also higher towers and wider right of ways are required for safety at higher voltages. Already 7×10^6 acres are used for high voltage transmission lines, but where space is available this will probably be the preferred technique because of the economic advantage.

Nonetheless, high unsightly towers and wide right of ways stretching across the countryside are under attack, and efforts are being made to develop underground lines at least for those areas where the lines make the worst intrusions. Another incentive for underground transmission is that right of way, especially in and near urban areas, is becoming extremely expensive. Unfortunately, underground cable is usually from 6 to 20 times more expensive than overhead lines. Also the power carrying capability of an underground line is limited because the heat generated cannot be easily dissipated. Even with oil cooling of the cables, which has already been tried in Russia, the maximum load is probably less than 600×10^6 w (600 Mw).

Two other possibilities are being actively studied, both of which attempt to decrease the resistance R of the conductor in an attempt to decrease the power losses. The more dramatic of the two makes use of the phenomenon of superconductivity. When certain metals are cooled below a critical temperature, usually near absolute zero, their resistance suddenly drops to zero. Thus, there are no losses and no heat dissipation problems if the conductor can be kept cold enough. Such cables, if they could be developed, could carry power levels as high as

10,000 Mw, enough to service the city of New York with a single cable only about 2 ft in diameter.

The metal niobium, which is superconducting below 9 K (−264°C), appears to be the strongest candidate for such cables at present although niobium requires cooling with liquid helium and is therefore very expensive. A niobium-tin alloy is superconducting below 18 K, but is more difficult to handle mechanically. A major advance would be to find a superconductor with a critical temperature above the boiling point of liquid hydrogen (20 K).

Because of the difficulties of working at such extremely low temperatures, an alternative proposal is simply to cool a conductor to around the temperature of liquid nitrogen (77 K). The resistance decreases significantly, though not to zero, by this point so that the power losses are decreased. However the heat created by the small power losses must be dissipated so that efficient refrigeration is also required, and this may prove difficult.

The vast majority of the electric power used is alternating current (ac) where the line voltage rises and falls 60 times per second. Direct current (dc), corresponding to a steady voltage, offers some advantages in transmission because the same diameter line can carry twice the average power. There are also magnetic effects in ac transmission that will give rise to power losses even in the case of a superconducting line. But if dc transmission were used, ac to dc converters would be needed at either end of the line, and these are expensive. For long distance transmission dc may still be worth the expense, especially if cheaper and more efficient converters could be built.

Although the ultra high voltage overhead lines will undoubtedly be with us for some time, some of the other possibilities look attractive, particularly large capacity superconducting cables. It is to be hoped that this research will continue and that it will not be left only in the hands of the manufacturers of current equipment who may be reluctant to see their present devices made obsolete too quickly.

15-9 Fuel Cells

Another attractive contribution to the solution of transmission and storage problems of electric energy may be the fuel cell. These devices have the advantage that they work equally well at comparatively small output, thus lending themselves to a more dispersed generation of electricity closer to consumer sites. This would help reduce electric transmission requirements. Such units could also be used to supplement base load power by providing peak load power to local areas.

A fuel cell is conceptually a simple device, rather like an electrolysis cell in reverse. Compounds such as hydrogen and oxygen or carbon monoxide and oxygen interact at electrodes to generate a voltage difference between the electrodes and support a current flow. A single hydrogen cell, for example, will produce a 1-v potential and can generate between 0.1 and 0.2 amp/cm^2 (ampere per square centimeter) of electrode surface. Many cells can be connected to produce voltages up to 1000 v and power output up to 100 Mw. A fuel cell thus provides a simple direct way of converting chemical to electrical energy.

Fuel cells have a number of obvious advantages both technically and environmentally. They are an extremely clean source of electricity producing no air pollution or noxious byproducts. They vent heat directly to the atmosphere and so do not require water cooling. Fuel cells are essentially quiet devices. All of these features make them extremely easy to site in a convenient spot near the demand. Fuel cells also readily lend themselves to modular construction so that, as the electric demand increased, new modules could be readily created.

Most fuel cells under test use natural gas as fuel. This could be a limitation as the supplies of natural gas run low. Fuel cells could be made using hydrogen as a fuel so that they make an excellent complement to the hydrogen economy concept. Both natural gas and hydrogen are cheaper to transport than electricity; thus it may be more economical to transport energy as hydrogen even if electric use is required by the consumer. Fuel cells are intrinisically efficient converters, particularly if the initial material does not require treatment. For hydrogen, efficiencies of 50 to 70% might be expected. In addition, these high efficiencies are maintained even at low output power, unlike conventional electric generating systems. This is an argument for using fuel cells with natural gas because the higher efficiency means that we make better use of a scarce resource.

Fuel cells have been used extensively in the space program and operate very satisfactorily. However, the criteria for success back on earth are somewhat different. In particular economics plays a much more significant role. Pratt and Whitney, a Connecticut company, has done the most extensive work on fuel cells and claim that they are within a factor of 2 in capital cost and lifetime of competing with alternative generating systems. At present these costs are about $400 per kw capacity and the lifetime is about 16,000 hr. Pratt and Whitney hope to reach the breakeven point within the next 3 years.

Fuel cells offer an exciting alternative generating system using either natural gas or hydrogen. They could serve as supplemental peak power suppliers with the advantage of being placed close to the consumer. They should also prove extremely useful for generation in remote areas. Whether they can compete as an alternative central power generation system is still unknown.

15-10 Summary and Conclusions

In addition to an energy problem with respect to total resources, we are also heading towards a power problem in providing energy as it is needed. New storage concepts such as hydro or compressed air storage will help peak power demands. Development of economical high capacity storage batteries also seems finally closer at hand. The use of hydrogen, either as liquid or gas or absorbed in a metal, both for storage and transmission of energy is an exciting new concept which will undoubtedly see more development.

The trend toward bigger and bigger power plants often at remote sites has emphasized the importance of the transmission of energy. New technologies learned from the basic research areas of solid state and, particularly, high energy physics may provide a needed breakthrough with the use of superconducting materials. Finally an alternative to large central stations is a more dispersed system of efficient fuel cells using pipeline hydrogen as fuel. This would minimize transmission problems and would be much less vulnerable to system breakdown. Hopefully some or all of these possibilities will help to solve the storage and transmission problems we face.

Questions

1. The suggestion has been made that power plants "store" energy as some form of potential energy during times of low demand. Discuss some of the options (gravitational, chemical, mechanical) and outline their advantages and disadvantages.

2. Why would superconducting cables be advantageous for transmitting electricity? What are the main problems in producing such a cable at present?

3. Argue the case for "the hydrogen economy." What special precautions would be needed if hydrogen were widely used as a fuel?

4. Hydrogen is being investigated as a transportation fuel to replace gasoline. Discuss the advantages of hydrogen as a fuel. Estimate the changes in electrical demand that this change might involve.

5. Mark the *incorrect* statement:
   (a) The use of hydrogen as a fuel may help to alleviate energy transportation and storage problems.
   (b) Hydrogen gas from dissociation of sea water could provide a major energy resource.
   (c) Hydrogen can be passed through the natural gas pipeline network with few alterations.
   (d) Hydrogen ignites with a much smaller energy input than natural gas.
   (e) Hydrogen can be stored as a liquid at 15K.

6. Why are fuel cells being considered as a source of electricity? What problems does fuel cell technology still face?

Bibliography

[1] J. McCallum and C. L. Farest: New frontiers in energy storage. *Battelle Research Outlook,* Vol. 4, No. 1, 1972.

[2] *Report of the Task Force on Energy.* 92nd Congress, December, 1972.

[3] R. B. Korsmeyer: Underground air storage and electrical energy production. Report ORNL-NSF-EP-11. *Oak Ridge National Laboratory, USAEC,* (Feb 1972).

[4] M. L. Kyle, E. J. Carious, and D. S. Webster: Lithium/sulphur batteries for off-peak energy storage. *Argonne National Laboratory Report ANL-7958,* March, 1973. This report gives an excellent survey of the status of all types of storage battery research and development.

[5] D. Gregory: The hydrogen economy. *Scientific American,* January, 1973.

[6] Hydrogen: synthetic fuel of the future. *Science,* November 24, 1972.

[7] W. E. Winsche, K. C. Hoffman, and F. J. Salzano: Hydrogen: its future role in the nation's energy economy. *Science,* June 29, 1973.

[8] D. D. Moore, G. B. Gaines, and D. Hessel: Getting energy to the user. *Battelle Research Outlook,* Vol. 4, No. 1, 1972.

[9] New means of transmitting electricity: a three-way race. *Science,* December 1, 1972.

[10] Fuel cells: dispersed generation of electricity. *Science,* December 22, 1972.

Thermal Pollution and Climate Changes

16-1   Introduction: Thermal Pollution: an Ultimate Limit to Growth

At the beginning of Chapter 15 we noted that, even if the problem of obtaining sufficient clean resources were solved, there might be other difficulties associated with an ever increasing growth of energy consumption. One of these was the transportation and peak power problems discussed in the last chapter. There is another problem associated with energy consumption, thermal pollution, that may pose a fundamental and ultimate limit to our use of energy. This limit follows directly from a simple application of physical laws, particularly the second law of thermodynamics discussed in Chapter 5.

Technology has proved extremely successful in the past 50 years in many fields. Medical science has conquered numerous diseases; agriculture has increased crop outputs many times; physics and engineering have revolutionized communications and placed men on the moon. As a result, there is a prevalent attitude of technological optimism which asserts that, given enough effort, scientists can solve any problem. Unfortunately this is not so. Scientists are constrained by the basic laws of physics. My observation is that technological optimists are usually not physical scientists but rather social scientists or economists, whose training perhaps does not fit them for the constraints imposed by immutable laws.

There has already been some reaction to the widespread use of technology caused, perhaps, by the observation of disasters produced by shortsighted "scientific" fixes. A recent example was the over-

209

zealous application of DDT for pest control. The DDT, a long lived chemical, gradually moved up the food chain, destroying wildlife and ultimately threatening man. The recent ban on the use of DDT in the United States will hopefully allow the environment to recover. As a result of this kind of misplaced technology, some people have become disillusioned with progress and long for a simpler life style. I believe that this view is also unrealistic. Scientific progress has generally improved life for most men and is necessary to support the population we already have. However, we must be careful to assess the impact of a particular technology before our human options are diminished. Science implies knowledge but it does not follow that we must implement all the technology that this knowledge allows.

Thermal pollution may be one of the insoluble problems with which we will have to coexist. There may not be any viable solution. We have already discussed thermal pollution by power plants in Chapter 11. There we referred to local thermal pollution, usually of the water of a lake or river, by the heated water from the condenser of a power plant. You will remember that the average efficiency of a fossil fuel power plant is at best about 40% and of a nuclear plant near 30%. This means that 60 to 70% of the total energy is dissipated as heat at the plant. What happens to this heat energy? Ultimately it gets transferred to the atmosphere, even without the use of cooling towers, either by evaporation from the water surface or by radiation.

The remaining energy output of a power plant is electric energy. We might ask what happens to this energy? Part of it is used to cook our food, to turn motors of various kinds, and for space heating. Nearly all the energy is ultimately transformed into heat which is simply dissipated. The same is true of almost all energy used, whether in manufacturing or in transportation. Imagine the energy consumed in driving your car to work and back. After you return home the car is parked in the same spot. Therefore it has the same potential energy and zero kinetic energy. Yet the car used up chemical energy from the gas in the tank in taking you to and from work. Where has this energy gone? The chemical energy ultimately heated up the atmosphere. This heat came variously from friction as the car moved along; from engine heat, which is first transferred to water in the radiator and then removed from the water by air at the radiator; from the brake linings as the car stopped; or simply from the hot exhaust gases.

The main point is that most of the energy we use is only transiently useful. Energy is not lost, but it is degraded into low level heat that cannot be readily recovered and converted to useful work. The effect is simply to heat up the atmosphere. This, then, is our problem. How much heating is taking place and how much can the atmosphere stand? These are complex questions, which we will now turn to in more detail.

16-2   Energy Balance of the Earth and Atmosphere

We noted in Chapter 6 that the earth has a dynamic energy balance between incoming solar radiation at short wavelengths and outgoing radiation at longer wavelengths. For a total albedo of about 36%, we showed that the effective temperature of the upper atmosphere was about 251K ($-22°C$) using the Stefan-Boltzmann relation that the radiation emitted by a black body per unit area, S, is proportional to T^4, where T is the temperature of the body in kelvin (or degrees absolute). That is

$$S = \sigma T^4 \qquad\qquad 16\text{-}1$$

where σ is a constant called the Stefan-Boltzmann constant which has a value of 5.67×10^{-8} w/(m²)(K⁴).

Let us now consider the more complex problem of calculating the temperature at the earth's surface. To do this we must first consider the structure of the earth's atmosphere.

The atmosphere is divided into three main sections, the troposphere, the stratosphere, and the upper atmosphere. (See Figure 16-1.) The **troposphere** is the layer closest to the earth's surface, stretching from ground level to a height of about 20 km (kilometer). The temperature decreases with height to about $-55°C$ at the **tropopause,** which is at the top of the troposphere. Essentially all weather takes place in the troposphere and about 75% of the mass of the atmosphere is contained

Figure 16-1

The generalized vertical distribution of temperature and pressure up to about 110 km. Note particularly the tropopause and the zone of maximum ozone concentration with the warm layer above it. [Information from R. G. Barry and R. J. Chorley: *Atmosphere, Weather, and Climate.* Holt, Rinehart and Winston, New York, 1970.]

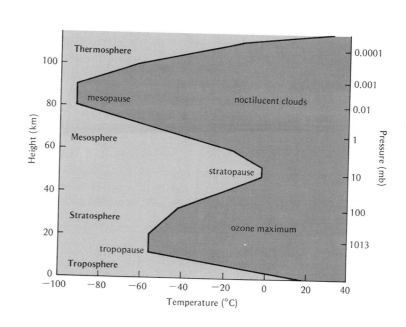

there. The troposphere has a comparatively rapid mixing and cleansing ability because rainfall can precipitate out many particles quite rapidly.

The next layer is the **stratosphere** stretching up from about 20 to 50 km and containing almost all the remaining atmospheric mass. The lower levels of the stratosphere contain the highest concentration of ozone (O_3). The temperature of the stratosphere rises from about -55 to $0°C$ at the **stratopause.** The stratosphere is a very stable region with little mixing with the lower layers. Dust particles or jet contrails can have very long lifetimes, up to some years, in the stratosphere.

The highest layer can be further subdivided, into **mesosphere** and **thermosphere** with the temperature falling in the latter as low as $-90°C$ and then rising to 25 or $30°C$ at 110 km. Some atmosphere extends much further, perhaps 1000 km, into space, but there are very few particles and these tenuous outer regions do not affect the present discussion.

Let us consider now in detail what happens to the incident solar radiation. Remember that radiation from the sun, because of the sun's high surface temperature, has a spectrum that consists almost completely of wavelengths less than 4 μ (microns). Cooler bodies emit at longer wavelengths. The total radiation from the sun just outside the earth's atmosphere is about 2 cal/(cm²)(min)* or about 1400 w/m². Because the total cross section for the earth to intercept this radiation is πr^2, where r is the radius of the earth, the total amount of radiation falling on the earth is $(1400 \times \pi r^2)$ w. (See Chapter 6.)

If we now call this total incident energy per second 100% or 100 units for simplicity, then we can trace its path to the surface in these same units. This is shown schematically in Figure 16-2. First 2 units are absorbed by ozone in the stratosphere; these 2 units are later returned as longer wavelength radiation to the troposphere. Clouds (23 units) and air molecules and dust (6 units) in the troposphere reflect short wave radiation and, together with 7 units reflected from the earth's surface, make up the 36 units reflected, giving a total albedo of 0.36. The troposphere has a net absorption of 15 units of short wavelength radiation. The earth's surface receives a total of 54 units of short wavelength radiation of which 7 is directly reflected, leaving a net absorption of 47 units. Approximately 31 units of the total 47 are from direct radiation and 16 units are diffuse radiation scattered by clouds or by air molecules and dust.

When we turn to the emission of long wavelength radiation by the earth, we find that this is also complicated by the presence of the atmosphere. The earth directly radiates 98 units to the troposphere. Most of this radiation is absorbed by water vapor and carbon dioxide in the troposphere, with only 7 units passing through radiation

212

Thermal Pollution
and Climate
Changes

---

* Recent measurements suggest a value of 1.94 cal/(cm²)(min) on the average. There remains the possibility of variations of a few percent around this average.

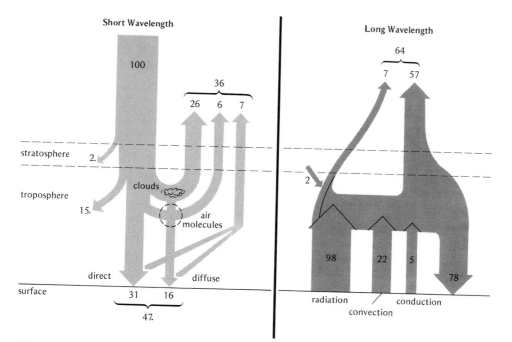

Figure 16-2

The balance of the atmospheric energy budget for short and long wavelength radiation. The total incident solar radiation is taken to be 100 units. The numbers refer to the net number of units absorbed or reflected or otherwise transferred. Note that in the troposphere there are 15 units of short wavelength radiation absorbed, which must be added to the 120 units of long wavelength radiation absorbed in the troposphere. Note also for the outer atmosphere 36 units are reflected (albedo = 0.36) and 64 units are reradiated, whereas at the earth's surface 98 units of long wavelength radiation are radiated to the troposphere.

windows to be directly emitted. Additional energy is also added to the troposphere from the earth's surface by convection (22 units) and conduction (5 units). The total energy input to the troposphere is made up of 15 units of short wavelength radiation and 120 units of long wavelength radiation (91 units radiated, 22 units from convection, and 5 units by conduction from the surface plus 2 units radiated from the stratosphere). The energy deposited in the troposphere is then reradiated, 57 units going into space which, together with the 7 units directly emitted, make up a total of 64 units radiated from the earth. Finally 78 units of long wavelength radiation from the troposphere are radiated back to the earth's surface.

A summary of the input-output situation for the three systems, earth, troposphere, and surface is given in Table 16-1. For the earth as a whole 100 units of short wavelength are incident, 36 units are reflected, and 64 units of long wavelength radiation are reradiated. For the troposphere, 135 units total are incident, with the bulk (91 units) of

213

16-2 Energy Balance
of the Earth and
Atmosphere

Table 16-1
Energy Balancing in the Earth's Atmosphere

	Total			
	Gain			**Loss**
outer edge of atmosphere		100		36
stratosphere		2		64
troposphere	from		to	2
	short-wave	15	space	57
	long-wave	91	surface (back radiation)	78
	stratosphere	2		135
	convection	22		
	conduction	5		
		135		
surface	short-wave	47	atmosphere (long-wave)	98
	long-wave	78	convection	22
		125	conduction	5
				125

Source: Data taken from Barry and Chorley [8].

long wavelength radiation being absorbed by water vapor and carbon dioxide; 135 units are also reemitted, 78 to the surface and 57 to space. For the surface, 125 units are incident, a mixture of both short wavelength (47 units) and long wavelength radiation (78 units); 98 units are reradiated by the surface, 22 units are carried off by convection, and 5 by conduction completing the balance.

The important point to realize is that, for all three systems, the total energy incident balances the total energy emitted. If this were not the case, there would be a net energy gain or loss and the system would either heat up or cool down, until a new equilibrium situation was reached at a new temperature.

The earth-atmosphere situation we have discussed may seem fairly complicated, but as you will realize with a little thought we have actually been treating the real problem in a very much simplified way. We have taken overall average conditions, whereas many factors influence the radiation incident on a particular place on the earth's surface. For example, variable cloud cover can clearly affect the balance conditions discussed since clouds are such important reflectors. Variation in water vapor, carbon dioxide, or dust in the atmosphere is also important. Latitude affects the amount of radiation incident on a given surface area, more radiation falling at the equator than at the poles (see Chapter 13). Finally the nature of the surface, whether land or water or the particular nature of the land surface, also affects the reflection properties.

Table 16-2 gives a list of the albedos of a number of surfaces. Note that we used an average value of 0.13 for the albedo of the surface of

Table 16-2
Percentages of Solar Radiation Reflected by Different Surfaces (Albedos)

Surface	Albedo (%)	Surface	Albedo (%)
new-fallen snow	85 (90% has been observed in Antarctica)	green grass	8–27
		grain crops, depending on ripeness	10–25
		clay (blue), dry	23
		ploughed fields, dry	12–20
old snow	70	pine forest	6–19
thawing snow	30–65	oak tree crowns	18
salt deposits from dried-up lakes	50	granite	12–18
white chalk or lime	45	other rocks, generally	12–15
yellow deciduous forest in autumn	33–38	stubble fields	15–17
quartz sands, white or yellow	34–35	clay (blue), wet	16
clayey desert	29–31	spruce tree crowns	14
parched grassland	16–30	wet fields, not ploughed	5–14
river sands (quartz), wet	29	fir tree crowns	10
green deciduous forest	16–27	water, depending on angle of incidence	2–78

Source: Lamb [9].

the earth in the preceding discussion because 7 units of the 54 units of short wavelength radiation incident on the surface were directly reflected.

16-3 Surface Temperature of the Earth

In spite of the simplifications made above, this overall picture can be used to calculate a reasonably accurate average temperature of the surface of the earth. Because we noted in the previous section that 98 units of energy were radiated from the whole earth, of surface area $4\pi r^2$, to the atmosphere, the total energy radiated per second per square meter is given by

$$\frac{98}{100} \times \frac{\pi r^2 \times 1400 \text{ w/m}^2}{4\pi r^2} = 343 \text{ w/m}^2 \qquad \text{16-2}$$

(Remember 100 units $= \pi r^2 \times 1400$ w/m²). Now using the Stefan Boltzmann relation (see Chapter 6)

$$343 = \sigma T^4 = 5.67 \times 10^{-8} T^4 \qquad \text{16-3}$$

that is

$$T = \sqrt[4]{\frac{343 \times 10^8}{5.67}} * \qquad \text{16-4}$$
$$= 279 \text{K (or 6°C)}.$$

* Note $\sqrt[4]{\dfrac{343 \times 10^8}{5.67}}$ means take the square root twice, i.e. $\sqrt[4]{x} = \sqrt{\sqrt{x}}$.

Thus for this simple calculation the average temperature of the earth's surface is around +6°C; for the earth's upper atmosphere, a similar calculation gave an average temperature of about −22°C, that is about 28°C colder. (The mean surface temperature is actually around 15°C.) If the surface were really 28°C colder, life as we know it would be virtually impossible. The atmosphere is necessary as a "thermal blanket," as well as being a source of oxygen for life.

Records of the earth's past climatic history show that there has been variation of the temperature of the earth's surface over long periods of time. There are three different factors that may produce a decrease in temperature. One is the amount of incident radiation. If the solar constant varied, this would cause a change in equilibrium temperature. There is some evidence of a small variation of the sun's radiation, correlated with sunspot activity, but whether there are long term cycles is still unknown. A full discussion of such variation is given in Lamb's book [9].

A change in the overall albedo could also change the overall temperature. For example, a change in cloud cover would have a significant effect because of the high reflectivity of clouds. Ice and snow have a very high albedo, which is partly responsible for the lower temperatures at extreme latitudes. Finally, a change in the atmospheric composition could affect the temperature by modifying the absorption or reflection properties of the troposphere. Additional amounts of water vapor or carbon dioxide would tend to raise the temperature by providing additional absorption of outgoing long wavelength radiation. The effect of dust is less clear because it depends upon the detailed composition of the dust. It is generally believed that an increase in dust at high levels will increase the albedo and lower the temperature.

16-4 Global Thermal Pollution

There is another change that could affect the overall temperature of the earth's surface, namely the addition of heat by human activities. First let us see how to calculate the temperature rise for a given heat input, assuming that there are no other secondary effects. Let us take the amount of heat added per second by human activities to be H J/(sec)(m²) (joule per second per square meter). Then instead of writing $343 = \sigma T^4$, we must write a new relationship,

$$343 + H = \sigma T_H^4 \qquad\qquad 16\text{-}5$$

As before we could simply solve this equation for T_H, the new, higher, temperature corresponding to an addition of heat H. Alternatively by dividing the two equations (16-5 and 16-3) we find

$$\frac{T_H^4}{T^4} = \frac{343 + H}{343} = 1 + \frac{H}{343} \qquad\qquad \text{16-6}$$

that is

$$T_H = T\sqrt[4]{1 + \frac{H}{343}}$$

or

$$T_H \approx T\left[1 + \frac{1}{4}\left(\frac{H}{343}\right)\right]^* \qquad\qquad \text{16-7}$$

The temperature increase $\Delta T_H = (T_H - T)$ is then given by

$$\Delta T_H \approx \left(\frac{T}{4}\right)\left(\frac{H}{343}\right)$$

that is,

$$\Delta T_H \approx \left(\frac{279}{4}\right)\left(\frac{H}{343}\right) \text{ (since } T = 279K)$$

or

$$\Delta T_H = 0.20 \times H \qquad\qquad \text{16-8}$$

Remember that H is given as the energy produced per second per square meter. If we have a measure of the total energy produced per year, then we must divide this by the surface area of the globe $(4\pi r^2 = 5.10 \times 10^{14}$ m$^2)$ and by the number of seconds in a year $(3.15 \times 10^7$ sec) to obtain H.

As an example, the total world energy used in 1970 was approximately 1.5×10^{20} J/year. Therefore the number of joules per second per square meter

$$H = \frac{1.5 \times 10^{20} \text{ J/year}}{5.10 \times 10^{14} \text{ m}^2 \times 3.15 \times 10^7 \text{ sec/year}}$$

$$= 9.3 \times 10^{-3} \text{ J/m}^2 \text{ sec.} \qquad\qquad \text{16-9}$$

Therefore

$$\Delta T_H = 0.20 \times 9.3 \times 10^{-3} = 2 \times 10^{-3} \text{ °C.} \qquad\qquad \text{16-10}$$

This is a very small rise in temperature. However if we now consider not the present use of energy but some estimates of future use, the picture is not so happy. There are a number of approaches to estimating the total energy needs. One is to consider a "reasonable" energy consumption per person and then estimate the world population at some time in the future to obtain the total energy use.

Bjerklie [7] has estimated a maximum world population assuming

$* \sqrt[4]{1 + x} = (1 + x)^{1/4} \approx 1 + \dfrac{x}{4}$ if x is much less than 1.

various constraints of food, water, and space. Although the numbers are admittedly not very accurate, all three limits come out approximately the same with an upper limit of about 40×10^9 people. Weinberg and Hammond [1, 12] in discussing limits to energy use assume an upper limit of 15 to 20×10^9 people. A recent article by Tonias Frejka in *Scientific American* claims that the most likely stable population will be about 8.4×10^9 people although it may go as high as 15×10^9 people. The 8.4×10^9 projection requires that a net reproduction rate of unity be achieved by the year 2005.

The energy consumption per capita in the United States in 1970 was about 3.7×10^{11} J (Figure 7-2) per person. The doubling time for this total is about 20 years. Increasing demands for clean water and clean air will undoubtedly increase this per capita consumption without any effective increase in the "standard of living." As minerals and fuels become scarcer, more energy will be required to extract them. The present nuclear reactors are less efficient than the fossil fuel plants they are replacing. There will almost certainly be an increased per capita consumption in the United States simply to hold the effective living standard at present levels.

When we discuss average energy consumption even in the United States, we do not take into account the large disparity between different segments of the population. Middle and upper class families undoubtedly use more energy than families with lower income. If we take energy use proportional to income, then we could anticipate an increasing demand simply as the less affluent groups reach up to achieve the same rate of energy consumption as the upper and middle classes now have. For these reasons, primarily pollution control, scarcity of resources, and removing inequalities, let us assume an increase in per capita energy consumption of about a factor of 10 above 1970 numbers. This probably allows very little change in the effective consumption of the upper middle classes in the United States. This would then imply a per capita consumption of about 3.7×10^{12} J per person per year.

If we now consider that eventually the rest of the world will attempt to reach this same living standard and energy consumption, we can calculate the effect on the earth's temperature. Let us assume a stable population of 20×10^9 people, using 3.7×10^{12} J/year. The total energy consumption per year would be 7.4×10^{22} J. The value of H is obtained by dividing by the total surface area of the earth (5.10×10^{14}) and the number of seconds in a year (3.15×10^7 secs); that is, H is about 4.6 J/(m²)(sec²). Thus using Equation (16-8), namely

$$\Delta T_H = 0.20 \times H \qquad \qquad 16\text{-}8$$

gives a temperature rise of about 1°C (1.8°F).

An alternative technique is to consider the number of doublings of the 1970 usage that will produce this same temperature rise. We noted that the 1970 world energy consumption implied a temperature rise of $2 \times 10^{-3}°C$. This would need to increase by about 500 to correspond to a 1°C temperature rise. Since $2^9 = 512$, a factor of 500 means about nine doublings. Nine doublings thus implies a temperature rise of about 1°C. Because the doubling time at the present is around 20 years, this implies that a time lapse of only 180 years would bring a rise of 1°C.

Although there are significant assumptions built into either of these estimation techniques, the main point is not the detailed time scale involved but rather the realization that a temperature increase is linked to an increasing energy use. This temperature rise, although negligible at present levels, is significant at consumption levels not too far from present per capita use in the United States. If we demand energy use above this level, then it may someday involve us in conflicts with other countries who are also increasing their energy consumption.

It should also be emphasized that the simplified calculation we have made of temperature increase neglects other secondary effects that may have an impact on the surface temperature. As temperature rises, evaporation will increase and the water vapor content of the atmosphere will rise, enhancing the increased temperature. On the other hand, cloud cover may also increase, which would change the total albedo and thus slow the temperature rise. However, an increase in cloud cover may not be an attractive solution for many people who enjoy sunny skies.

Making some allowance for these effects, Bjerklie [7] estimates that, for total energy consumptions between 12×10^{18} btu/year and 40×10^{18} btu/year (this maximum is rather similar to the estimate of 7.4×10^{22} J made above), the temperature rise could be between 0.4°F and 9°F!

Let us now turn to the possible effects of increased temperature on climate.

16-5 Climate and Weather

Weather and climate must be among the most widely discussed subjects in the world, but it is only comparatively recently, with the advent of satellites, that forecasting has become fairly accurate. Climatologists distinguish climate and weather. Weather is a more local phenomenon in time and place. Hull defines weather to mean the totality of atmospheric conditions at any particular place and time. Climate, he sees as the sum total of the weather experienced at a place in the course of the year and over the years. This definition implies a set of conditions that can be called normal or near average and change rather slowly. Over thousands of years the world's climate has changed. At various times in the past there have been periods where huge ice sheets have covered large areas of the globe. It is interesting to note that comparatively small temperature changes are involved even during these glaciation periods. For example the temperature of the Caribbean Sea changed by only about 5°C between the ice ages and the warm periods in between.

Although the reasons for these long term climate changes is still not clear, it is known that there are many factors which affect the overall climate. So far we have been discussing the average temperature of the earth's surface. It is clear, of course, that the actual temperature varies widely from place to place on the earth surface and even with the time of year at the same place. One of the factors producing these differences is the dependence of the incident radiation upon latitude, which we noted in Chapter 13. Changes of the surface albedo can also change the amount of radiation deposited as can cloud cover. The presence of large expanses of water or land have an effect on the energy deposited. The oceans tend to be excellent absorbers of radiation. Figure 16-3 shows the global distribution of annual net radiation over the surface of the globe. The largest changes are around large land masses.

The other general feature one can note is that the amount of radiation being received on the average, near the equator, is about $2\frac{1}{2}$ times

Figure 16-3
Global distribution of the annual net radiation, in kilocalories per square centimeter. Note 1 kcal/cm² = 4.2 × 10⁷ J/m². Thus 60 kcal/cm² (year) is 2.52 × 10⁹ J/m² per year or approximately 80 w/m² averaged over 1 year. [Information from R. G. Barry and R. J. Chorley: *Atmosphere, Weather and Climate.* Holt, Rinehart and Winston, New York, 1970.]

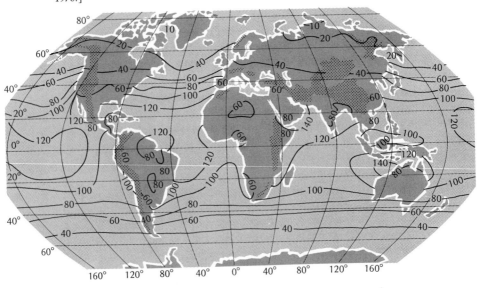

that received at the poles. This is because of both the latitude effect and the high reflectivity of the snow and ice near the poles. Some of this energy is transferred from the tropical regions to more temperate regions. The main source of the transport is through the atmosphere by winds which move large masses of warm air from near the equator to higher latitudes. About 80% of the total energy is transferred by this method. There is also a significant transfer of energy by warm ocean currents which sweep large quantities of warm water from tropical regions to cooler areas.

The overall pattern is quite complicated, and detailed understanding of climate changes is not available. There are a number of factors that are known to affect the climate. Sea ice is one of these. Increase in the quantity of sea ice tends to cause cooling because ice has a higher albedo than water. Suggestions have been made to decrease the albedo of the ice by scattering dust and so producing warming. Ocean temperature also has a significant effect on climate because the ocean has a large heat storage capacity and also because the amount of evaporation from the ocean depends upon the temperature. Increased evaporation means an increased water vapor content, possibly more clouds, and more circulation.

Another notable effect on climate is the presence of particles in the atmosphere. A reasonably close correlation has been established between large volcanic eruptions, which can hurl dust particles into the stratosphere where they may remain for 2 years or more, and short term cooling trends. Dust can also get into the atmosphere by other means, such as storms in the desert or large scale mechanical farming or mining operations. Normally these do not get dust as high as the stratosphere so that they have somewhat shorter term effects. The effect of carbon dioxide (CO_2) in the atmosphere has been discussed earlier (see Chapter 6).

A final suggestion that has been made to account for climate changes is the output of the sun. We know that the sun is really not a stable body. For example there is a well known 11-year cycle of sunspot activity which has been studied for many years. This sunspot activity is probably coupled to a change, albeit small, of the radiation emitted by the sun. Whether there has been any long term variation of the output of the sun, giving rise to long term climatic effects, is not well determined. Hopefully further studies, especially by satellites outside the earth's atmosphere, accurately measuring the solar radiation will give a much better understanding of this problem.

The important point to realize is that climate is a complex problem. There are a number of interweaving effects that are not well understood. Comparatively small changes in temperature can have quite a significant impact. Suppose, for example, that the temperature rise were sufficient to change the overall amount of land ice significantly. The amount of ice between the last ice age and the present era is about a factor of 2. At present, there is approximately 32.8×10^6 km^3 of ice, most of it in the Antarctic. The Arctic ice is largely sea ice on the surface of water. It is estimated that during the last ice age there was approximately 70×10^6 km^3 of land ice in the Antarctic, in North America, in Scandinavia, and in Siberia. If all of the present land ice melted, the sea level would rise about 82 m. Many of the major cities in the world, including New York, London, and Paris, are built close to the ocean and at fairly low levels so that a rise in water level would cause catastrophic damage to many of these cities. If one looks at a map of Europe or North America, very large areas of land are less than 82 m above sea level.

Although the total melting of the Antarctic ice cap is unlikely and also a rather slow process, the preceding discussion indicates some of the dramatic effects temperature change can cause. Even melting of the Arctic sea ice could produce a feedback effect. The difficulty is the interrelation between all the problems. As water is warmed, its ability to retain carbon dioxide decreases and it evaporates more readily. An increase of carbon dioxide and water vapor will produce an increase in temperature from the greenhouse effect, which in turn causes more heating of the ocean, releasing more carbon dioxide and water vapor, and so on. This feedback effect is hard to estimate and the interplay between the different factors is hard to consider.

The important point is that, if we do continue to use more energy, this will increase the temperature of the earth. Increasing the temperature by even a comparatively small amount could have significant and far reaching effects on the earth's climate.

The only form of energy that does not produce this problem is earth-based solar energy. If we made use of some of the solar energy incident on the earth from the sun, the overall balance could be preserved. Even in this case we would still probably have local problems if we had a concentrated area of use such as cities. We are already beginning to see the effects of concentrated energy use in urban centers.

16-6 The Climate of Cities

As the world's population has grown so have cities. People have tended to concentrate in cities both for economic and for cultural reasons. The presence of a city has a significant effect on the climate in that area. The effect on the climate comes about from a number of different reasons. There is the effect of pollutants produced in the city. Factory smoke and automobile exhausts both obviously affect the composition of the atmosphere and therefore the climate. Buildings also modify the albedo of the region. In addition, concrete and stone have a large heat capacity so that they retain heat longer and only slowly release heat during the evening. A visit to Manhatten Island in the evening after a warm summer day gives dramatic confirmation of this phenomenon.

Because of the drains and concrete roadways, rain tends to run off more quickly and there is less evaporation. Because evaporation carries heat off, the decrease of evaporation produces a warming trend. Finally, the concentration of energy use in this small area adds a significant heat input to the solar input in the region of the city. This can have the effect of raising the temperature of the city. Such effects have already been observed. Heat islands around cities are well known.

In this section we will concentrate on this latter problem. Let us make a simple calculation to indicate the temperature rise to be expected in a city. Suppose we use as an example the city of Detroit with a population of about 4.2×10^6 people and an area of say 900 mi² (2.33×10^9 m²). Let us assume that each person in Detroit uses the annual per capita energy consumption of the United States in 1970 which is 3.7×10^{11} J per person per year. To find the number of joules per square meter per second released in Detroit, we must divide 3.7×10^{11} J by the area of Detroit (2.33×10^9 m²) and by the number of seconds in a year (3.15×10^7 sec) and multiply by the number of people (4.2×10^6).

That is

$$H(\text{Detroit}) = \frac{(3.7 \times 10^{11} \text{ J/person}) \times (4.2 \times 10^6 \text{ people})}{(3.15 \times 10^7 \text{ sec}) \times (2.33 \times 10^9 \text{ m}^2)} \qquad \text{16-11}$$
$$= 21 \text{J}/(\text{m}^2)(\text{sec})$$

If we assume that Equation 16-8 applies to smaller regions than the whole earth, then we can use this value of H, to find the temperature rise for the city of Detroit

$$\Delta T_H \text{ (Detroit)} = 0.20 \times H \qquad \text{16-8}$$
$$= 0.20 \times 21 = 4.2°C$$

Obviously 4°C (7°F) is a very noticeable temperature rise. A similar calculation by Porter, Hagler, and Kristiansen [6] using rather high values of the solar input for the New York City metropolitan area (7000 mi²) calculated that, by the year 2000, a temperature rise of about 12°C could be expected.

It is already possible to observe these effects in urban areas. For example, the distribution of minimum temperatures in the city of London in May, 1959 (Figure 16-4), shows a marked increase from the edge of the built up area towards the center of the city by about 12°F, that is, about 7°C.

The reason that the effect is not as bad as the simple calculation

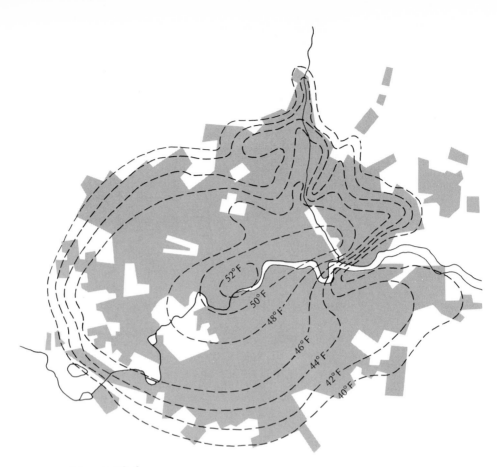

Figure 16-4
Distribution of minimum temperatures (°F) in London on May 14, 1959, showing the relationship between the urban heat island and the build-up area (shaded).
[Information from R. G. Barry and R. J. Chorley: *Atmosphere, Weather and Climate*. Holt, Rinehart and Winston, New York, 1970.]

would suggest is because the calculation assumes a static situation, whereas in practice energy is transferred to the surrounding, cooler countryside mainly by convection. Although the increased temperature does often have a stabilizing effect and the winds are generally less, there is a smoothing effect. Nevertheless the heat island of a city is already clearly observable for most large cities.

In this situation also there may be feedback effects in operation. For example, in summer with increased use of air conditioning, more energy is used and therefore the temperature will rise in the city. This prompts even more use of air conditioning, which in turn raises the temperature even more. In winter, some heating economies may be realized in cities. Already however summer peak uses, at least of electricity, are higher than winter peaks (Figure 15-1). These peaks will be magnified because of the increased heating of the urban environment.

The increased heating effect in the cities will be present whether solar energy is used or not because the solar energy used in the urban area would undoubtedly be produced elsewhere and transported to the city. If the energy use per capita continues to grow and if the concentration of people in cities also continues to grow then, temperature rises and local climate changes will undoubtedly continue.

16-7 Summary and Conclusions

Although climatic conditions are difficult to predict and many interrelating factors are not well understood, we can simply say that, because most of the energy we use finishes up as heat, an increasing energy consumption will have an impact on the overall temperature of the earth. At present, the effect is extremely small (2×10^{-3}°C). However in only nine doublings this would increase to almost 1°C. A similar effect would be noted if the rest of the world was brought up to the living standard of the upper and middle classes of the United States and if allowances are made for water purification, air pollution control, and increased energy consumption to extract metals from depleted reserves.

One may disagree with particular assumptions, but the basic point of a significant temperature increase, at *some* level of energy use cannot be disputed. This follows simply from the basic laws of physics. Only if we generate a significant portion of our energy from the solar energy incident on the earth can this problem be avoided. Even in that case, we will have problems in urban centers, where energy use is concentrated. Already cities are significantly warmer than their surroundings. These urban heat islands will be the first indication we have of the overall problem of global thermal pollution. Although the urban problem could in principle be solved by the transfer of energy to a wider area, it should give us pause, because it may be an early warning of an even more significant problem some years ahead.

Questions

1. Assume that world energy consumption is increasing at 4% per year. How long will it be before the surface temperature of the earth increases by 2°C?
2. Why would increased carbon dioxide concentration in the atmosphere lead to higher surface temperatures on the earth?
3. The earth has been undergoing a cooling phase recently. However, energy

use increases the earth's surface temperature. How long will it be before there is a significant impact on the earth's average temperature? Make your assumptions clear.

4. Estimate and discuss the temperature changes likely in a large urban area like New York, Los Angeles, or Chicago over the next 50 to 100 years.

5. If the temperature rise due to present global thermal pollution due to man's use of energy is $2.5 \times 10^{-3}°C$ and the use of energy continues to increase with a doubling time of 20 years, how long would it be until the temperature rise was $2.5°C$?

6. Mark the best answer.
   Which of the following contributes to global thermal pollution when used steadily over several decades?
   (a) a hydroelectric generating station
   (b) a wood fireplace fire
   (c) an automobile
   (d) a windmill
   (e) a solar house

7. Calculate the expected temperature rise in the greater New York area (population 20×10^6 people, area 10^4 square miles) assuming an average per capita energy use of 3.7×10^{11} J/year.

8. In the text a temperature rise of $4.2°C$ was calculated for the city of Detroit, compared to its surroundings. Why is the observed temperature rise not as great as calculated?

Bibliography

[1] A. M. Weinberg and R. P. Hammond: Limits to the use of energy. *American Scientist*, **58** (4): 412 (1970).

[2] Man's Impact on the Global Environment. Report of the Study of Critical Environmental Problems. Massachusetts Institute of Technology Press, 1970.

[3] The Study of Man's Impact on Climate: The Summary Report. Massachusetts Institute of Technology Press, 1971.

[4] Inadvertent Climate Modification. Study of Man's Impact on Climate. Massachusetts Institute of Technology Press, 1971.

[5] H. E. Landsburg: Man-made climatic changes. *Science*, **170**: 1265 (Dec. 18, 1970).

[6] W. A. Porter, M. O. Hagler, and M. Kristiansen: Global temperature effects of the use of fusion energy and the fusion torch. *IEEE Transactions on Nuclear Science*, Vol **18**, Number 1, page 31 (1973).

[7] J. W. Bjerklie: Engineering of energy effects with an expanding world population. *Intersociety Energy Conversion Conference*. Energy 70 Las Vegas, Nevada, September 1970, Paper 6-1.

[8] R. G. Barry and R. J. Chorley: *Atmosphere, Weather, and Climate*. Holt, Rinehart and Winston, 1970.

[9] H. H. Lamb: *Climate, Present Past and Future*, Vol. 1. Metheun and Co., 1972.

[10] A. M. Weinberg and R. P. Hammond: Global effects of increased use of energy. *Bulletin of the Atomic Scientists,* March, 1972.

[11] C. Barus: Energy limits. *Bulletin of the Atomic Scientists,* February, 1973, p. 4.

[12] A. M. Weinberg and R. P. Hammond: Energy limits. *Bulletin of the Atomic Scientists,* May, 1973.

227

Bibliography

PART FIVE

FURTHER IMPLICATIONS OF ENERGY USE

Energy Conservation

17-1 Introduction

Thus far this book has emphasized the difficulties associated with the rapid increase in the use of energy. These problems include the lack of satisfactory long lasting resources and the pollution of air and water by many of the current energy sources. Even if these problems are met, we saw in Chapter 16 that at some point there will be an ultimate limit to the amount of energy used because of the heating problems associated with the use of energy. Although it is possible to minimize and perhaps to solve some of these resource problems, the long term solution must involve a stabilization of energy demand. One important element in stabilizing demand is energy conservation.

Up till now little thought has been given to energy conservation. In 1964 the United States government point of view, as reflected by the Federal Power Commission, was that we should rapidly develop our resources, keep energy costs to a minimum, and encourage the growth of energy use. Even in June, 1973 as was pointed out in the Report of the Task Force on Energy [2], there was no federal office that was primarily responsible for energy conservation. This point is underscored by President Nixon's energy messages in 1972 and early in 1973 which were criticized because of their lack of emphasis on energy conservation. Only very recently, and in the face of obvious shortages, has there been any emphasis on energy conservation in messages from the White House. Prof. David White of the Massachusetts Institute of Technology stated in his testimony before the Task Force on Energy that "Conservation to slow down growth while satisfying the needs of society has a greater societal payoff than any other single factor today including new energy supply developments and new resource discoveries."

It is important first to examine where energy is used so that conservation measures can be directed to those areas where substantial savings can be made. There are a number of ways of displaying energy demands. In Chapter 7, energy use was divided into four major categories: electrical utilities, industrial, transportation, and household/commercial. Each of these used approximately one quarter of the total demand in 1967. The detailed breakdown from 1963 to 1967 is given in Table 7-1. Department of the Interior projections of energy consumption through the year 1990 are shown in Figure 7-6. The main point to note from these projections is the anticipated large growth in the electrical production fraction of total energy consumption from 25% in 1971 to 38% in 1990. This suggests that careful consideration should be given to the efficiency of electrical generation in the next few decades.

On the other hand, electrical energy is generally used either in manufacturing (57% in 1971) or in residential/commercial (43% in 1971). An alternative breakdown of total energy use, after dividing up the electrical load, would be, for example, in 1971, industrial 42%, residential/commercial 33%, and transportation 25%. When these sections are further subdivided, we find that a few specific uses take up a significant amount of the demand. These subdivisions will be discussed in later sections.

It is important to realize that, when we divide energy use into various categories, this involves a major simplification because these categories are not independent. There is generally a significant correlation between use in one area and in another. The requirements for electric generation would probably be decreased if energy use was curtailed in either the residential/commercial or industrial sectors. Another example of this interrelation is provided by the automobile, which is generally considered to use energy in the transportation sector. However, there are large amounts of energy used in mining and producing steel for the automobile, in manufacturing the automobile, and in building roads for use by automobiles; all of this uses significant amounts of energy. If automobile use were curtailed, it might well have repercussions not only in transportation but in other areas as well.

A slightly more mundane example is the electric toothbrush, which is often caricatured as being a completely unimportant aspect of energy conservation. Certainly if we consider only the electric energy used by electric toothbrushes, the impact on energy consumption if people stopped using them would be insignificant. On the other hand, electric toothbrushes have to be manufactured, transported from one place to another, and sold. All these operations require energy.

Perhaps, even more important, the "electric toothbrush syndrome" represents an attitude towards energy use that is anticonservationist. People are encouraged by advertising to substitute electric energy for their own effort, even in simple tasks like brushing teeth and opening cans. Whether these add to the quality of life is, I think, very much open to question.

This brings us to a final point on energy use. Ultimately *people* use energy. While we make divisions into industrial, residential/commercial, and transportation, in a very real sense all energy use is personal. Because we are the people who use energy, we are also the people who can have an impact on limiting its use. Therefore education of people about the problem should be an important part of any conservation program. Awareness of the issues and taking what may seem like small steps are part of the solution. If many people took many small steps, there would be a significant impact on overall consumption.

Let us now turn to each of the different sectors and examine the possibilities of energy conservation in detail. The first area to consider is transportation.

17-2 Transportation

Transportation is the single largest user of energy; 25% of all the energy consumed in the United States is used to move people or freight from one place to another. When historians look back at America in the period from 1910 to the 1970s, one of the dramatic changes they will see is the tremendous increase in mobility and in transportation use. At the moment 1% of the United States is covered with roads: 1% of the total land area is roads! The automobile in particular has permeated our culture. Its use has significantly changed our whole way of life. The reasons are fairly clear. The automobile is a relatively rapid and very convenient form of transportation. Perhaps even the idea of individual transportation reflects the concept of individual freedom which, at least philosophically, is an integral part of the American way of life. Certainly in the past, and perhaps even now, there has been a good deal of status associated with a man's automobile.

Dan Horvath, an urban geographer at Michigan State University, has called the automobile America's sacred cow. He points out that more and more of our central cities are being given over to automobiles and their related services. More Americans have been killed and maimed on our highways than in all our wars, and yet we continue to give up more land and more of our scarce resources to pre-

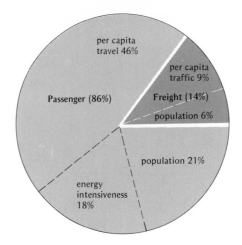

Figure 17-1

Factors accounting for the increase in transportation energy use between 1960 and 1970. (Numbers do not add up to totals because of rounding.) [From E. Hirst: Transportation energy use and conservation potential. *Bulletin of the Atomic Scientists*, November, 1973.]

serve the automobile. Horvath's point is that, although we readily criticize other countries for their apparently irrational beliefs, Americans are blind to their own folly.

The increased consumption of energy in transportation has a number of causes. Figure 17-1 shows a summary of the factors contributing to this increase in both passenger and freight transportation between 1960 and 1970. First, the increasing population has accounted for about a quarter of the increase in the passenger sector and about

Table 17-1
Passenger Transport Data for 1970

Passenger Mode	Energy Intensiveness* For Load Factor of 100%	Energy Intensiveness* For Actual Load Factor	Load Factor (%)	Revenue†	Fatality Rate‡
Intercity					
bus	1600	740	46	3.6	0.10
railroad	2900	1100	37	4.0	0.09
automobile	3400	1600	48	4.0	3.25
airplane	8400	4100	49	6.0	0.13
Urban					
mass transit					
bus	3700	650	18	9.5	—
electric	4100	1100	26	6.2	—
average	3800	760	20	8.3	0.26
automobile	8100	2300	28	9.6	2.11

SOURCE: E. Hirst: *Bulletin of the Atomic Scientists*, November, 1973 [11].

* btu per passenger mile.
† Cents per passenger mile.
‡ Deaths per hundred million passenger miles.

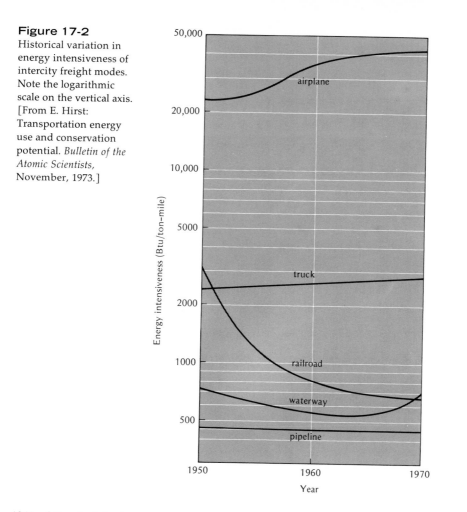

Figure 17-2
Historical variation in energy intensiveness of intercity freight modes. Note the logarithmic scale on the vertical axis. [From E. Hirst: Transportation energy use and conservation potential. *Bulletin of the Atomic Scientists,* November, 1973.]

40% of the freight increase. Even more important has been the growth in the level of mobility. More goods are being shipped. More people are traveling both for business and for pleasure. Over half of the rise in passenger travel is due to the increase in miles traveled per person.

Finally there has been a shift to less efficient forms of transportation. A decreasing fraction of freight is now moved by rail and waterway as the percentage of road and airplane use increases. These latter methods are less efficient energy users in terms of energy consumed per ton-mile of freight carried. (Figure 17-2 and Table 17-1). One reason that a change to less energy intensive systems is possible economically, is because of what is essentially a government subsidy of these modes. The federal government subsidizes roads and airports, and without this assistance, road and air transportation would be much more expensive. The freight handling sector, however, is very sensitive to cost as well as convenience and speed especially in handling large amounts of material so that it would probably be rather

235

17-2 Transportation

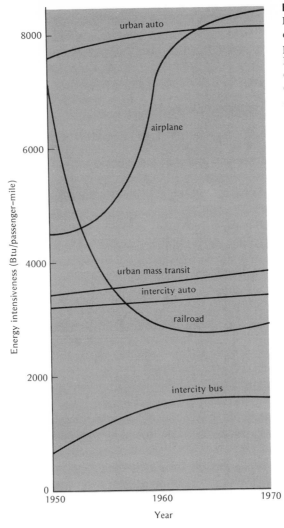

Figure 17-3

Historical variation in energy intensiveness of passenger modes. [From E. Hirst: Transportation energy use and conservation potential. *Bulletin of the Atomic Scientists*, November, 1973.]

responsive to measures designed to promote less energy intensive freight transportation.

Passenger travel has also become more energy intensive both because of the shift to more energy intensive modes of travel like the automobile and the jet airplane instead of the train and bus and also because both automobile and air travel have become less efficient (Figure 17-3). Environmental and safety concerns have been blamed for the decrease in energy efficiency (decreased miles per gallon) especially by representatives from the big automobile manufacturers and the oil companies. Certainly as people have become more aware of the air pollution caused by the automobile, political pressure has resulted in the passage of pollution control legislation like the Clean Air Act. As a result, air pollution control devices are being installed on new cars.

These, in turn, have led to a decrease in energy efficiency of the automobile in terms of energy consumed per passenger mile. Russell Train, administrator for the Environmental Protection Agency, estimates that pollution control devices presently add about 10% to gasoline consumption. Estimates of increased gasoline consumption in post 1976 cars as high as 30% have been made, but the figure more commonly accepted is around 20%.

Another fairly recent policy change by the federal government has been to have stricter safety standards to try to decrease the devastation caused by automobiles and to minimize the economic burden of personal injuries and property damage. For example, bumpers are now required to withstand greater shocks than before, and there is a general emphasis on safety features. The way the automobile manufacturers have tackled these problems has resulted in additional weight. Automobiles are getting heavier. On the other hand, to supply the performance requirements the public wants, or at least thinks it wants right now, heavier automobiles must consume more energy.

Although it is true that pollution control equipment and safety features have contributed to increased gasoline consumption, it is important to put this in perspective. Table 17-2, for example, lists the consumption of the most efficient 1974 models and shows clearly the very strong dependence of gasoline consumption on the weight of the car. A 4500-lb car used over twice as much gasoline as a 2000-lb car.

There are also extra options going into automobiles, like air conditioning and automatic transmission, that also reduce gas mileage. These two options, for example, probably cause about the same increase in gas mileage as do the air pollution control devices. Therefore, before blaming safety features and pollution control for the increased gas consumption, the effect of other less necessary options should be made clear. If cars were made smaller and lighter, and particularly if their performance characteristics were allowed to slacken, they could

Table 17-2
Gasoline Consumption for "Most Efficient" 1974 Models

Vehicle Weight (lb)	Vehicle Type	Average Gasoline Consumption (mpg)
2000	Honda Civic	29.1
	Toyota Corolla–1 Coupe	27.1
2250	Datsun B-210 (manual transmission)	24.9
	Toyota Corolla–2 Sedan	22.6
3000	Chevrolet Vega Kammback	20.0
	Ford Pinto Wagon	19.6
4500	Chevrolet G-20 Sportvan	12.4
	AMC Matador SW	12.3

SOURCE: Environmental Protection Agency.

be made much more efficient in energy consumption. Let us hope that this will be the future trend in automobile purchases and manufacture.

Considerable energy savings could also be realized by the use of more efficient components particularly more efficient engines. The use of radial ply tires, overdrive and constant speed accessory drives would all improve fuel economy. New engine types such as the stratified charge engine or high temperature gas turbine would also be advantageous but these are somewhat longer term propositions. The Department of Transportation [12] suggests that the use of more efficient components could lead to a reduction of 11.5% to 12% in transportation energy use.

There have been a number of proposals made to try to force lower fuel consumption by automobiles. Lowering speed limits to 50 mph can produce savings of between 20 and 30%. Keeping the engine tuned and driving without rapid acceleration can produce further savings. Some more general approaches are either to tax gasoline and thus raise the price or to ration gasoline. Rationing is fraught with bureaucratic problems, but a high tax on gasoline would be unfair to poor people who are forced to drive. A better approach might be to have a progressive tax on engine size, where cars with large engine and heavy weight would pay a very large tax each year. An even more drastic step is being considered in Wisconsin, where legislation is being considered that would ban the sale of automobiles which do not achieve 25 mpg. Although this proposal is unlikely to become law, it indicates a growing attitude against wasteful use of gasoline, especially as supplies run short.

After realizing that the private automobile as well as trucks and airplanes are large energy consumers, the question arises — what are our alternatives? One suggestion is that mass transit systems, especially for urban and suburban transport, would reduce the need for private automobile trips. The Bay Area Rapid Transport (BART) system has recently been completed in the San Francisco Bay Area, and this will be an interesting experiment to observe. New York City has had a successful subway system for many years and now even smaller communities are beginning to experiment with local bus systems.

It has been estimated that mass transit would save a significant amount of energy in terms of energy used per passenger mile. Hirst (see Table 17-1) estimates that a fully loaded bus is 3.5 times less energy intensive than a fully loaded private automobile. (The factor decreases to about 2.2 for average loadings of 18% for the bus and 29% for the car). If the transit system was able to attract commuters, it might produce the additional savings of decreasing traffic snarls, which waste a significant amount of gasoline.

Rapid mass transit systems also lend themselves to alternative fuel sources more readily than private automobiles. Electric powered ve-

Energy Conservation

hicles are used for example in New York City and in Melbourne, Australia. If cheap plentiful sources of electricity can be developed (see Chapters 13, 14), then electric powered mass transit systems could help save significant amounts of fossil fuels.

Serge Gratch, of the Ford Motor Company, in a talk delivered at Michigan State University pointed out a number of problems with a mass transit system. One problem is that the basic design of most cities does not permit simple transportation solutions. One reason for the success of mass transit in New York City and Melbourne is the layout of the urban development. In Melbourne, for example, residential development has followed the arms of the train lines (Figure 17-4). Unfortunately most cities do not readily lend themselves to mass transit development. This should be a major consideration in new urban planning.

A second difficulty in mass transit is to convince people to use it. This will involve not only making sure that it is reliable and fast but may also include negative incentives for private automobile use. Unless mass transit systems are loaded to a reasonable capacity and reduce automobile traffic, they will not provide significant energy savings.

Another proposal for reducing automobile use is to make more extensive use of bicycles. The bicycle is an extremely energy efficient form of transportation, essentially using only the food energy we eat, most of which we would use anyway. Because 50% of automobile trips are of 5 miles or less, a good fraction of these could be made by bicycle or by walking—a very significant reduction in automobile traffic would result (and the health of the population would improve). Some cities, such as Davis, California, are beginning to develop a bicycle path system that would help to remove the dangerous situation which exists when bicycles compete with cars. Building more extensive bicycle path systems should further encourage bicycle use. One major, and I believe increasing, use of the automobile, is by the mother who drives her children to one or more activity—piano lessons, swimming instruction, or dancing class. If a safe bicycle system was available, many of these trips could be made by the children alone saving gasoline as well as wear and tear on mother.

The number of bicycles has been growing rapidly in the United States in recent years, but many of these are used only for recreation. This application is admirable, but it might be even better if we learned to use our bicycles, and our legs and lungs, for more of our "necessary" business trips as well. A test in East Lansing showed that bicycle travel at peak time was quicker up to 3 miles from campus. Even up to 6 miles the difference in time would be very small and a valuable reduction in traffic congestion and gasoline consumption would result.

So far we have tried to suggest less energy intensive ways of doing the same amount of travelling. A different approach to the problem is

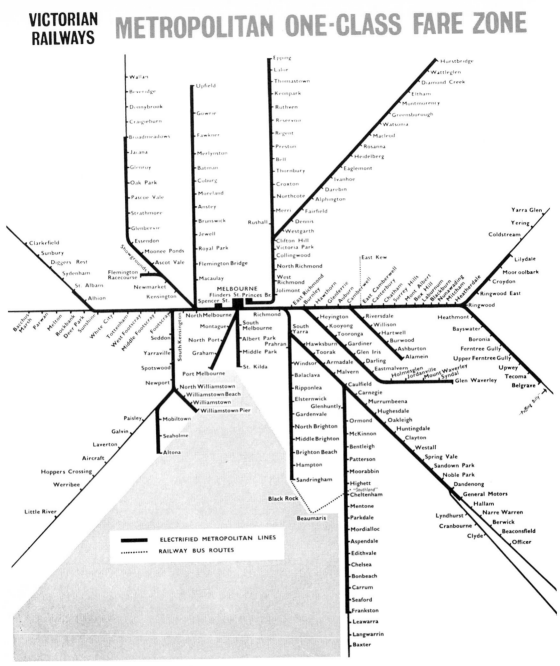

Figure 17-4
Electric train map for the City of Melbourne, Australia. Note that urban development has been along train lines making mass transit easier to use. [Courtesy of Victorian Railways.]

to ask whether we need to travel as much as we do? Arthur Clarke, the well known science fiction author, points out that electronic communication has now reached a point where many of our needs could be met by a communication center in our homes. With two-way or multiple linkup sight and sound communication with anywhere in the world available in the home, much business and entertainment could be provided right there. Libraries of books, music, and films could be made available. People would not have to live so close together. The cultural stimulation of urban living could thus be provided in smaller communities. Such electronic systems using transistors or even more sophisticated solid state microcircuitry use very little energy so that this approach would provide a very small drain on energy sources. This is an interesting suggestion, worth pondering especially by people who spend an hour or more each day traveling to and from work.

17-3 Conservation in Industry

When total energy use is divided by its three end users, industry becomes a major user, accounting for approximately 42% of the total energy use of the United States. Industrial energy use is primarily in three areas: steam production, which uses 17% of the total; the production of heat, which uses 11% of the total; and finally 8% of the total goes to operating electric motors of one kind or another. These three processes account for 36% of the total energy use; the remaining 6% goes into a variety of other uses.

If we now turn to the particular industries, we find that six main areas use over two thirds of the total energy. This is shown in Table 17-3 where we see that three of the extremely large users of energy are

Table 17-3
Industrial Fuel Consumption by Major Users (10^{12} btu)

Industry Group	Coal	Natural Gas	Petroleum Products	Electricity	Total Energy	Percentage
primary metal industries	2,838	863	306	1,291	5,298	21.2
chemicals and allied products	666	1,219	1,426	1,626	4,937	19.8
petroleum refining and related industries		1,012	1,589	225	2,826	11.3
food and kindred products	263	593	134	338	1,328	5.3
paper and allied products	467	341	211	280	1,299	5.2
stone, clay, glass, and concrete products	406	449	87	280	1,222	4.9
Subtotal	4,640	4,477	3,753	4,040	16,910	67.7
all other industries	976	4,781	721	1,572	8,050	32.3
Total	5,616	9,258	4,474	5,612	24,960	100

Source: Stanford Research Institute using Bureau of Mines data.

primary metal industries, the chemical industry and petroleum refining and related industries. We notice that the primary metal industry is one of the main users of energy. This is an extremely important industry which has effects throughout the whole economy because many secondary processes use metals such as steel, aluminum, and copper. Curtailment of their production would have far reaching consequences.

In the past industry has been very conscious of costs in order to make a profit, and rightly so. Because energy has been fairly cheap, energy intensive processes have generally also been the least expensive. Undoubtedly successful managers are continuing to look for less expensive techniques of manufacture and production. Manufacturers will attempt to use processes that are, overall, the least expensive. This means that, in order to provide an incentive for reducing energy in industry, it will be necessary either to make energy more expensive to the user or to have some other penalty or tax on those processes that are particularly energy intensive.

There is one advantage in attempting to introduce conservation measures in industry. Because the free market is a competitive situation, industry is generally fairly responsive to economic pressures. The companies that see some economic advantages in a new and cheaper process will be the ones that change over to the new process. Those companies that do not change will be left behind and will eventually be eliminated by the competition, unless they too change their methods.

One place where energy costs would probably have an immediate impact is in the recycling process. It has been estimated that the energy requirements for recycling, particularly the nonferrous metals, are about 20% smaller than the primary production process. Aluminum in particular requires a good deal of energy to produce. Recycling aluminum containers would require much less energy. Therefore, if energy becomes more expensive, energy consuming processes would be economically disadvantageous and it would pay companies to encourage recycling. A similar situation holds in the glass container industry.

More expensive energy costs would also have the result of decreasing wasteful energy use practices. Generally these occur in industries that do not use large amounts of energy because the large users already are concerned about their energy use problems. However, even for these small users it is advisable to encourage good energy use practices.

Another important advance that could have an even larger impact and has not been used very extensively is the recycling of energy. As we have seen many times, much of the energy that is used to do work finishes up as waste heat. If this waste heat, at lower temperatures, could be recycled and used for preheating or in some other process, or if a total system could be designed that made use of this waste heat, improved overall efficiencies would certainly result.

These are all ways in which industrial use of energy could be decreased. Undoubtedly other energy saving techniques are possible. A conservation program together with an educational program would be very useful in industry, particularly if professional engineers and managers were educated by their professional societies, trade journals, or managerial schools to become more energy conscious.

17-4   Electric Utilities and Energy Conservation

The utilities have an impact on energy conservation both as users of energy and as providers of electric energy. Because fuel costs are a significant proportion of the total cost of operating a power plant, the electric utilities have generally been very conscious of the efficiency of their systems. The efficiency of central power plants has climbed from $\approx 10\%$ in 1920 to a little above 40% at present in a well maintained modern system. Recently, however, the average efficiency has begun to decrease. Some of this reduced efficiency is due to the installation of pollution control devices, some to the use of peaking systems that are inherently less efficient, and some simply by the decreasing efficiency of older plants. If the use of nuclear power plants grows as anticipated, then the average efficiency, at least initially, will be even lower because the present nuclear plants have efficiencies of around 30%. Presumably this efficiency will increase with improved engineering, particularly if the breeder reactor is developed.

The use of magnetohydrodynamics (MHD) topping (see Chapter 14) could, in principle, raise the efficiency of fossil fuel plants from the present 40% to between 50 and 70%. This technique is still being developed but should be seriously considered as an energy conservation measure as soon as possible.

However, electric utilities can probably have their main impact on energy consumption, in their role as provider of electric power, both by their advertising policies and especially by the rate structure of electric pricing. The maximum profit margin for electric utilities is controlled by law, and the profit is based on the amount of capitalization of the company. It therefore pays the company to build new facilities. But to justify these new facilities, it is necessary to point to increasing consumption. Thus it pays the utilities to increase consumption not only because this increases the sale of their product but also because an increasing rate of consumption enables them to justify building new plants.

An indication of the success of advertising is seen in the seasonal peak load. Some years ago, even in the south, the peak electrical demand occurred in winter with increased heating and lighting requirements. Then the utilities decided to level out the peak by encouraging the use of air conditioning. This campaign was so successful that, at present, the peak demand in almost all areas in the United States is now in the summer instead of the winter, and air conditioning is one of the most rapidly growing uses of electricity.

There is another aspect to electric consumption that has a large effect on energy conservation — the rate structure. At present the pricing of electricity is such that small users pay a higher rate than larger users. Thus, small users subsidize larger ones. If the rate structure were changed so that larger users paid at the same or even higher rates for electricity, there would be a great incentive for conservation. Because most of the large users are in industry, this could have a large economic impact and would probably have to be implemented slowly. However, as mentioned previously, industry is very responsive to economic considerations and probably has the capability of changing practices fairly rapidly. At present, on the average, energy accounts for only 1.5% of production costs in industry so that a significant price increase could probably be handled in most industries without too serious an economic impact.

17-5 Reduction of Commercial Energy Consumption

Commercial energy use is usually combined with residential use, but the problems of conservation are sufficiently different that we will consider them separately. One feature of commercial operations that has been changing over the years is size. Large office buildings are becoming more common, even in comparatively small towns, and the ubiquitous shopping center is becoming larger and larger.

Energy requirements are very seldom a consideration in the design of an office building. One of the reasons for this is that the initial cost and operating costs for a building are usually financed separately. It often pays to minimize initial cost at the expense of operating cost. The very size of office buildings makes them large consumers of energy. Elevators both for people and freight are required particularly if buildings more than five or six stories are considered. The World Trade Center in New York City uses 8×10^4 kw of power, which is approximately the same as the power requirements of a city of 100,000 people.

There are many other examples of the lack of energy consideration in an office building. The large glass walls, particularly when coupled to a lack of careful siting, place very large additional requirements on both the heating and cooling systems of the building. Commercial buildings are often overheated and are provided with excessive air exchange with outside air. This infiltration of outside air may account for approximately 25 to 50% of the heating or cooling requirements of a large building. Special areas, for example toilets, kitchens, or heavily used conference rooms need large amounts of ventilation, but it is wasteful to apply these same standards to the whole building. Most buildings are also completely sealed so that artificial cooling is always required in warm weather. This is especially noticeable when the air conditioning breaks down. Even if the air is fairly cool outside, there is essentially no way of getting a breeze into the building which steams in its self-generated heat waste.

Lack of natural air flow also means that the building is subject to greater wind stresses. R. G. Stein, a New York architect, points out [9] that for this reason buildings must be more massive, using more materials, whereas if the wind were allowed to enter the building the stresses would be reduced as well as providing some natural ventilation.

While dealing with the subject of economical air conditioning, it is interesting to note how air conditioning is engineered. The outside air is usually cooled to a much lower temperature than is required and then heated before being passed through the building. Extra energy is thus used both to overcool the air and to rewarm it again. This is a clear case when energy conservation plays a negligible role in design.

Another wasteful use of energy, again quoting Stein [9], is the excessive lighting used in many commercial buildings. This can run between 10 and 25% of the total electrical requirements. The standards for lighting are much higher in the United States than in Europe although it is not clear that brighter lighting is an advantage. In fact, some eye complaints are treated by exercising the eye muscles by forcing them to adjust to bright and dark stimuli alternatively. Uniform lighting means that the eye muscles work less. Stein finds also that uniform bright light can be exceedingly dull from an aesthetic point of view and suggests much more variation, as well as reduction, in our use of lighting. In many large office buildings, the lights are left on during nonworking hours, again giving rise to wasteful use of electricity.

Another aspect of energy consumption is in building design where materials that require a large amount of energy in production are commonly used. A good example is aluminum. Perhaps architects could use more imagination and try other less energy intensive materials like wood in their structures.

The large shopping center or mall is another feature of commercial energy use that contributes to excess energy consumption. Because these malls are very large, they must draw customers from a fairly large area. This means that the average customer has to travel a considerable distance to shop, thus adding to transportation costs.

Both the size of many buildings and the lack of concern about energy requirements, especially in design, are some of the difficulties in commercial energy conservation. More expensive energy and an education program, especially among architects, may help to alleviate these problems.

17-6 Savings in Home Heating

The breakdown of energy use in the residential sector in 1960 and 1968 is shown in Table 17-4 together with the respective growth rates. The total residential use accounts for about 19% of total United States energy use, and space heating alone is responsible for about 11% of the total. Clearly space heating is a primary place to undertake energy conservation measures.

The two main sources of space heating are direct heating by burning oil or gas and electric heat. Furnaces are typically 75% efficient when operating well, but it requires only about a half a millimeter of soot to degrade their performance by 50%. Electric heat is very efficient in the home, but the central power plant is at best 40% efficient, and there are additional losses in transmission. On the other hand, there is likely to be better maintenance in a central plant so that the efficiency will probably remain near its peak value, unlike the situation for many home furnaces. Pollution control is also more easily installed, maintained, and supervised in a central power station. Nevertheless a well maintained furnace is typically twice as efficient overall as electric heat.

Table 17-4

Total Fuel Energy Consumption in the Residential Sector in the United States by End Use (Electric Utility Consumption Has Been Allocated to Each End Use)

End Use	Consumption (10¹² btu)		Annual Rate of Growth (%)	Percent of National Total	
	1960	1968		1960	1968
space heating	4,848	6,675	4.1	11.3	11.0
water heating	1,159	1,736	5.2	2.7	2.9
cooking	556	637	1.7	1.3	1.1
clothes drying	93	208	10.6	0.2	0.3
refrigeration	369	692	8.2	0.9	1.1
air conditioning	134	427	15.6	0.3	0.7
other	809	1,241	5.5	1.9	2.1
Total	7,968	11,616	4.8	18.6	19.2

An attractive alternative to a furnace is a heat pump which uses energy to pump heat from one place to another. Perhaps the most common example of a heat pump is an air conditioner, which pumps heat from inside a room to the outside world. Basically a heat pump can be thought of as a heat engine in reverse. In a heat engine, useful work is obtained as the engine transfers heat from a hot reservoir to a cold reservoir. The maximum efficiency of such a heat engine (note Chapter 5) is given by Equation 17-1.

$$\text{max. eff.} = \frac{\text{work out}}{\text{heat transferred from hot reservoir}} \qquad \text{17-1}$$

$$= \frac{W}{Q_{\text{hot}}} = \frac{T_{\text{hot}} - T_{\text{cold}}}{T_{\text{hot}}}$$

where T_{hot} and T_{cold} are the temperatures of the hot and cold reservoirs in kelvin (or degrees absolute).

In a heat pump, work is put *in*, to transfer heat from the cooler reservoir to a hotter one. In an air conditioner, for example, the maximum efficiency is given by Equation 17-2.

$$\text{max. eff.} = \frac{\text{heat removed from cool reservoir}}{\text{work in}} \qquad \text{17-2}$$

$$= \frac{Q_{\text{cold}}}{W} = \frac{T_{\text{cold}}}{T_{\text{hot}} - T_{\text{cold}}}$$

Suppose we have an air conditioner operating in a room at 68°F while the outside temperature is 86°F

$$T_{\text{cold}} = 68°F = 20°C = 293K$$
$$T_{\text{hot}} = 86°F = 30°C = 303K$$

$$\text{max. eff.} = \frac{T_{\text{cold}}}{T_{\text{hot}} - T_{\text{cold}}} = \frac{293}{10} = 29.3$$

Therefore in principle a rather high efficiency could be achieved so that comparatively little work need be done to obtain a large transfer of heat. In practice, however, present commercial air conditioners have efficiencies of only about 1.7 to 3.5.

If we turn to the case of a heat pump for heating in the winter, then heat must be pumped from the cool outside to the warm inside. In principle the maximum efficiency is given by Equation 17-3.

$$\text{max. eff.} = \frac{\text{heat added to warm reservoir}}{\text{work input}} \qquad \text{17-3}$$

$$= \frac{Q_{\text{hot}}}{W} = \frac{T_{\text{hot}}}{T_{\text{hot}} - T_{\text{cold}}}$$

If, for example, the outside temperature is just at freezing (32°F) and the room temperature is again 68°F

$$T_{\text{cold}} = 32°F = 0°C = 273K$$
$$T_{\text{hot}} = 68°F = 20°C = 293K$$

$$\text{max. eff.} = \frac{T_{\text{hot}}}{T_{\text{hot}} - T_{\text{cold}}} = \frac{293}{20} = 14.6$$

Thus ideally, even under the fairly severe conditions considered above, a heat pump could operate quite efficiently. If electric energy is used to power the heat pump, an efficiency of 2 for the heat pump would mean a system with the same total efficiency as a furnace, (because at present electric heating has an overall efficiency of between 30 and 40% compared with a furnace with a typical efficiency of around 70%). Any higher efficiencies would place electricity ahead of direct burning of oil or gas for home heating.

The main problem with heat pumps has been their poor reliability, but hopefully further engineering work will make these devices commercially available with satisfactory performance characteristics. This could be a major boon to space heating both in homes and commercial buildings.

Perhaps the biggest savings in home heating can be realized by better insulation of homes. A study of homes in Atlanta, New York, and Minneapolis with floor area of 1800 ft² concluded that most homes were greatly under insulated. Even the new (F.H.A.) standards established in 1971, although an improvement, do not yet achieve optimum insulation conditions. Table 17-5 lists the old and new standards together with the optimum considered for a house in New York. An average of about 48% of the total energy for heating could be saved for a home complying with the new F.H.A. standards. (The national average is slightly less, about a 42% energy saving.) However, with better insulation, other sources of waste heat such as lights, stoves, and other appliances become a significant fraction of the total heat required so that actual savings may be even more. The advantage of

Table 17-5
Comparison of Insulation Requirements and Monetary and Energy Savings for a New York Residence

Insulation Specification	Unrevised MPS*		Revised MPS*		Economic Optimum	
	Gas	Electric	Gas	Electric	Gas	Electric
wall insulation thickness (in.)	0	$1\frac{7}{8}$	$1\frac{7}{8}$	$1\frac{7}{8}$	$3\frac{1}{2}$	$3\frac{1}{2}$
ceiling insulation thickness (in.)	$1\frac{7}{8}$	$1\frac{7}{8}$	$3\frac{1}{2}$	$3\frac{1}{2}$	$3\frac{1}{2}$	6
floor insulation	No	No	Yes	Yes	Yes	Yes
storm windows	No	No	No	No	Yes	Yes
monetary savings ($/yr)	0	0	28	75	32	155
reduction of energy consumption (%)	0	0	29	19	49	47

* Minimum property standards (MPS) for one and two living units.

good insulation was noted recently by a military installation buried in a hill in New England. The building has never required any additional heating, the heat from the lights being sufficient to warm the building.

The F.H.A. standards, of course, only apply to new homes. It is much more difficult to install insulation in older homes. It may be even more difficult to legislate standards for such older homes. Education is again required perhaps emphasizing the long term dollar advantages of insulation. People generally resist large capital outlays even though these may bring later returns. One suggestion to solve this problem is that insulation costs could be paid initially by the fuel supplier and then paid for by a small surcharge on a customer's monthly fuel bill. The cost of fuel should decrease after the installation of the insulation so that if the payment for the insulation is made over a long enough period, the average monthly bill may be immediately decreased.

Similar considerations also apply to storm windows. These will also be of assistance in insulation and are simpler to install in older homes. Again the capital costs of installation could be absorbed by the utility company and added to the fuel bill to ensure more rapid installation. Another simple technique in winter is to draw curtains across windows because these also give some additional insulation.

There is one other way in which heating costs could be reduced immediately with no installation required. The amount of energy to heat a home and the amount of heat lost to the outside depends upon the temperature difference between inside and outside (See Chapter 5, Example 5-1). If thermostats were run a little lower in winter and a little higher in summer substantial savings in both heating and cooling costs could be realized. It has been estimated that a change of 4°F in the thermostat settings in summer and winter could save 10% or more of the total heating and cooling costs. In many countries the temperatures of homes are allowed to fluctuate much more than in the United States and people dress accordingly. In the United States we insist on dressing in summer clothes all year round and compensate by heating homes to summer temperatures. It may even be healthier to keep one's home at a lower temperature in winter.

17-7 Other Energy Conservation Measures in the Home

Although air conditioning at present is a fairly small fraction of total energy demand (see Table 17-4), it is the most rapidly growing area of residential energy use. If this growth rate continues, space cooling will shortly be a more significant fraction of total residential use. As with space heating, one simple way of reducing the air conditioning load is simply to set the thermostat a little higher and adjust to a slightly warmer room. Insulation of the house will also help to decrease the air conditioning load. Shades or awnings to stop direct sunlight streaming in through a window are another useful load reducer. An aesthetically pleasing solution, though generally not quickly implemented, is to use a deciduous tree that shades the roof and windows in summer but in winter sheds its leaves and allows winter sunlight to help warm the house.

In the previous section, in discussing heat pumps, we noted that an air conditioner had an ideal maximum efficiency of almost 30. Figure 17-5 shows some examples of the efficiency of current air conditioners. These are usually quoted in British thermal units per watt hour. Since 1 btu = 0.3 wh, an efficiency rating of 10 btu/wh means a dimensionless efficiency of 3, which is about 10 times less than the theoretical maximum value of about 30. Two features are noticeable from Figure 17-5. For 115-v units the efficiency rapidly increases with cooling capacity, whereas for 230-v units the change with cooling capacity is very small. This is probably because total cooling capacity is easier to achieve with the 230-v unit, and little effort is required to engineer higher efficiencies. Typical efficiencies for a 230-v unit are around 2 (about 6 btu/wh). In contrast, the 115-v units generally have much higher dimensionless efficiencies, up to 3.6 (equal to 12 btu/wh) although still far from ideal. If greater concern was displayed for energy consumption, it seems clear that greater efficiencies could be achieved, especially for 230-v units.

Just as in commercial buildings, there are sometimes alternative cooling methods. An attic fan that brings cool air in from outside in the evening is a very useful cooling technique. The basement is usually one of the coolest places in the house in summer and activities could be carried on there in hot weather. In Australia, which is generally much hotter than most of the United States in summer, air conditioning is used very little. Windows are kept open at night to let in cool air, and then the house is shaded during the day which keeps it fairly cool. Another design feature that is widely used there is a veranda surrounding the house to help insulate it. Other cultures, including the Indians in the southwest United States, have developed different designs using the natural properties of materials as temperature controllers. For example the use of thick adobe brick insulates the house during the day and then reradiates the heat during the cooler evening. Modern architects seem to have forgotten these lessons and instead must provide artificial energy sources to make a house livable.

The second highest user of energy in the home is water heating, which used almost 3% of the total United States energy budget. Some immediate ways of saving energy here would be to use lower temperature water, have shorter showers, and use a minimum of hot water for

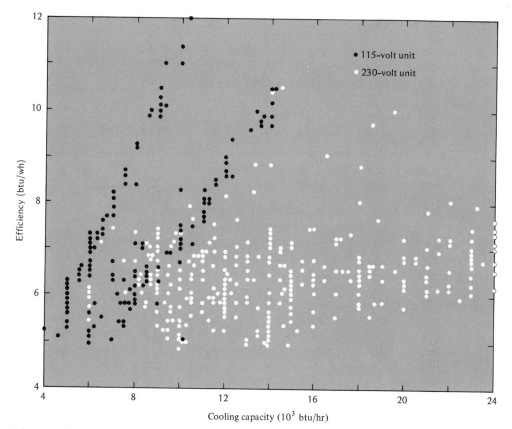

Figure 17.5

Efficiency of room air conditioners as a function of unit size. [From E. Hirst, et al.: Efficiency of energy use in the United States. *Science,* **179**:1299–1304 (30 March 1973). Copyright 1973 by the American Association for the Advancement of Science.]

washing dishes and clothes. Longer term aids include better insulation of the heater tank and pipes and a redirecting of used hot water to preheat the incoming water for the hot water system. Hot water heaters powered by solar energy are already available and are widely used in other countries. These would represent a saving of present energy resources.

Lighting in the home is an area where a technical breakthrough could be extremely valuable. Most residential lighting uses incandescent light bulbs which are 4 times less efficient than fluorescent bulbs. A small screw-in fluorescent bulb would represent a large saving in energy used for lighting.

The average energy consumed by a number of common household appliances is shown in Table 17-6. Note that convenience options such as quick recovery hot water service or a frost-free refrigerators are costly in energy use. An automatic drier uses almost ten times as much

Table 17-6
Electrical Energy Consumption in the Home

Appliance	Approximate Average Energy Consumed Per Year (kwh)
hot water heater	4200
"quick recovery" hot water heater	4800
standard 14 ft³ refrigerator	1140
"frost free" 17 ft³ refrigerator	2000
automatic washer	103
automatic drier	1000
black and white TV (3.6 hr/day)	120
color TV (3.6 hr/day)	440
air conditioner (on "high" for 24 hr/day for 1 month)	1440 (per month)
garbage disposal	30
carving knife	8
electric toothbrush	0.5
Total average electrical energy used per household in 1972	8000

energy as an automatic washer. In other cases, an improved convenience has added energy conserving features. A self-cleaning oven, which operates at very high temperatures, requires the use of additional insulation, which means that energy requirements in regular operation are decreased. Gas pilot lights on stoves and water heaters have also been shown to be extremely wasteful of energy. Electronic ignitors are much less wasteful and should be replacing pilot lights.

The design of other home appliances for cooking, refrigeration, clothes washing, and drying could probably be improved to help conserve energy. In many of these appliances, lifetime costs have been sacrificed to minimize initial costs. If overall energy consumption, efficiency, and operating costs were prominently displayed on an appliance and if the public could be educated to consider these long term costs, this trend might be reversed. Many cases, less than optimum materials are used which contribute to the lack of efficiency.

Finally, in discussing home appliances, the point should again be made that, although any one appliance may use a small amount of energy, the number of appliances represents an anticonservation attitude. Is the quality of one's life improved by being able to open a can with an electric opener, which is necessarily more elaborate than with a hand opener? Does bread or meat taste better if sliced with an electric knife?

One final aspect of residential energy conservation that should be discussed, relates to the growth of the mobil home industry. Mobil homes typically have thin walls and roof and very poor insulation. Therefore, they require large amounts of energy both to heat them in winter and cool them in summer. Improved standards of insulation for these homes would decrease these requirements and help limit the energy requirements of this rapidly growing segment of the residential market.

17-8   Urban Design and Energy Conservation

Although some of the energy conserving steps we have noted lend themselves to fairly immediate or short term application, others require more basic changes and longer time scales. For example, to make really significant changes in transportation patterns, it may be necessary to change the design of the cities themselves. Most cities now operate on a plan where people are forced to commute from surrounding areas to the central city for business or commerce. Workers typically live in homogeneous social groups while industry is located elsewhere.

Alternative designs, where smaller groups of business centers cater for local areas and where less homogeneous suburbs allow people to live closer to their place of work, would minimize commuting time and transportations costs. The city of Canberra, Australia, is attempting urban development along these lines (Figure 17-6) where various business centers are located in adjacent valleys surrounded by a group of suburbs. Each suburb also has its centrally located shopping center within walking distance of essentially every home. Roadways are cut by underpass walkways to make it safer for children to walk or bicycle to school or playgrounds. There are difficulties in the design and it has not been optimized for minimum transportation costs. Nevertheless, Canberra may provide an interesting guide for future planners.

Another feature that should be incorporated into future urban design is the concept of total energy system planning. In this system whole blocks of buildings or residences could draw on a centralized heating and air conditioning system. Waste heat could by recycled and possibly waste heat from nearby industrial plants or utilities could be used. It has been estimated in the Intertechnology Corporation report that such centralized systems could save up to 50% of space heating costs, even without waste heat recycling.

Perhaps even more radical solutions will be required in the future, such as limiting city growth to some optimum size determined by sociological, cultural, economic, ecological, and energy considerations. In a smaller, self-contained, and well designed city of, say 200,000 people, local transportation could probably be handled by bicycle and small electric buses. Intercity transportation could use fast trains.

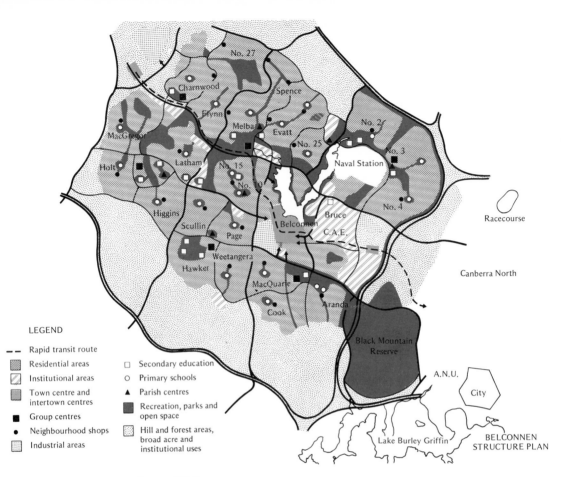

LEGEND

- - Rapid transit route
▨ Residential areas
▨ Institutional areas
▨ Town centre and
  intertown centres
■ Group centres
• Neighbourhood shops
▨ Industrial areas

☐ Secondary education
○ Primary schools
▲ Parish centres
■ Recreation, parks and
  open space
▨ Hill and forest areas,
  broad acre and
  institutional uses

Figure 17-6
Urban planning around central areas: part of the city of Canberra, Australia, population 150,000. This is one of the independent "cluster" developments in the Belconnen valley which is part of the total city. Business, industrial, residential, and commercial areas in each cluster help to minimize commuting. [Courtesy of National Capital Development Association.]

Heating and electric requirements could all be centrally planned, with a constant recycling of waste heat and minimum total expenditure of energy. At present such a concept is purely a dream, but perhaps we are at the stage where such planning should be started.

17-9 Summary and Conclusions

Energy conservation is a many faceted question. There are a few areas such as transportation, space heating, and some industrial processes that use a high proportion of the total United States demand and should therefore be emphasized in any conservation program. However, small savings in many areas should also be encouraged. Conservation will be most successful when both large and small items are given consideration. Many people being aware and tackling the problems in their own locality will make a significant national impact. Education is therefore an extremely important aspect of energy conservation. A report prepared by the Subcommittee on Energy of the 93rd Congress entitled *Individual Action for Energy Conservation* [3] is included as Appendix I.

Figure 17-7 taken from the Office of Emergency Preparedness [1] indicates the total savings that could be realized by 1980 in various areas. Some of the main contributions to these savings could come from the following steps.

Transportation. Conduct educational programs to stimulate public awareness of energy conservation in the transportation sector; establish government energy efficiency standards; improve airplane-load factors; promote development of smaller engines/vehicles; improve traffic flow; improve mass transit and intercity rail and air transport; promote automobile energy efficiency through low loss tires, engine tuning and reduced speed limits. *Savings: 10%.*

Improve freight handling systems; support pilot implementation of most promising alternatives to internal combustion engine; set tax on size and power of autos; support improved truck engines;

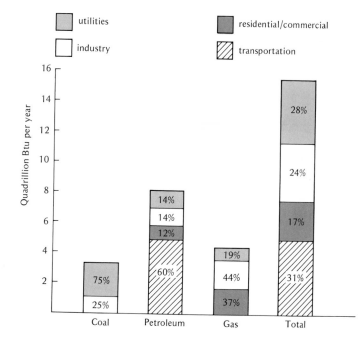

Figure 17-7
Projected annual savings possible by 1980 through conservation measures. [From *The Potential for Energy Conservation.* Staff Study Office of Emergency Preparedness, October, 1972.]

require energy-efficient operating procedures for airplanes; provide subsidies and matching grants for mass transit; ban autos within the inner city; provide subsidies for intercity rail networks; decrease transportation demand through urban refurbishing projects and long range urban/suburban planning. *Savings: 21%.*

Electric Utilities. Smooth out daily demand cycle by means of government regulations; decrease electricity demand. Restructure rates for heavy uses to smooth out demand cycle; facilitate new construction. *Savings: 8%.*

Industry. Increase energy price to encourage improvement of processes and replacement of inefficient equipment; provide tax incentives to encourage recycling and reusing of component materials. *Savings: 6–11%.*
Establish energy use tax to provide incentive to upgrade processes and replace inefficient equipment; promote research for more efficient technologies; provide tax incentives to encourage recycling and reusing component materials. *Savings: 12–17%.*

Residential/Commercial. Establish upgraded construction standards and tax incentives and regulations to promote design and construction of energy-efficient dwellings including the use of the "total energy concept" for multifamily dwellings; provide tax incentives, research and development funds and regulations to promote energy efficient appliances, central air conditioning, water heaters, and lighting. *Savings: 14%.*

A detailed breakdown of savings in homes is given in Table 17-7. Conservation in space heating and air conditioning represent the largest savings.

Many energy uses are interrelated; therefore, energy conservation

Table 17-7
Annual Energy Savings Possible in the Residential/Commercial Sector 1980

Residential	Savings (10^{12} Btu/year)	Percent of Total Residential/Commercial Sector*	Percent Total Consumption All Sectors†
space heating and cooling:			
(a) existing homes	1100	3.1	1.1
(b) new homes	1100	3.1	1.1
water heating	250	0.7	0.3
cooking	50	0.1	0.05
refrigeration	100	0.3	0.1
air conditioning equipment	500	1.4	0.5
other, including lighting, clothes drying, etc.	500	1.4	0.5
Residential Total	3600	10.1	3.7

* Percentages calculated on basis of a denominator of 35.6×10^{15} Btu. This is the energy consumption of the residential/commercial sector including electrical energy, expected in 1980.
† Percentages calculated on basis of a denominator of 96×10^{15} Btu which is the total national consumption for all sectors expected for 1980.

applied in one area can also be effective in other areas. We have already noted this effect with the automobile and the electric toothbrush. Perhaps even more important to stress is the attitude of conservation. This relates very much to one's values and how one judges quality of life.

Let me conclude this chapter with a personal story that I think relates to this question. I enjoy camping with my family. A number of times we have been sitting by a fire in a state forest, the children already in bed in the tent behind us, when along the narrow rutted forest trail will come, bouncing and squeaking, a huge motor home, with a power boat coupled behind and with trail bikes strapped to the sides. After a good deal of maneuvering, and usually cussing, the caravan is parked. The owner then starts up his motor generator, shattering the peace of the still evening to supply himself with light and possibly a television program. I wonder whether this extravagant consumption is adding to the quality of his life. It is certainly detracting from that of all the other people enjoying the forest that evening.

Questions

1. How long can the gasoline consuming automobile survive in the United States? What changes in transportation might be seen in the next 40 years?
2. Outline some suggestions for decreasing energy consumption through improved urban design.
3. What are ten ways *you* could save energy in the next year? Estimate the effect on the United States energy budget if everyone followed your example.
4. Suppose you came in from skiing extremely cold. You had to choose a means of warming up, either a hot bath, an electric heater (1.5 kw) or an electric blanket (300 w). Estimate the relative energy efficiency of using one of these three methods. Mention some alternatives of lower energy consumption.
5. Air conditioner efficiencies are usually given in British thermal units (btu) of heat moved from inside to outside per kilowatt-hour of electricity consumed. Convert btu to kilowatt-hours or vice versa to estimate the percentage efficiency of an air conditioner rated at 10 btu/kwh.
6. Over a period of about a decade, the largest energy savings in transportation can be achieved through
   (a) small cars and increased component efficiency.
   (b) small cars and urban mass transportation.
   (c) increased component efficiency and urban mass transportation.
   (d) urban mass transportation and intercity busses.
   (e) increased component efficiency and intercity busses.
7. The largest savings in total energy in the home in Michigan are attainable in
   (a) air conditioning
   (b) home heating

(c) cleaning

(d) refrigeration

(e) washing

8. The order of importance (high to low) of activities in energy consumption in the United States is

   (a) commercial, household, transportation, industrial.

   (b) transportation, industrial, household, commercial.

   (c) household, transportation, industrial, commercial.

   (d) industrial, transportation, household, commercial.

   (e) household, industrial, commercial, transportation.

9. Recently, we have been asked to "dial down" our thermostats to 68°F and to drive under 55 mph. Discuss the effects of these conservation steps. Suggest other methods of conserving energy. Estimate how much we can reduce energy consumption if we make an all-out effort to conserve energy.

Bibliography

[1] *The Potential for Energy Conservation.* Staff Study of the Office of Emergency Preparedness, October, 1972.

[2] *Energy Research and Development.* Report of the Task Force on Energy 92nd Congress, December, 1972.

[3] *Individual Action for Energy Conservation.* Prepared by the Subcommittee on Energy, 93rd Congress, June, 1973. (See Appendix I.)

[4] Conservation of energy: the potential for more efficient use. *Science,* December 8, 1972, p. 1079.

[5] E. Hirst and J. C. Mayers: Efficiency of energy use in the United States. *Science,* March 30, 1973, p. 1299.

[6] G. A. Lincoln: Energy conservation. *Science,* April 13, 1973, p. 155.

[7] C. A. Berg: Energy conservation through effective utilization. *Science,* July 13, 1973, p. 128.

[8] Constance Holden: Energy: shortages loom but conservation lags. *Science,* June 15, 1973, p. 1155.

[9] R. G. Stein: Energy 5: waste. *Intellectual Digest,* April, 1973, p. 21.

[10] Energy and conservation. *Time,* Nov. 26, 1973.

[11] E. Hirst: Transportation energy use and conservation potential. *Bulletin of the Atomic Scientists,* November, 1973.

[12] A. C. Mallianis and R. L. Strombotue. "Demand for Energy by the Transportation Sector and Opportunities for Energy Conservation." Conference on Energy: Demand, Conservation and Institutional Problems. Massachusetts Institute of Technology, Cambridge, 1973.

CHAPTER

The Economics of Energy Use

18-1 Introduction: Economics as a Science

Many times already in this book there have been economic dimensions to a number of the issues discussed, and it is now time to face these questions more directly. Economic considerations are clearly very important to most of us. How much something costs is a large factor in determining whether we will purchase it or not. Economic policy, which can affect costs, is, therefore, one effective way of changing both buying and usage patterns. In this chapter the economic implications of some of the issues raised thus far and proposals for solving some of the problems involved in these issues will be discussed explicitly.

Economics is concerned with the market place, with costs, pricing, and economic growth, and not generally with physical laws or concepts. Sometimes physical laws do impinge upon economic considerations because the materials dealt with by economists are still subject to these basic laws. It is my impression that some economists at least tend to be rather more cavalier about such laws than may be warranted.

The science of economics, like all sciences, deals with models. These models are based on particular assumptions about economic conditions and people's response to specific circumstances. The models can be developed with great mathematical sophistication. Ultimately, as with physical science, the models would not only explain what has happened in the past but also be able to tell us what will happen in the future. This predictability is the acid test of a good model or theory. Unfortunately, in economics and other social sciences, the variables are difficult to control. This makes it impossible, for example, to repeat experiments precisely. The social sciences, therefore, are faced with a very difficult task in predicting the results of any experiment using a particular model and, as a result, are inherently less accurate than the physical sciences. It is sometimes difficult to get economists to agree even on the direction in which a particular policy, such as a tax increase, will influence the economy to say nothing of the precise magnitude of the change. Hopefully the situation will improve as these sciences become more refined. With this understood, let me turn to a discussion of some basic economic principles.

18-2 The Concept of the Pure Competitive Market

One of the basic concepts in economics is the operation of the pure competitive market to control prices by supply and demand. In its simplest form, the assumption is made that, in a competitive market, a group of individuals, called sellers, make free choices about the price and quantity of a particular commodity to be offered for sale. Commodities can be either manufactured goods such as toothbrushes and automobiles, resources such as oil and electricity, or even services like a haircut. The assumption is also made that the prices of other commodities stay the same and that the income of the buyers remains constant.

It is now possible to plot a demand curve for this item as shown in Figure 18-1. The axes of the plot are the price and the quantity of the product demanded. For simplicity, the demand curve has been drawn as a straight line, implying a linear relationship between price and quantity. This assumption of a linear relationship between price and

Figure 18-1
A demand curve. The higher the price per unit, the smaller the quantity demanded. As the price per unit decreases, the quantity demanded increases. The point x refers to a situation of high price per unit and low demand. A straight line (linear) relationship between price per unit and quantity demanded is shown for simplicity.

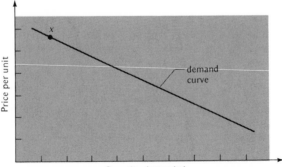

Price per unit

demand curve

Quantity demanded

Figure 18-2

A supply curve. The higher the price per unit, the greater quantity a producer is likely to supply. Point y refers to a situation with a low price per unit and, therefore, a small quantity supplied. A linear relationship between price per unit and quantity supplied is shown for simplicity.

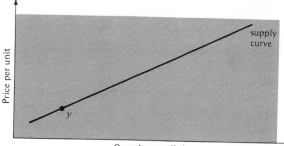

quantity is not fundamental to the argument, and a nonlinear demand curve would probably be more realistic. A linear relationship is chosen only for simplicity. The important point to note is that the demand curve slopes down. If the price of an item is high, the quantity demanded will be small (point x in Figure 18-1). As the price decreases, the quantity demanded by buyers will increase, assuming that all other market conditions remain the same. This is, of course, a very simple model and neglects many other factors that might affect the demand for a particular commodity. Some of these factors might be a change in the consumer's income or taste, the price of similar goods or the consumer's expectation of future prices. These factors may cause a shift of the whole demand curve to the right or left in Figure 18-1.

On the same set of axes it is also possible to plot a supply curve (Figure 18-2). This gives a relation between the quantity of a commodity which a supplier is willing to supply and the price of the commodity. A supply curve usually, but not always, slopes upwards to the right (Figure 18-2). If the price for a particular item is low, a supplier will be willing to supply only a small quantity of the item (point y in Figure 18-2). As the price rises, suppliers will be willing (even eager) to supply more of the commodity at the higher price. This is the basic thinking behind the view that an increased price for natural gas will stimulate producers to provide larger quantities of natural gas to consumers.

The upward slope of the supply curve also implies that if the supplier undertakes to provide a greater quantity of a particular item, the cost of producing the item will rise so that the price per item which he must charge also rises. There may be a number of reasons why it is more expensive for a manufacturer to produce more quantity of a particular item. For example, he may be competing with other manufacturers for a limited quantity of raw materials. He may have to pay a higher price for these materials if other manufacturers are also competing for them. Or he may have to employ unskilled labor to produce more, which may be less efficient and raise his costs.

As for the demand curve, the supply curve in Figure 18-2 also shows a linear relationship between quantity supplied and price. This is probably an even more simplified model than for the demand curve, particularly if the manufacturer's plant is not operating at its full capacity. The linear relationship, however, serves to illustrate the gross features of the supply curve in this ideal model.

The supply curve discussed here may appear to contradict one's instinct that the *greater* the amount of a commodity supplied the *lower* will be the price. The upward slope also appears contrary to the idea of economies of scale discussed in Section 18-4. It is true that in certain cases, due to economies realized by large size operations, there may be a decrease in the price per item as the quantity supplied is increased. All supply curves need not have the simple slope shown in Figure 18-2. Nevertheless the simple curve does illustrate the ideal market situation clearly and has some validity in practice. Certainly if the price of an item falls too low, the supplier will eventually not find it worthwhile to supply any significant quantity of that commodity.

If both supply and demand curves are now plotted in the same figure (Figure 18-3), the model states that the market price for a particular item will occur where the quantity demanded exactly matches the quantity supplied. In other words, the market price is obtained from the point where the supply and demand curves cross. Suppose initially the manufacturer supplies too great a quantity, z, of the item, then he will be forced to charge a higher price, s, for it. But for this same quantity, z, on the demand curve, buyers would be willing to pay a price, d, much smaller than that required by the seller. The latter would then reduce the quantity supplied, lowering his price to the point where supply equals demand, at which time the selling price will equal the buying price, m, and the item will sell. A similar argument can be made if the manufacturer supplies too small a quantity of the required item. Thus the establishment of the market price makes sense in this world.

Although this is an extremely simplified picture of market operation, it does illustrate the general economic principle. The closest

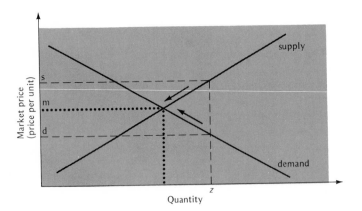

Figure 18-3

Establishment of the market price. The market price, m, (price per unit) and the quantity supplied (or demanded), is determined by the point at which the supply and demand curves intersect (dotted lines).

approximation to the pure competitive market discussed above is probably the commodities market for agricultural products. Most other markets are more complex and require more sophisticated models.

Without further discussing these complexities, I will turn to the areas where economics has impact on environmental questions, particularly some of the energy issues we have discussed so far. There are three topics that I shall consider; the question of externalities, economies of scale, and the limit to economic growth. All of these subjects are extremely large and already have a substantial literature associated with them. I can only hope to raise some issues that seem particularly important without claiming to be able to give definitive answers.

18-3 Externalities

Externalities are external effects or costs that are not taken account of in determining the market price of a commodity as discussed in the previous section. Positive externalities are additional good effects which arise from the sale of particular items or the development of a specific resource. Negative externalities are harmful effects associated with the sale or use of certain commodities.

Gerald Garvey in his book *Energy, Ecology, Economy* [2] points out that even the most adamant free enterprise proponents believe in government assistance to help exploit resources because they believe in positive externalities. They argue that encouraging the development of resources helps the whole economy as well as benefitting the individual developer. Only recently has the concept of negative externalities, particularly as regards environmental issues, been raised.

Consider, for example, the difference between the purchase of air pollution equipment and an air conditioner for an automobile. The price and quantity of air conditioners are determined, more or less, by the market conditions discussed above. Air conditioners are items many people want to make their travel more pleasant, and they are willing to pay the necessary price. Air pollution control devices, on the contrary, are of very little direct advantage to the buyer. Air pollution is a cost to society as a whole, a cost not reflected in the market place. If everyone else installed air pollution devices on their cars, the air would be much cleaner for a particular individual whether he purchased that equipment or not. It would be to his economic advantage, in fact, not to purchase this equipment. Although there is a bumper sticker that reads: "The pollution you breathe may be your own," in general this is not true; at least one's pollution is only a small fraction of the total pollution one breathes.

There are many examples of negative externalities associated with particular products. For example, production of electricity involves many negative externalities. One is the air pollution produced by most generating plants which only now is beginning to be included (or internalized) in the market price by regulations that set emission standards for power plants and force companies to spend money on control technology. Thermal and chemical pollution of waterways is a similar situation. Perhaps a less well recognized externality in power plant operation is the using up of resources. This means that less of a resource, say coal or oil, is available in the future as a result of our present use, particularly if the present use is inefficient. Garvey [2] has called this effect depletive waste. He also characterized another negative externality of resource use, namely, the adverse effect of the extraction or conversion of the resource. Strip-mining of coal and oil spills are examples of this effect.

Nuclear-generated electricity is not free from externalities either. Many of the problems associated with nuclear energy which were discussed in Chapter 11 fall into this category. Particular examples are the safety problems associated with the transportation and processing of nuclear fuel elements and especially the difficulties associated with disposal or storage of long-lived radioactive wastes.

Why are these costs not properly accounted for in the market place and what can be done about it?

Garrett Hardin explains the problem in an article entitled "The Tragedy of the Commons" in *Science* magazine [10]. He points out that, for commonly held property, such as a common meadow used for grazing, it benefits any individual to exploit this resource as far as he is able. The destructive effects of his exploitation will be spread over all the people who use the meadow whereas the benefits accrue to him alone. We noted a similar example in discussing the purchase of air pollution equipment for an automobile. The common resource, clean air, is a common benefit to all. It will pay an individual if he can convince everyone else to buy pollution control equipment, because then the air will be cleaner, while he does not pay the money to buy such equipment himself.

The problem of resource use provides another example. Not only does the price of electricity not reflect the cost of the environmental damage *produced* in mining the coal necessary to *generate* it but also the people who suffer most, both in terms of health and of environmental disaster, are the miners and their families. The users are often far removed both physically and mentally from the ravages of the coal mining process while enjoying its benefits.

How can the problem of negative externalities be tackled? Two general approaches have been suggested, taxation or government regulation. The most common one so far has been by regulation. Various federal agencies have made regulations to control emissions by automobiles and by power plants. Thermal emissions have likewise been regulated in many states. Realizing the significance of the depletion of oil by automobiles, there has even been a proposal in Wisconsin to ban the sale of all automobiles that do not have a gasoline consumption of at least 25 mpg. The difficulty with the regulation approach is that it is often not enough to insist that emission control devices be installed; they must also be maintained in good working order to be effective.

Many economists prefer the alternative system of taxation as a more flexible way of attempting to internalize the cost of a negative externality. If the market price of the item was made to correspond more closely to the true cost, including the societal cost, then regular market factors of supply and demand could once again operate. Many particular proposals for taxation have been suggested.

One simple technique is to impose a linear tax on a particular pollutant. The amount of tax paid is directly proportional to the amount of pollutant emitted. For example, a firm whose plant emits x tons of sulfur dioxide each day must pay $\$y$ tax. The greater x becomes, the greater y will be. This system, while having the advantage of simplicity, suffers from a lack of flexibility. The taxation rate would also have to be very carefully adjusted so that it is not cheaper for an individual simply to pay the tax and continue to pollute as before.

A more sophisticated and probably a more realistic approach has been suggested by Dr. Herman Koenig, professor of Systems Science at Michigan State University. Dr. Koenig and his collaborators point out [3] that, in order to set a sensible taxation rate, it is necessary to know how much of a certain pollutant any particular region or body of water can tolerate. If small enough quantities of a pollutant are added, then natural processes can handle the waste products without harmful effects. At some level, the system is no longer able to cope with these foreign elements and begins to be destroyed as a useful resource for other purposes. For example, although a river or lake may be able to dissipate a certain level of heat input without impairing its overall ecological balance, at some point, depending on the size of the body of water and the heat added, this ecological system will begin to break down. Determination of the limits of a particular system require measurement and study and will never be completely certain.

Once the limits have been determined as accurately as possible, the suggestion is to impose a nonlinear tax (see Figure 18-4). For small amounts of pollutants a small tax is charged. As the amount of pollution approaches the limit the system can safely handle, the taxation rate rises steeply. Any uncertainty in the capacity of the system to deal with a particular pollutant (shown shaded in Figure 18-4) will also be internalized by shifting the taxation curve to the left until it becomes the dotted curve shown in the figure. The greater the uncertainty, the more quickly will the taxation rate become prohibitively high. The

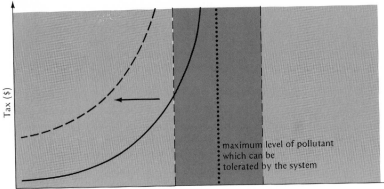

Figure 18-4

Nonlinear taxation of pollution. The dotted line gives the maximum level of pollution a given system can tolerate. The shaded area represents the uncertainty in this level. The tax curve (solid line), therefore, moves to the left (dashed curve) to allow for uncertainty.

Tax ($)

maximum level of pollutant which can be tolerated by the system

Amount of pollutant

smaller taxes associated with smaller uncertainties may even encourage private support for studies of pollution limits in ecological systems so as to reduce the uncertainties.

This system has the advantage that it can be used on a regional basis and adjusted to local differences. If the Los Angeles basin is particularly sensitive to air pollution, then the taxation rate could be set much higher there than in Des Moines, Iowa, which has fewer problems. By adopting a regional approach, one also avoids the criticism that it is unfair to tax someone, for instance a farmer, who is not contributing substantially to the pollution problem in a large city. The regional approach will be able to discriminate in this situation and at the same time provide a financial incentive to encourage people and industry to move away from particularly pollution-sensitive areas.

There is one further point to be made regarding nonlinear taxes. Because they can have such a dramatic impact on price, they should be introduced gradually. This is illustrated in Figure 18-5. The horizontal line labeled (1) represents a linear tax. The slightly upward curve (2) shows a small nonlinear effect. The impact can gradually be made more dramatic by increasing the upward slope (3) while being careful that the system does not become unstable.

Any system imposing tax on pollutants tends to be unfair to the poor in society. A uniform taxation system would be especially burdensome because it would have to be set rather high to deter upper and middle income buyers. A nonlinear taxation system, which was applied gradually, would probably be more equitable because there would be time to adjust to the new requirements and the tax rate could be low. In an extreme case, direct compensation of some kind might be required for people who are especially hard-hit economically. Such problems do not mean that we should refuse to act because

Figure 18-5

Graduated nonlinear taxes. Curve (1), a straight horizontal line, represents a completely linear tax. Curves (2) and (3) represent nonlinear taxes with a gradually increasing slope from (2) to (3).

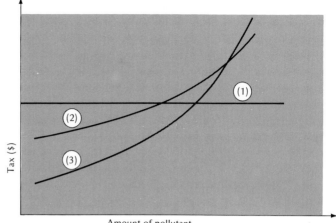

eventually the situation may become even worse. Even now the poor generally suffer most from pollution. For example, air pollution is usually worst in the center of a city, precisely the same area in which the poor are forced to live.

The flexibility of a regional nonlinear tax means that it can be more easily adjusted to achieve the optimum balance of cost versus benefit. The cost of reducing the emissions from a power plant becomes much greater as the quantity of emissions decreases. It may cost as much, for example, to remove the last 5% of sulfur dioxide emissions as it did to remove the first 95%. To insist on zero pollution is, therefore, extremely costly and probably unnecessary. The amount of pollution, or any other externality, should be set by the capacity of the environment to preserve whatever quality society values. In the real world this is best achieved by a compromise between cost and benefit.

One other interesting sociological question related to taxation is whether people are deterred from consuming more by paying a lump sum in the beginning, such as a large outlay for control equipment or by a continuing cost such as a tax on gasoline use. Both methods are probably fairly effective in industry because proper accounting is usually made. For personal consumption, however, it would seem that an initial lump sum has much more impact than a continuing small cost. Experience with home insulation bears this out. Most people prefer to pay higher heating bills than to make an investment in better insulation for their home.

Both regulation and taxation systems have the disadvantage that they require policing. Unfortunately this generally leads to a larger bureaucracy, but this may be a price society will have to pay for a more livable environment.

18-4 Diseconomies of Scale

One of the features of technical change has been the phenomenon of an economy of scale. If a plot is made of the cost per unit against the number of units produced (Figure 18-6), for many cases this curve slopes down from left to right. (Note that this effect is neglected in the supply curve discussed in Figure 18-2.) This scaling effect is observed in many areas. In agriculture for example, farms have become progressively larger and larger. Power plants have increased in size, and even larger ones are being planned. Even in the retail business, supermarkets are gradually replacing smaller specialist stores often operated and owned by a family. The lesson in many of these areas is—grow bigger or get out!

One of the main reasons for economies of scale in an industrial society is that labor costs are a very large part of the cost of production. Large scale operations, although they may be very costly in terms of initial capital costs, are much less labor intensive and therefore less expensive than a small scale operation. In other cases, in a nuclear reactor for example, there are certain fixed costs independent of size.

While the economic optimum may be in the direction of very large size, there may also be significant costs associated with this growth. Energy consumption per unit of production, for example, usually rises dramatically in large operations. Some Texas rice farmers require 20 cal of energy to produce 1 cal of food energy, whereas a Chinese rice farmer expends 1 cal of energy to produce 50 cal of rice. The Texas farmers are basically converting fossil fuel energy into food energy at a very inefficient rate.

Figure 18-6
Economies of scale. **(A)** The curve represents the usual situation of an economy of scale where the cost per unit may often decrease with the number of units produced. **(B)** However, if the externalities associated with size are internalized in the cost, the cost per unit may slope upward beyond a certain quantity of units produced. The minimum cost per unit will then occur at the minimum (low point) of the curve at a particular value of the quantity of units produced (dashed lines).

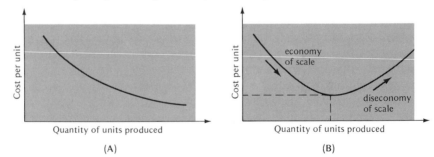

One can also see many diseconomies associated with very large power plants. First, the air pollution effects of a large plant are concentrated in a small area. Even if a plant is set far from population centers, the effects can be very objectionable. An obvious example is the Four Corners Power Plant in New Mexico discussed in Chapter 10. Thermal pollution effects will also be more serious from a single large plant than from many small plants. A large plant which necessarily serves a larger area is usually further from more consumers so that transportation costs are therefore greater. Finally a single large plant serving a large area creates many more problems in the case of breakdowns. When Con Edison in New York had technical difficulties in installing their new large generator, Big Allis, significant delays in servicing their customers resulted because this single unit was a large fraction of Con Edison's total capacity.

Diseconomies of scale may even be associated with very large cities. Crime may be a societal cost of the impersonal nature of large urban areas. Certainly air and thermal pollution are endemic to cities because of the highly concentrated energy consumption.

If the externalities that size gives rise to are treated, therefore, as externalities and an attempt is made to internalize their cost by one of the devices discussed in the last section, then the cost per unit versus quantity curve seen in Figure 18-6A will take a different shape (Figure 18-6B). The curve will first decrease as before but then will rise at some point due to the imposition of specific costs related to size. The minimum (low point) in the curve, corresponding to the smallest unit cost, would then determine an optimum size. Of course, this method should be introduced slowly and with a pragmatic attitude while studying the advantages and disadvantages of a particular size.

18-5 Growth

The notion of growth in America has been one of the things, like motherhood, that has traditionally been a self-evident value. Economic growth, growth of the use of resources, growth in energy use, even population growth were regarded as intrinsic to the American way of life. It is only fairly recently that these assumptions have been challenged. Of course, Malthus made dire predictions about the results of population growth over a century ago. The predictions have failed to come true in the developed countries primarily because technological developments increased productivity even faster than population growth. However, not all countries have been so fortunate and semi-starvation is today a state of existence for a large portion of the world's population.

More recently a new challenge to the concept of continued growth has been raised by Meadows, Meadows, Randers, and Behrens in their book *The Limits to Growth* [5]. This book is a popular presentation of the results of a project on the future of mankind (sponsored by an international organization called the Club of Rome). The authors have developed a computer model of world growth based on a model first proposed by Professor J. Forrester of the Massachusetts Institute of Technology. Various assumptions about five major factors, resource development, population growth, industrialization, pollution levels, and food production can be introduced. This world model then takes into account the various interactions and dependencies of these variables and predicts the world development that will follow. This is an extremely ambitious project and the authors point out that great accuracy cannot be expected.

The model we have constructed is, like every other model, imperfect, oversimplified, and unfinished. We are well aware of its shortcomings, but we believe that it is the most useful model now available for dealing with

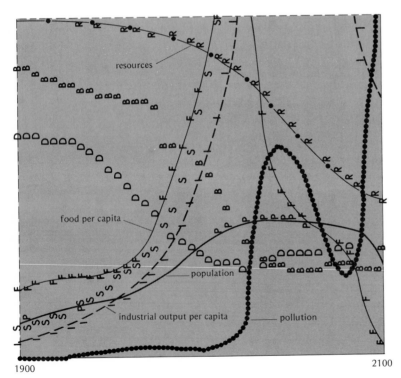

Figure 18-7

World model with "unlimited" resources, pollution controls, increased agricultural productivity, and "perfect" birth control. Four simultaneous technological policies are introduced in the world model in an attempt to avoid the growth-and-collapse behavior of previous runs. Resources are fully exploited, and 75% of those used are recycled. Pollution generation is reduced to one fourth of its 1970 value. Land yields are doubled, and effective methods of birth control are made available to the world population. The result is a temporary achievement of a constant population with a world average income per capita that reaches nearly the present United States level. Finally, though, industrial growth is halted, and the death rate rises as resources are depleted, pollution accumulates, and food production declines. [From D. H. Meadows, et al.: *The Limits to Growth.* Universe Books, New York, 1972.]

resources

food per capita

population

industrial output per capita

pollution

1900

2100

Figure 18-8

Stabilized world model. Technological policies are added to the growth-regulating policies of the previous run to produce an equilibrium state sustainable far into the future. Technological policies include resource recycling, pollution control devices, increased lifetime of all forms of capital, and methods to restore eroded and infertile soil. Value changes include increased emphasis on food and services rather than on industrial production. Births are set equal to deaths and industrial capital investment equal to capital depreciation. Equilibrium value of industrial output per capita is three times the 1970 world average. [From D. H. Meadows, et al.: *Limits to Growth.* Universe Books, New York, 1972.]

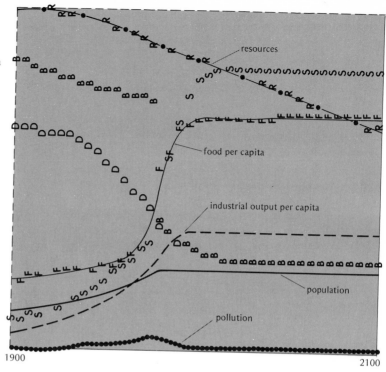

problems far out on the space-time graph. To our knowledge it is the only formal model in existence that is truly global in scope, that has a time horizon longer than thirty years, and that includes important variables such as population, food production, and pollution, not as independent entities, but as dynamically interacting elements, as they are in the real world.

This model has the advantage that the assumptions are made very explicit and thus the interaction of the variables can be carefully traced. Neither of these characteristics is true in any existing qualitative predictions of where the world is going.

The results of this analysis are presented as a series of computer outputs for a wide range of assumptions including for example "unlimited" resources, pollution controls, increased agricultural productivity, and "perfect" birth control (Figure 18-7). The result, even with these optimistic assumptions, is that the population declines as industrial growth is halted, pollution rises, and food production declines. It would seem to indicate that only if overall growth limiting policies are introduced into our society fairly soon can stability be achieved (Figure 18-8).

Realizing the possible inaccuracies in the time scale, the authors state their conclusions explicitly.

1. If the present growth trends in world population, industrialization, pollution, food production, and resource depletion continue unchanged, the limits to growth on this planet will be reached sometime within the next one hundred years. The most probable result will be a rather sudden and uncontrollable decline in both population and industrial capacity.
2. It is possible to alter these growth trends and to establish a condition of ecological and economic stability that is sustainable far into the future. The state of global equilibrium could be designed so that the basic material needs of each person on earth are satisfied and each person has an equal opportunity to realize his individual human potential.
3. If the world's people decide to strive for this second outcome rather than the first, the sooner they begin working to attain it, the greater will be their chances of success.

These conclusions have been criticized by economists on a number of different grounds. The critics point out that, a sophisticated computer model is not needed to see that if one assumes both an exponential growth of one or more variables like population, food production, or pollution, and a slower growth of technology, the system will inevitably blow up. The crux of the contentions, therefore, center on these assumptions. Economists generally fall into the "technical optimist" camp which believes that with enough effort and money all problems have a technical solution. More economists than scientists seem to hold this view. Up till now it must be admitted that the "technical optimists" do have a good historical argument at least in the industrialized countries. Whether this will continue indefinitely into the future is a difficult question.

Another point often made by economic critics, such as Solow [6], of the *Limits to Growth* is that the authors did not take into account market forces. As a particular commodity becomes scarce, the price will rise and, therefore, less of it will be used and also other alternatives will be developed. If we are running out of oil, then another energy source will be found as oil becomes scarce and, therefore, more expensive. This is a variation of the technical optimist position because it also assumes that technology will always find alternatives to all scarce resources.

Another issue on which Meadows and coauthors are brought to task is that, although economic growth, as measured, for example by an index like the gross national product (GNP)* may continue, the direction of production and spending may shift in a more ecologically sound direction. For instance, pollution control devices will add to the price of an automobile and so will contribute to the growth of the GNP. But this growth will be in the direction of reducing, not increasing, the pollution of the environment. Or there may be an increase in service oriented industries that may consume many fewer resources while still increasing the GNP.

* GNP is a measure of the total goods and services produced by a country.

While these arguments have considerable validity, technical development must also be seen to have limits. Earlier advanced societies such as the Roman Empire have declined in the past due to overtaxing their resources. Whole regions of the earth have been despoiled and the inhabitants have been forced to move on. The world is now too small and interdependent to allow this escapist solution for mankind.

Another reason for a lack of overwhelming optimism is the time lapse in effecting technical progress. The scientific principles underlying the breeder reactor have been understood for about 30 years and still no commercial system is in operation. The basic concepts of the fusion process are known, but a working reactor is still a project to be realized in the future. And, at present, the amount of federal research funding on which technology depends is being decreased in many of the basic sciences. Time is an important commodity, and few politicians are used to planning for long-term gains. Congressman John Davis, Chairman of the House Committee on Science and Astronautics, pointed out that while 30 years may seem a short time in scientific terms, most Congressmen think in terms of 2-year cycles. Whether the massive technical progress required to alleviate the problems associated with growth can be brought about under these conditions is far from clear.

My main concern about the limit to growth stems, however, not so much from the five factors discussed by Meadows and his coauthors but rather from the consideration of energy limitations. There is a well known relationship between GNP and energy consumption that holds true for many countries (see Figure 7-1). In the United States, energy use has grown at least as fast as the GNP (Figure 7-2). All the suggestions made about changing the direction of the GNP will not obviously change this correlation. Antipollution devices, for example, increase the use of energy in both transportation and electric power production. Service-oriented industries are probably as energy intensive as other industries, even if they do not consume other resources very rapidly.

As was noted in Chapter 16, there is an ultimate limit to energy use. Nearly all energy consumed releases waste heat, which raises the temperature of the earth. Although the temperature at which environmental problems will arise is not well determined, it is generally agreed that a rise of more than a few degrees centigrade would have a very significant effect on climate. At current energy growth rates, this level will be reached in about 150 years. The impact of temperature rise in urban areas will be noted even sooner, even if a large increase in solar energy use helps to minimize the overall global thermal effect.

Thus, unless we are able to dissociate a rise in GNP from increasing energy consumption, the ultimate limit on energy use will limit the growth of GNP within the next two centuries. This conclusion is independent of technical innovation or increases in productivity. Both of these developments tend to increase the growth of energy consumption—remember the Texas rice farmer! The heating effect simply follows from fundamental physical laws which cannot be repealed.

One technical possibility to help solve this problem might be to move rapidly in the direction of large increases in solar energy use. However, this would not solve the problem of urban heat islands and, in any case, the solar input in any given year is also finite. The other possibility is by deliberate climate engineering, such as altering the albedo of the earth. Apart from the social, psychological, and political difficulties of deciding how little sunshine people are willing to tolerate, the uncertainties are so great that it would seem best to avoid such a possibility.

By far the best solution would appear to be to gradually turn down the rate of economic as well as population growth and learn to live with a more static system.

18-6   A "Static" Economy

Being forced to live with a slow or zero economic growth rate has its own problems. In fact, these problems have been so great that most economists shut their minds even to the possibility and look for other solutions to the problems of growth. Perhaps the greatest difficulty is the fact that a static economy tends to preserve the status quo. Because most societies have significant disparities between rich and poor at present, a freezing of this situation would perpetuate such an unfair situation. A similar problem occurs on an even larger scale between rich countries and poor countries. It is hard to imagine a stable society with such built-in inequities and with little chance to change. Few people, I think, would postulate such a society as ideal.

In order to change the distribution of goods in a static economy, it would be necessary for the "haves" to be willing to give up some of their wealth to the "have nots." This is clearly an extremely difficult thing to bring about either within a particular society or especially on an international scale.

The economists' solution to this problem of redistribution is to continue economic growth. In such a growth situation, it is possible to imagine a more rapid improvement of the poorer segment of society, thus narrowing the gap between rich and poor. Even if this does not happen, it is easier to live with a situation where the lot of the poor is at least improving on some absolute scale even if it is not approaching that of the rich.

The difficulty is evident and appreciable, but the continued growth solution has even more problems. Fortunately, there remains some time, albeit short, in which to make adjustments while continuing to grow. Conservation policies might buy us a little more time. A decrease in the population growth rate will buy even more time and both population control and conservation of energy should be strongly encouraged. However, economic and political policies that aim toward static economic growth should now be seriously considered while facing squarely the problems of redistribution both nationally and internationally. Advertising and much of our education has trained us for consumption. Perhaps these same tools can be used to train us instead for conservation.

In the absence of any economic models, it seems appropriate to consider examples that may be found of societies which have lived or still do live in equilibrium with their environments. In the anthropological literature, studies have been made of many such societies. Economists have tended to ignore this material, or when cited, equilibrium societies are seen as negative examples of stagnation, a state that must generally be avoided. These "primitive" peoples are viewed as backward holdouts in an age of progress, worthy of curiosity but not of serious consideration.

One example of such an equilibrium society is that of the !Kung Bushmen of Botswana. The !Kung Bushmen inhabit a portion of the Kalahari Desert of southern Africa, an area that receives 6 to 9 inches of rainfall each year and would be considered marginal to human existence by any standards. Contrary to popular conception, these people do not live on the edge of survival. In fact, they live an abundant, leisurely, and secure existence. Their adaptation is so successful in this environment that they have continued a hunting and gathering existence for many thousands of years. (Compare this with the 200–300 years it has taken us to bring an immensely richer environment to the point of ecological crisis.)

In his 15 months of field study, Richard B. Lee, a young American anthropologist, has found a surprising degree of prosperity among the !Kung Bushmen [9]. For a people of small size and stature but vigorous activity, it has been determined that they would need 1975 cal daily including 60 g of protein per person per day. The !Kung Bushmen average 2140 cal/day and 93 g of protein. This adequate diet is provided for all by an average of 2 to 3 days of work per adult each week; the children and elderly are not made to contribute at all. At least 10% of the population is over the age of sixty. This figure compares favorably with that of industrialized nations. Some of the old are blind, but they are considered important members of the community for their wisdom and are well respected. Leisure time, of which there is an abundance, is spent visiting and receiving friends and relatives, dancing, and performing religious rites. Their security of life was seen during the third year of one of the worst droughts in southern Africa's history.

Most of the 376,900 people of Botswana are farmers and pastoralists. After the crops had failed for 3 years in succession and over 100,000 head of cattle had died for lack of water, the United Nations instituted a famine relief program which included over 30% of the people of Botswana. The !Kung Bushmen live in an isolated area in the extreme northwest of the country where they were not reached by the relief program. They were able to survive well on their wild foods, and they were joined in foraging by the women of many of the farming Bantu peoples. Even in this time of drought the natural resources were able to support a much higher population than they would have to if the Bantu harvest had been sufficient. Yet this added pressure on their resources did not adversely affect the Bushmen.

The point of this example is not that the American population should return to a hunting and gathering existence. Our population is too large and our society too complex to make a retreat to the primitive life possible. However the !Kung do show us that a "static" society can be prosperous and can exist stably for long periods of time. The security of the !Kung Bushmen's way of life perhaps has something to say to us about a people who can live in harmony with their environment without destroying it. They have a much different view of the meaning of life and work than we do in this country. Once all needs are provided for, the rest of the time is spent enjoying oneself. In the United States pressure is put on all to achieve, to be able to buy every new and ingenious gadget. With a high rate of mental diseases, heart conditions, and ulcers, not to mention all of the pollution and waste disposal that material achievement brings, it would seem that we should at least consider alternative systems.

The question that we must eventually face is what ultimately are our values, what does make people happy? One of the staff members in our laboratory recently went to India after an absence of almost ten years. On his return, he discussed the changes he had seen but also the extreme poverty, widespread disease, and short lifespan he had observed especially in the rural villages. I asked him whether he felt that the people were happy. Without hesitation, he replied that he was certain that they were much happier than Americans. He went on to say that family life was still very important to the villages and that he himself had felt a tremendous sense of security while in India even though he had not been there for 10 years and had felt that he might be too much a stranger.

The point is not that we should therefore refuse to aid the Indian people or discourage their technical advance, but rather that in contrast to many of our imagined beliefs, happiness is not only, if at all, found mainly in material possessions and conspicuous consumption. Such a lesson could have a profound effect on our society and it may be one which is forced upon us.

18-7 Summary and Conclusions

Economics plays an extremely important role in the energy problem both in resource development and in pollution control. Only recently has the concept of the negative externalities associated with energy use been realized, and methods of internalizing these costs are still being developed. Market forces may have a significant impact on various kinds of energy use when the market price reflects the true cost including societal costs.

While economies of scale have played an important part in industrial development, in some cases size too may be a negative externality. It may be necessary also to consider the extra costs of large power plants, supermarkets, even cities and, if necessary, impose a diseconomy of scale to reach a totally optimized size.

Finally, although economic growth gives one solution to the problem of national and international inequities, this growth may ultimately be limited by constraints on the use of energy. If this is true, consideration should be given to deriving models of more static economic systems which can still face the problems of redistribution to bring about a stable, happy, and yet creative society. As E. J. Misham of the London School of Economics writes:

As producer, affluent-society man has little choice but to adapt himself to the prevailing technology. No provision is made by industry enabling him, if he chooses, to forego something in the way of earnings for more creative and enjoyable work. Nor, as a citizen, has he been presented with the choice of quieter and more humane environments, free of noise and motorized traffic.

Questions

1. Explain why government regulation or taxation is necessary to supplement the law of supply and demand for certain products whose manufacture involves the use of public resources.
2. How realistic is a "static" (nongrowth) economy?
3. Why are nongrowth economic policies not favored by most economists? Can you counter any of these arguments?
4. Large scale operations are usually less expensive per unit than smaller ones. Discuss some of the energy problems posed by large scale systems and suggest solutions. Use examples to illustrate your points.
5. Many economists believe that only by increasing prices substantially can energy use be curtailed. Justify or attack this point of view. Suggest methods for implementing such a policy in practice.

Bibliography

[1] M. H. Spencer: *Contemporary Economics.* Worth Publishers, 1971.

[2] Gerald Garvey: *Energy, Ecology, Economy.* Norton & Company, 1972.

[3] H. E. Koenig, W. E. Cooper, and J. M. Falvey: Engineering for ecological, sociological and economic compatibility. *IEEE Transactions on Systems, Man and Cybernetics,* Vol. SMC-2, No. 3, July, 1972.

[4] J. Forrester: *World Dynamics.* Wright-Allen Press, 1971.

[5] D. H. Meadows, D. L. Meadows, J. Randers, and W. W. Behrens: *The Limits to Growth.* Universe Books, New York, 1972.

[6] R. M. Solow: Is the end of the world at hand? *Challenge,* March/April, 1973, p. 39.

[7] R. Wilson: Tax and integrated pollution exposure. *Science,* October, 1972, p. 182.

[8] R. Boyd: World dynamics: a note. *Science,* August, 1972, p. 516.

[9] Richard B. Lee: *Subsistence Ecology of Kung Bushmen.* Ph. D. Thesis, University of California at Berkeley. 1965.

[10] G. Hardin: The tragedy of the commons. *Science,* **162,** p. 1243, (1968).

CHAPTER 19

Energy Policy

19-1   Introduction: Political Pressures

We noted in the previous chapter that economics has a large impact on many energy issues. However, the implementation of any economic theory depends upon political decisions. Energy policy is determined by legislators either in Congress in Washington, D.C., in state legislatures, or possibly in city or town councils throughout the country. It is important, therefore, to gain some appreciation of the problems faced by such legislators, particularly if we hope to help influence their decision making.

Every politician, whether the President of the United States or a city councilman in East Lansing, Michigan, is continually bombarded by a whole series of issues each clamoring for immediate attention. Pressure groups of many kinds are all eager to influence the legislator to support their point of view. Ideally he is trying to be responsive to his constituents whose votes keep him in his present position. Elected officials generally have to face the voters as often as every 2 years. As a result, politicians are frequently more responsive to immediate or short term issues rather than those requiring more foresight.

Many questions concerning energy policy are long term ones, however, sometimes requiring planning that may only come to fruition after 20 or 30 years. The issues are often complex and interrelated. It is to be hoped that long term effects will be considered as present energy policy is formulated.

In one way we are perhaps fortunate that the present "energy crisis" has descended upon us. Summer gasoline shortages, winter heating oil shortages, and electrical brownouts in both seasons have forced

both the public and their legislators to consider the problems of energy very seriously. The danger, however, is that legislators may overreact to the present problems and seek solutions to immediate shortages with policies that may neglect, for example, their environmental results.

An example of this hasty mood has been the recent passage of a number of bills introduced in the United States Congress to prevent further legal action to delay the trans-Alaskan pipeline. Oil shortages have apparently convinced a majority of lawmakers that it is necessary to move rapidly on the pipeline. However, as pointed out by Luther J. Carter in *Science* [2]

The case to be made for an independent evaluation of the merits of a trans-Canadian pipeline by the National Academy of Sciences is substantial. The Department of the Interior already has issued a nine million dollar, nine-volume environmental and economic impact study of the pipeline, but the adequacy of such a study is not best measured by its cost and its bulk. An early draft said that shipment of the oil across Canada would present fewer environmental drawbacks than the movement of the oil from the North Slope to Valdez (on the Gulf of Alaska) by the pipeline, then from Valdez to West Coast Markets by tanker. This important conclusion was unaccountably left out of the final report. The report also failed to answer convincingly competent opinion that not before the late 1980's will the West Coast be able to use all of the Alaskan oil, with the result that part of the oil will have to be marketed in Japan. A trans-Canada pipeline would bring the oil both to the West Coast and the fuel-short Midwest.

Furthermore, there is evidence that both the Administration and Trans-Alaska Pipeline (TAP) supporters in Congress have made a deliberate effort to obfuscate rather than clear up the question of whether Canada would be receptive to a trans-Canada pipeline proposal. Indeed, Representative Anderson, who visited Ottawa in early June, 1973, to learn directly of Canadian attitudes, has reported that the Department of State in effect told Canada's Ambassador to the United States, Marcel Cadieux, to stop meddling when his government sought to correct some misimpressions. The Mondale-Bayh amendment called for immediate U.S.-Canadian discussions of the pipeline question.

It is to be hoped that safety and other environmental issues will not be forgotten in order to provide energy at all costs!

To appreciate the present energy policy situation better, let us begin by reviewing the situation up to the middle of 1972.

19-2   Previous Energy Policy

Much of the United States energy policy has been characterized by a division of responsibility among various agencies which have issued conflicting statements. As the *Federation of Atomic Scientists Newsletter* states [3]

> Fourteen Congressional committees, six White House offices, nine departments of the Executive Branch, six independent commissions—in all about sixty-five government agencies are devoted to it (energy). Whether, in fact, their recommendations are coherent or contradictory, adequate or inadequate, no one knows.

This spreading of responsibility with no overall policy leads to a number of problems. One of these problems is that a good deal of important research does not get done. For example, in a comprehensive report prepared by an interdepartmental group of federal agencies, entitled *Energy Research and Development and National Progress* and published in 1964, it was concluded that several long term deficiencies in United States energy research and development were apparent [4]

1. Lack of a long-range integrated plan for civilian energy research and development.
2. Delay in initiating essential research with distant payoffs.
3. Insufficient support of devices and systems whose promise has not yet been demonstrated.
4. Neglect of certain "old" resources.

These conclusions have gone largely unheeded, however, so that many of them are echoed by the more recent report of the Task Force on Energy published in December, 1972, and entitled *Energy Research and Development* [5].

Another result of the lack of a single responsible agency has been a marked imbalance in the energy funding picture. Table 19-1 gives a list of energy research and development funding by program. The clear message is that nuclear energy has been receiving a massive share of total funding with coal running a poor second. In 1972 the total solar and geothermal funding was only about 0.5% of the total. A fivefold increase since then has now brought these to about 2% of the total energy research and development funding, still far below the level of nuclear reactor funding.

Other reasons for the large imbalance of funding in favor of nuclear energy have been investigated in a study by Bruce Mocking entitled, "Electrical Power Research and Development and Federal Government Support Policy: Two Case Studies [1]." Dr. Mocking identifies four factors that explain why some research is supported at the expense of other research. The first is that legislators are aware only of the possibilities of a certain line of research. To broaden their awareness may require a substantial educative effort because congressmen are often lawyers by profession and, therefore, have little scientific and technical background. The second factor is the amount of national prestige

Table 19-1
Energy Research and Development

Program	Obligation (millions of dollars)*		
	1972 Actual	1973 Estimate	1974 Estimate
fossil fuel energy			
production and utilization of coal	74	94	120
production of other fossil fuels	13	13	9
nuclear energy			
liquid metal fast breeder reactor	236	272	323
nuclear fusion	53	66	88
nuclear fuels process development	35	42	62
other nuclear power	87	98	90
solar and geothermal energy	3	8	16
other energy related programs	37	50	63
Total	537	642	772

* Includes funds for conduct of research and development and related facilities. Detail may not add to totals due to rounding.

associated with a particular project. The example used by Mocking is atomic energy for which terms like "national security" and "United States prestige" can readily be invoked. A third cause is simply the effect of government functions: If a program has no powerful supporters, such as a congressional committee or government agency, then its chances of support are reduced. Finally, it is easier to have funding continued than to begin funding. Therefore, it is advantageous to request funds early in the project before the costs are known. If the costs escalate later, more money will usually be made available.

One can see the operation of some of these factors when examining the total United States research and development budget (Table 19-2). Defense receives over 50% of the total funding whereas the National Science Foundation, which supports primarily basic research in universities, receives less than 3% of the total.

All of these factors have favored the cause of nuclear energy which has both its own particular agency, the Atomic Energy Commission (A.E.C.), and its own congressional committee, the Joint Committee on Atomic Energy. Although the A.E.C. has grown more powerful and nuclear energy has received a good deal of funding, a number of problems have arisen within the structure of the A.E.C.

One basic problem has been that the A.E.C. has two separate purposes which are sometimes conflicting. On the one hand, the A.E.C. has the responsibility of encouraging the use of nuclear energy, but, as well, it is also responsible for the safety and licensing of nuclear reac-

Table 19-2
Conduct of Research and Development (numbers are in millions of dollars)

Department or Agency	Obligations	
	1973 Estimate	1974 Estimate
Defense—military functions	8,338	8,808
National Aeronautics and Space Administration	3,383	2,995
Health, Education, and Welfare	1,832	1,969
Atomic Energy Commission	1,339	1,411
National Science Foundation	461	516
Transportation	367	425
Agriculture	378	351
Interior	259	262
Commerce	214	211
Environmental Protection Agency	117	138
Veterans Administration	76	78
Housing and Urban Development	43	71
Justice	39	54
all other	184	141
Total conduct of research and development	17,110	17,430

tors. There are occasions when these two responsibilities conflict. In these cases, the lack of separation of responsibilities and particularly the lack of clear priorities has cast doubt on the reliability of certain safety precautions. In the past, the A.E.C. has not been particularly sensitive to environmental concerns and under the previous chairman, James Schlesinger, the A.E.C. was brought to court for a lack of response to the National Environmental Protection Act, in particular for not providing environmental impact statements for the breeder reactor program. Under the new chairman, Dixie Lee Ray, this action was settled out of court with the A.E.C. agreeing to provide the required impact statements. Dr. Milton Shaw, the head of the breeder development program, retired shortly afterwards.

A major aspect of previous policy has been the belief that we must have cheap energy to stimulate industrial development. This emphasis on cheap energy has led to a number of anomalies, perhaps the most striking being the federal controls placed on prices for domestic oil and natural gas shipped across state boundaries. The price of natural gas is still controlled at about 26¢ per 1000 scf (standard cubic foot) at the wellhead and has not changed significantly for many years. Oil prices are in a similar position. This means that domestic production is discouraged because not enough profit can be realized to justify further exploration and development.

19-3 Recent Changes in Energy Policy

Recently there has been a number of indications that the climate of thinking is changing in energy policy and that the seriousness of the situation is receiving some attention. The Task Force on Energy of the 92nd Congress under the Chairmanship of Representative Mike Mc-Cormack, from Richland, Washington, has completed an extensive series of hearings on energy and published a comprehensive report in December, 1972. The conclusions and recommendations contained in this report are given in Appendix II. Basically these recommendations call for a greatly increased research and development effort and organizational reforms to deal better with energy questions. The report also emphasized environmental protection and energy policy and stressed a number of areas of particular importance including solar, geothermal, breeder reactors, coal, and fuel oil. The 93rd Congress has now appointed a separate subcommittee on energy which will be chaired by McCormack to continue investigation and suggest legislation on this important issue.

Senator Henry Jackson has also been largely instrumental in focusing attention on energy questions both on the floor of the U.S. Senate and also through his influence as Chairman of the Committee on the Interior and Insular Affairs. He is particularly concerned with the danger of a growing United States dependency on foreign oil and he, therefore, favors rapid expansion of domestic oil supplies. However, Senator Jackson has also sponsored the National Environmental Protection Act (NEPA) and sometimes these two concerns conflict.

A nongovernmental group that is also concerned with questions of energy policy is the Energy Policy Project, supported by the Ford Foundation at a cost of $3 million. The project is headed by S. David Freeman, who is a former presidential advisor on energy problems. This Energy Policy Project is supporting a number of studies on various aspects of energy policy and will publish a summary volume probably within the next year. Such independent considerations should be of value to government policy makers.

The most important impact on energy policy, however, will almost certainly be from the Administration. On June 4, 1971, President Nixon sent an energy message to Congress, but very little was done about it. On February 19, 1973, a message on Natural Resources and Environment also made brief mention of energy questions [6]. This was followed by a more extensive energy message on April 18, 1973, which outlined some general policy statements and was followed by specific pieces of legislation aimed mainly at immediate problems such as the Santa Barbara channel operation and land reclamation. The message differed in one major respect from previous statements in that much more stress was placed on conservation as a necessary part of any solution to our energy problems.

President Nixon recently followed his April message with a further statement on June 29 [7], which outlined some administrative changes and presented in more detail some of the areas in which the Administration will propose legislation. The administrative changes included the appointment of John Love, former governor of Colorado, as Assistant to the President for Energy and Director of the Energy Policy Office (EPO)*. The President has also asked Congress to create a Cabinet-level Department of Energy and Natural Resources (DENR) and a new Energy Research and Development Administration (ERDA).

The DENR would bring together a number of federal programs that are concerned with energy or natural resources, mainly from the Department of Interior, but also from the Departments of Transportation, Agriculture, Commerce, and the Department of the Army. The new department would have responsibility for balancing the use and conservation of the nation's natural resources and assure that future demands for water, timber, minerals, and energy resources are met without sacrificing forests, lakes, wilderness, beaches, and the general environment.

The proposed Energy Research and Development Administration would be a completely independent agency that would be responsible for overseeing the nation's energy research and development. The A.E.C. functions of nuclear materials production, reactor development, military applications, physical research, biomedical and environmental research, and controlled thermonuclear research would all be transferred to ERDA. In addition, ERDA would assume responsibility for research on fossil fuels, power transmission, and other nonnuclear energy research and development. The A.E.C. would then be responsible only for the licensing and regulation of nuclear energy and would be renamed the Nuclear Energy Commission (NEC).

These proposals have a number of obvious advantages. First, the allotment of the A.E.C's regulation and promoting responsibilities to different agencies removes the problem of conflicting interests and should allow both new agencies to pursue their respective goals more freely. The creation of ERDA, bringing all energy research under the one agency, should also help to correct the imbalance of funding for nuclear energy that presently exists. It remains to be seen whether Congress will approve these proposals.

As well as the organizational changes discussed above, President Nixon also proposed a $10 billion budget for energy research and development funding over the next 5 years. Although this falls short of Senator Jackson's hope of $20 billion over the next 4 years, it never-

---

* Governor Love only lasted a few months, when he was replaced by William Simon as Energy Czar.

theless represents a major advance in government thinking on energy research and development. Among the projects to receive immediate funding, with a $100 million grant, would be research in coal liquification and gasification, sulfur oxide removal, magnetohydrodynamics, and geothermal energy research. Additional funds for an alternative reactor project—the gas cooled reactor would also be provided.

Finally, the President's message emphasised an energy conservation program to attempt to reduce personal energy consumption by 5% over the next 12 months. He is adding weight to his proposals by instituting steps to reduce government energy use by as much as 7% in the next year by reducing air conditioning and lighting in government buildings. Business trips by federal employees will be decreased and more attention will be given to energy efficiency in automobiles and government-operated facilities.

Although all of these measures are valuable steps in the right direction, it is to be hoped that both Congress and the President will have the courage to take the further difficult steps necessary to preserve environmental concerns while promoting energy use. For example, some of these steps might include decisions to reduce growth if necessary for conservation purposes and to fund basic research in energy projects which may not have an immediate payoff.

19-4 Local Issues

As well as the national concerns discussed in the previous section, many energy issues are joined at the local level, and it is of some interest to see how these are resolved. An example of such an issue is the Calvert Cliffs case where the court of appeals decision required for the first time that the A.E.C. weigh environmental factors in reaching its decision. Professor D. A. Bronstein, an environmental lawyer, in an article in the *Ecology Law Review* [9] discussing this case points to a number of problems in current licensing procedures. These include (a) the fact that the Advisory Committee on Reactor Safety (ACRS) has no power to enforce remedies to its objections, (b) the ambiguity and consequent difficulty in enforcement of the phrase "radioactive discharge from each reactor as low as practical," and (c) the question of guarantees of relative safety. Bronstein also stresses that

> The most fundamental problem, however, is one that is almost completely hidden. Lawyers trained in the common law are taught that the adversary system is the best means of determining an issue. Reflection on this hearing, however, should indicate that the adversary method might fail to provide for the safety of people and the environment.

In the Calvert Cliffs case, the Weather Bureau, the Army Coastal Engineering Center, and the ACRS all found fault with the proposed plant. Yet none of their objections was raised by the Chesapeake Environmental Protection Association (CEPA) at the Atomic Safety and Licensing Board hearing because the CEPA was unable to secure experts in these fields and because the attorney for the CEPA felt these issues could not be won.

This type of tactical decision must be made whenever the adversary system is used. In making such tactical decisions, a lawyer simplifies the issues. Trial lawyers frequently ignore weak points to concentrate on strong points. The question is whether this type of thinking is apposite to a nuclear power decision, where one small design or operation error can spell disaster. In an extremely technical area such as nuclear power, however, there is the danger that simplifying the issues will result in oversimplification of the scientific problems—and an error of this type could lead to disaster.

In dealing with legal questions related to government agencies, it is important to realize that, in administrative law, the court does not have to weigh evidence and decide on the preponderance for a particular point of view. All that is required is that the agency provide some evidence in support of its position to win the case. This assumes that the government agency has access to a great deal of technical expertise, which simply requires confirmation in court.

As a result, local groups of intervenors, as they are called, seldom hope to win a particular legal battle if pitted against an agency or even a private company supported by a particular agency. Instead, they often resort simply to delaying a particular project by a series of legal maneuvers. These consequent delays are often so expensive to a private firm that a settlement with the intervenors might be reached out of court.

Precisely this situation arose in Michigan over the Palisades Park controversy between Consumers Power Company and a number of groups of concerned citizens, known collectively as the intervenors, over thermal pollution problems from a new power plant on Lake Michigan. The delay was costing Consumers Power millions of dollars so that they finally agreed to build cooling towers for the plant without the case coming to court at all.

Citizen groups concerned about environmental protection were given a new weapon in 1969 with the passage of the National Environmental Policy Act (NEPA). The most famous section of this act, Section 102, requires all federal agencies to prepare an environmental impact statement before taking any major action or recommending or reporting on any legislation that would significantly affect the environment. This environmental impact statement is then to be circulated for comment to other federal agencies with relevant expertise and to state and local environmental protection units. This act and particularly its famous Section 102 has come under fire from utilities as delaying the construction of power plants while environmental impact statements are prepared. There was even discussion of repeal of Section 102 to help electric shortages. Fortunately, however, this useful tool is still with us.

Both the NEPA and the use of delay are powerful tools in the hands of concerned citizens, but they must be used with care and restraint. Energy-environment questions are complex and usually multifaceted. In particular, reasonable alternatives to a problem should be proposed rather than mere negative opposition. One must also be sure that the alternative proposal will not cause more damage than good. Often technical experts must be consulted, and, even then, difficult questions may remain.

If intervenors are found to be causing harmful and unnecessary delays, this would finally serve to alienate both the public and the Congress, which might then remove some of the legal methods that now exist for protecting the environment.

Any environmental issue should involve an educational experience both in instructing the public to increased awareness of the problem and a learning process to find what are the viable alternatives. This should be true both on a local and a national level.

19-5 International Issues*

Much of the current energy crisis discussion has dealt with gasoline shortages that reached significant proportions (most gas stations kept shorter hours, or at least limited the amount of purchases) in the summer of 1973. This shortage has, in turn, focused attention on the importation of oil particularly from the Middle East. There has been considerable discussion as to whether the United States should encourage or discourage such oil imports.

On the one hand, using oil from the Middle East saves United States reserves of oil. Being basically cheaper to produce, oil from the Middle East has been the least expensive oil available to the consumer. As a result, import restrictions have been placed on oil to help protect the domestic oil producer. There may soon be little or no choice but to import oil until new liquid fuels are available, because United States oil reserves, even including Alaskan oil, are insufficient to meet present and growing demands. Estimates suggest that we well may be importing as much as 50% of our requirements by 1980. Realizing this, the President, in April, 1973, removed restrictions from importing oil. He has also encouraged building increased refining capacity and deep

* This section was written early in the fall of 1973 before the 1973 Arab-Israeli War and before the cutoff of Middle East oil to the United States. Rather than continually attempt to update this section as the situation changed, it was left as written, especially since many of the basic concerns raised are still valid and perhaps even more pointed.

sea port facilities to ease the importation and distribution of oil and oil products.

Many people, however, among them Senator Henry Jackson, point to a number of disadvantages with such an unrestricted import policy. First of all, if the domestic petroleum industry stagnates, it may not be easy to revive production facilities quickly if this ever proves necessary. Exploration and production facilities require capital investments to keep them up to date. These investments will only be made if a reasonable return can be anticipated.

There is also the balance of payments problem. At present the United States has an annual deficit of $3 billion in balance of payments due to fuel imports. If these imports increase as anticipated, then by the early 1980s this deficit could be as large as $20 to $30 billion per year. Such a trade deficit would be hard to compensate for by other exports. The eleven main oil producing countries* have formed the Organization of Petroleum Exporting Countries (OPEC) to raise prices and are growing more powerful and more confident. Many of these countries are in the Middle East, with strong Arab nationalist ties. They may well be tempted to use their power to influence United States foreign policy, especially toward Israel. In any event, if we imported 50% of our oil requirements, national security would be very dependent on such supplies from a comparatively unstable and vulnerable region of the world.

As the OPEC countries increase their revenues, they will also be able to use these reserves in the world money markets with unknown effects. Such large reserves of capital would enable these countries to outwait the oil dependent countries in any showdown over oil supply or prices.

Finally, the amount of oil, even from the Middle East, is finite both in total supply and especially in rate of production. The industrial countries of Western Europe and Japan are at least as dependent as the United States on Middle East oil. They will, therefore, be competing with the United States for oil, forcing the price higher, and generally making for conflicting relations between the United States and other oil hungry countries. We do not want to be put in a position of going to war to fight for oil in the Middle East.

The oil question is an important one and looms particularly large over the next 10 years, but there is another fact about our energy use that may have even more important implications. The United States has approximately 6% of the world's population but uses about 35% of the world's energy. As other countries begin to develop economically, they will demand an increasing share of the available energy resources. We will find it hard to deny such demands without retreating to a new colonialism.

* The eleven members are: Abu Dhabi, Iran, Iraq, Kuwait, Qatar, Saudi Arabia, Algeria, Libya, Indonesia, Nigeria and Venezuela.

Table 19-3
Economic and Population Growth

Country	Population (1968) $\times 10^6$	Average Annual Growth Rate of Population (1961–1968) (%/year)	GNP per capita (1968) (U.S. %)	Average Annual Growth Rate of GNP per Capita (1961–1968) (%/year)	Extrapolated GNP per Capita in Year 2000 (1968 U.S. $)
Republic of China	730	1.5	90	0.3	100
India	524	2.5	100	1.0	140
U.S.S.R.	238	1.3	1,100	5.8	6,330
United States	201	1.4	3,980	3.4	11,000
Pakistan	123	2.6	100	3.1	250
Indonesia	113	2.4	100	0.8	130
Japan	101	1.0	1,190	9.9	23,200
Brazil	88	3.0	250	1.6	440
Federal Republic of Germany	60	1.0	1,970	3.4	5,850

Even if energy resources are sufficient for all, when the total world population approaches the present per capita energy consumption of the United States, we will be approaching the upper limit to total world energy use (see Chapter 16). If the United States energy consumption has continued to grow, so that we still use more than our share, this again may pose a problem in international relations. Japan is already on an extremely rapid economic growth curve and may surpass the United States per capita GNP by the year 2000. A number of other countries are growing economically more rapidly than the United States, and others, like China and India, are also attempting expansion (see Table 19-3). If we are forced into a position of attempting to constrain the growth of other nations to limit energy consumption, this will also be an extremely unattractive and probably unstable situation.

19-6 Summary and Conclusions

Political as well as technical or economic considerations affect energy policy. Fortunately, previously stagnating energy issues are being revived both in Congress and by the President. One danger to be avoided is that the response may be too concerned about short term issues and not take account of the longer term implications.

Political action at a local level is growing in importance and effectiveness, particularly with new legislative support such as the NEPA. Such power, however, needs to be excercised with responsibility and restraint. Tilting at windmills may simply allow a real menace to go unheeded.

Finally, the international implications of many energy questions are extremely important. The present oil shortage has forced the United States into an unhealthy reliance on foreign imports. Alternative sources need to be developed to minimize this dependence. Longer term questions of allocation of energy use coupled to economic growth should also be faced before they reach critical proportions.

Questions

1. What are the main elements of a United States energy policy which you would propose?
2. Discuss a number of steps which you think would be feasible politically to reduce United States energy consumption by at least 20%.
3. Argue the case for or against the Alaskan pipeline as presently proposed, including the anticipated contribution to the total United States energy needs. Discuss alternative routes and make recommendations concerning these alternatives.

Bibliography

[1] Bruce Mocking: Electrical power research and development and federal government support policy: two case studies. Preprint
[2] Luther J. Carter: Alaska pipeline: Congress deaf to environmentalists. *Science*, 27 July, 1973, p. 326.
[3] *Federation of Atomic Scientists Newsletter*, Vol. 26, No. 2, February, 1973.
[4] *Energy Research and Development and National Progress.* U.S. Executive Office of the President, Office of Science and Technology, Prepared for the Interdepartmental Energy Study by the Energy Study Group under the direction of Ali Balent Cambell. June 5, 1964.
[5] *Energy Research and Development.* Report of the Task Force on Energy. 92nd Congress, December, 1972.
[6] National resources and environment. *Message from the President of the United States, 83-011 0.* February 19, 1973.
[7] *President's Statement on Energy, June 29, 1973.* White House Press Release by Charles DiBona, and *New York Times*, June 30, 1973.
[8] John N. Irwin, II: The international implications of the energy situation. *Department of State Bulletin*, May 1, 1973.
[9] Daniel A. Bronstein: The AEC decision-making process and the environment: a case study of the Calvert Cliffs Nuclear Power Plant. *Ecology Law Review*, Fall, 1971, p. 689.

[10] *The United States Energy Outlook and its Implications for National Policy.* John G. McLean, Chairman, Continental Oil Company. September, 1972.

[11] James R. Schlesinger, Chairman, AEC: The energy dilemma. *Oak Ridge National Laboratory Review,* Summer, 1972.

[12] P. H. Abelson: Energy and national security. *Science,* 2 March, 1973.

[13] *New York Times,* April 16, 17, 18, 1973.

[14] David J. Rose: Energy policy in the United States, *Scientific American,* Jan, 1974.

292

Energy Policy

CHAPTER

Overview

20-1 Growth

Unfortunately, most of the questions raised in this book do not lend themselves to easy answers. It would be very satisfying if I could sit down now and solve all the problems in this final chapter. I hope that the reader does not feel like the student who left the university after one term because the professors kept asking him questions whereas he had come to be given answers. Hopefully what this book has done is to eliminate some nonanswers and to help the reader to face up to the real issues involved in the energy question.

This is the reason for the quantitative approach taken whenever possible and justifies the technical chapters in the early part of the book. Not that I believe that all problems have quantitative solutions. Value judgements are extremely important, and these are difficult if not impossible to quantify. However, a quantitative approach helps to isolate the more important problems and to eliminate the trivial. Familiarity with technical terms and the ability to "put in some numbers" also shields one from being overwhelmed by "experts" who may be tempted to push one particular point of view. Many energy problems are not confined to a single discipline, and a broad overview of the issue is usually required. Many "experts" lack this ability.

One of the recurring issues we have discussed is the question of the growth of energy use, and on this question there are many conflicting views. The fact of growth, however, is inescapable. Whether future growth will be at the same rate as past growth is open to question. Most projections of energy growth rate made so far have usually erred on the side of predicting a slower growth than in fact took place. The

293

growth rate of electric energy use is about twice the total energy growth rate, and electric energy is taking over a larger proportion of total energy use.

Concerns with the environment will almost certainly tend to increase energy use, at least in the short term. Air pollution control devices on automobiles and power plants increase the use of fuel. Fresh water requirements, especially with the eventuality of a sea water distillation system, will also be energy consuming.

To achieve a decrease in growth rate will require a conscious decision on the part of society and its leaders to take deliberate steps to reduce growth.

Russel Peterson, ex-Governor of Delaware and presently chairman of the executive committee of the United States Commission on the Future of Man,* in discussing growth and development, writes [1]:

My whole career had been devoted to long-range planning. I began extrapolating into the future and realized that we were headed for a really serious problem if we didn't make some different decisions right now, especially in the energy field, because what's decided will affect all our future generations, perhaps irrevocably . . . We should shift from unlimited growth, particularly of energy-consuming items like cars and electric gadgets and turn our attention to the quality of life instead of quantity.

20-2 Resources

Perhaps the first place where the rapid growth rate of energy consumption is having an impact is in the present shortages of oil and natural gas. This has brought home to many Americans the finiteness of their nation's reserves of these valuable substances and has raised the problem of dependence on foreign suppliers for an energy source which, at present, seems vital to the security and way of life of this country. Estimates of even the world's reserves of oil and natural gas suggest that these also will last only a comparatively short time, certainly less than 50 years at current growth rates. In addition, petroleum is such a valuable source of chemicals for synthetic materials that it will be a great pity if the remaining petroleum is squandered to provide energy for power plants and automobiles.

The remaining fossil fuel, coal, is much more abundant and considerable reserves are available in the United States. But both mining and burning coal are damaging to people, to the land, and to the quality of the air. Underground mining is dangerous not only because of the

* Dr. Peterson became Chairman of the Council on Environmental Quality in Sept. 1973.

high probability of accidents but also because of the health hazards to miners exposed to coal dust year after year. Strip-mining is less expensive and less dangerous but is only useful if the coal seam is fairly close to the surface. Strip-mining is also so destructive to the land and streams that some states are considering banning it completely. Whether strip-mined land can be reclaimed, particularly in the hilly, water-short west, is presently unknown.

The burning of coal is also environmentally damaging. Both sulfur oxides and particulates are emitted. Technology has apparently almost solved the problem of sulfur oxide emission and the removal of large particulates from smoke-stack gases, although strict regulation or taxation with careful inspection will be required to ensure the continued use and effective operation of air pollution control devices. The small particles still cannot be readily removed and may pose one of the long-term problems in the increased use of coal.

The most promising use of coal may be after it is subjected to a liquefication or gasification process, preferably at the mine site, with pollution control devices to limit the emissions as much as is technically feasible. Ideally, the coal could be mined underground by automated machines which are now beginning to be developed, especially in Europe. Where surface strip-mining is required, the mine operators should be required to restore the land to its original state and to demonstrate that this is possible before mining is permitted. Much of the technology for reclamation, gasification, and pollution control remains to be developed, and research and development on these important projects should be strongly encouraged by both industry and government.

The other alternative resource, about which much optimism has been expressed, is nuclear energy. Compared to coal or even oil, nuclear energy is comparatively clean. Although at present nuclear power plants produce only a small amount of the nation's electricity, much higher fractions are expected within the next 10 years. However, nuclear power is not without its problems, too.

The low level emissions from nuclear reactors can be controlled to a sufficient extent that they probably will be a very minor health or genetic hazard. Recent stricter A.E.C. regulations encourage minimum emissions. However, careful monitoring is required at each reactor to ensure adherence to the law. In addition, stricter regulations are required on the fuel-processing plants to minimize emissions there also. Operations in these plants have been more careless and less controlled than in the power plants themselves.

Apart from low level emissions, there is also the danger of radioactive spillage from some catastrophic accident that could cause rupture of the containment vessel of the reactor. With the light water reactors (LWRs) in present use, the greatest question seems to be with core meltdown and the efficiency and reliability of the emergency core cooling system. The A.E.C. has been rather tight lipped on this question, although safety tests are continuing. This is a difficult problem, but one which must be solved before LWRs are allowed to proliferate. Any accident of this kind could do major damage both to people and property and would set back any nuclear program for many years.

Even if accidental disasters can be eliminated, a high level nuclear power generation capacity brings with it other problems. Sabotage or theft at the plant is an ever-present possibility. In transporting highly radioactive and potentially dangerous material from reactor to processing plant and back, accidents, sabotage, or theft are all possible and the first is even probable. Finally there is the question of storing long-lived, dangerous substances for tens of thousands of years. Arctic ice caps and salt mines have been suggested as storage sites for these wastes, but neither has been demonstrated to be without problems. Nevertheless, nuclear reactors continue to produce radioactive materials requiring storage even though a satisfactory solution to the waste disposal problem is not yet available.

Another difficulty with the LWRs is that they use only the rare isotope U^{235} which will become increasingly scarce if nuclear energy becomes more widely used. The usual estimates suggest that U^{235}, at acceptable prices, will only be available for another few decades. The solution to this difficulty is the fast breeder reactor which can use the much more abundant isotope U^{238} and which also produces more fissionable material as it operates. Present breeder technology is still in the experimental stage. A commercial pilot plant which is planned to be operational in the late 1970s is now being built by the Tennessee Valley Authority.

Even if the breeder technology is successful in developing a safe, reliable, and economic reactor, this will not solve but rather only enhance the dangers of living with plutonium. The element plutonium is extremely dangerous biologically. It is cancerogenic in minute quantities. It is insoluble in water and, therefore, is difficult to remove from an area and has a half-life of 24,000 years. Problems of handling and storage of this material are extreme. Although the breeder can conceivably provide practically unlimited energy resources, the dangers of living with a very large nuclear energy system are by no means negligible. At best, extreme care must be insisted upon.

Many of the proponents of the breeder program see it only as a bridge to cleaner, long-lived energy sources to be developed in the future. Two prime candidates are fusion and solar energy. Fusion has many attractive features. It offers, for example, an essentially infinite energy resource from the deuterium in the sea and is intrinsically a much cleaner system than the fission reactor. Unfortunately, although it appears that the demonstration of the scientific feasibility of fusion is drawing closer in the laboratory, probably either by the tokomak principle or by laser implosion, the construction of a working fusion reactor still seems a long way off. The breeder concept was demonstrated more than 30 years ago, and there is still no working commercial breeder reactor available. The problems of building a fusion reactor are even greater. Nevertheless, this is one avenue which must be explored with all due speed.

In some ways an even more attractive possibility, which so far seems to have escaped major consideration, is solar energy. The sun's rays can be used directly either for heating or electricity production. Other sources, such as wind or ocean thermal gradients that are driven by the sun, could also be used for electricity generation. The main disadvantages in utilizing energy from the sun is the large scale of solar collection systems required because of the diffuse nature of the source and the difficulty of transmitting and storing the power so gathered. But with technological development of more efficient collectors these problems do not seem insurmountable. The advantages of clean power, minimal environmental impact, and a potentially large and renewable resource suggests that a substantial increase in research and development funding is required to speed the utilization of solar energy.

Of the other major energy sources, only geothermal energy offers the possibility of any significant impact on total energy requirements. Even for this to be true, the development of a technology which is able to use hot rock sources and further advances in low temperature turbines will be required. Geothermal energy is more likely to remain a suitable local resource whereas long-term, widespread use will be made of either solar energy or the fusion process.

20-3   Storage and Transportation

As well as straining the earth's current energy resources, the rapid growth of energy use in the past few decades has also created problems with energy storage and transmission. Peak power demands mean extra generating capacity, which is both capital intensive and often inefficient if not used at near full capacity. Hydro storage has been used to help smooth out peak demands but suffers from a lack of available sites. Storage of compressed air in underground caverns, either natural or artificially created, has been suggested as an answer to the site problem. This technique also has the advantage that greater overall efficiency of energy use can be achieved using compressed air storage than with hydro storage.

The electrical transmission capabilities of the United States are also being increased rapidly, particularly to handle increased loads in urban centers. Superconducting transmission lines, which operate at very low temperatures but can handle very large currents, are one possible way of transmitting electricity with small losses. Other suggestions presently being pursued are ultra high voltage lines, cooled but not superconducting underground lines, and direct current (as opposed to conventional alternating current) transmission. Some combination of these techniques may prove useful for various conditions.

A less conventional approach suggests that energy may best be transported not along electric transmission cables at all but rather along pipelines. At the moment, natural gas is carried throughout the United States by a vast network of such pipelines. If hydrogen gas could be readily and cheaply produced at an electric generating station, for example, by the decomposition (hydrolysis) of water, it could then be readily pumped to a wide variety of sites, even into homes and commercial buildings. Hydrogen can readily replace natural gas as a clean fuel for heating and cooking. Liquid hydrogen, at low temperatures, has even been suggested as a possible transportation fuel to replace gasoline. Finally, with the use of fuel cells to convert hydrogen to electricity, whether in local centers or perhaps even in individual homes, the need for transmission of large amounts of electricity over long distances would be eliminated.

Although this may seem like a "far out" approach, it appears to offer an environmentally clean alternative to the spread of high voltage transmission lines. There remain technical problems, particularly with producing reliable fuel cells, and economic questions about producing hydrogen at competitive costs. However, the system has many attractive features, including a widely dispersed generating system. Such a system is probably more reliable and less vulnerable to accident or sabotage than a single large generating system with the large transmission lines then required.

20-4 Conservation

As well as developing new energy resources and providing better ways of storing and transporting energy, another important approach is to conserve energy. This has two complementary aspects. The first is to use energy more efficiently, particularly in those areas where the greatest use occurs. In the United States, industrial processing, transportation, and space heating are the major users. Better insulation of buildings is one way in which major energy savings could be realized. Recent federal regulations for new homes will help in years to come, but imaginative ways are needed to encourage better insulation of present structures. Industrial use of energy is probably fairly well optimized, although changes in the price structure could cause changes in operation away from particularly energy-intensive processes. The electric price-rate structure presently subsidizes the large users.

About one quarter of the total energy use in the United States is in transportation. The ease and convenience of the automobile has made us a nation of individual transport users with attendant large inefficiencies in energy use. Smaller cars, the use of bicycles for short trips, and mass transit for longer trips would all help to solve this problem and also relieve the extreme air quality problem in urban centers.

Unfortunately, existing cities often do not lend themselves to efficient transportation solutions. Cities generally are designed, or simply spring up, with little thought to transportation, and, as a result, commuting by automobile is almost a necessity for most workers. Architects and city planners should attempt to find solutions to this problem, at least in the newer cities that are growing up.

Better insulation, mass transit, and more efficient processing will reduce energy use, but there is another important aspect to energy conservation. The very term "conservation" implies a spirit of stewardship, of caring for and not squandering one's resources. This is an attitude which, unfortunately, is not particularly common in America, either about energy use or about the environment as a whole. It can perhaps be fostered by education, and a number of concerned groups are attempting such education.

Because people are the ultimate energy users, only people can reduce the use of energy. This may involve many people taking small steps that can add up to significant savings. This will require a change of attitude toward consumption of energy and of goods (whose production accounts for most of the industrial and commercial energy use). It raises questions concerning values and what makes people happy. At present, I feel that many of these values are set by advertisers, motivated primarily by the need to sell a product and make a profit. Perhaps the values of a society have too far reaching a consequence to be determined this way.

20-5 Thermal Pollution

Conservation may relieve the pressure on resources but, even with essentially infinite resources, there may be an ultimate limit on energy use imposed by the second law of thermodynamics. Eventually, as most energy is used, it is degraded into low temperature heat and cannot be recovered for useful work. Even the term energy "use" implies that, although the total amount of energy remains constant, it can be turned into a form that is not readily converted back into "useful" forms. The low grade heat produced by energy use is an additional input into the earth's heat balance equation.

The temperature of the earth is determined by a precise balance between the amount of radiation absorbed from the sun and the amount of longer wavelength radiation reradiated from the earth. As heat is input by man's activities at the earth's surface, more radiation must be radiated into space, and a new equilibrium situation will be reached at a higher temperature.

At present, man's energy use is only a very small fraction of the energy input from the sun (about 1 in 30,000). However, with population increase and with increased per capita energy consumption in the United States and particularly in countries just now developing, this fraction will increase. When the energy use generated by man becomes 1% of the sun's input, the temperature rise will be about 0.7°C. Projections of current growth rates suggest that this stage will be reached in less than 150 years!

The point I wish to stress is not whether this will come about in 100 years or even 500 years but rather that waste heat puts an ultimate limit on energy use. We live in a comparatively narrow range of acceptable temperatures and could not tolerate large departures. What the precise temperature limits are and whether feedback effects will accelerate the problem is presently unknown. It does seem quite certain, however, that we will ultimately be forced to limit energy use, perhaps in the not too distant future.

There are probably only two technical solutions to this problem. The first is an artificial alteration of the earth's energy balance by some kind of weather control. If, for example, the average cloud cover of the earth were increased, thus changing the albedo, the total amount of solar radiation incident on the earth's surface could be changed. However, the technical difficulties not to mention social or political problems with such attempts at widespread weather modification are enormous, and, to me, this does not offer a satisfactory approach.

A more attractive alternative is a vastly increased use of the solar energy incident on the earth. Since solar energy heats the earth already, tapping even a large fraction of it for useful work before it is degraded as heat, will not have any effect on the earth's overall energy balance. This seems a more reasonable possibility and appears much less likely to get out of control. Such an approach provides even more motivation for increased development of solar energy. However, it must be stressed that even the sun's radiation falling on the earth is limited, and that vast amounts of surface area are required to collect the energy. Therefore, this will also pose an ultimate limit, albeit a somewhat higher limit than if other energy resources were used.

The first place where such thermal effects will be noticeable is in urban centers with large concentrations of people and industry and a consequently high total energy use. Many cities already use a substantial fraction of the solar radiation input and their average temperatures are often 5°F or more hotter than their surroundings. Only heat transfer to the surrounding countryside prevents even larger temperature rises. As cities become larger and heat transfer becomes consequently more difficult, even larger temperature rises will be observed. The use of solar energy will not solve this problem because it is primarily a problem of concentrated use. Either energy use per capita must be decreased, or limits on cities' size may be required.

20-6 Energy Policy

Although the technical aspects of the development of new energy resources, energy conservation, and thermal pollution are significant, these issues also have important dimensions in the market place and in Congress. The realization of the impact of negative externalities on the true cost of many items including energy use is a valuable step forward. Pricing that reflects societal as well as labor and material costs should have a beneficial effect on many environmental issues and on energy use. The concept of regressive taxation based on the ability of a system to handle pollution is another useful concept which could also be fruitfully employed in energy pricing.

One of the significant challenges that I see facing economists is to develop models of satisfactory economic systems based on slow or static growth rates. At present, such systems appear to have a great disadvantage, since they "freeze" the status quo and perpetuate societal inequities. However, if at some point growth of energy use and, therefore, probably growth in gross national product are limited, such solutions will have to be found. More interaction between economists, engineers, scientists, and perhaps even philosophers may be needed to face these complex cross-disciplinary questions.

One of the most important places where energy questions should be faced is in the political arena. Until very recently energy policy questions were essentially neglected by federal policy makers. However, gasoline and electric shortages have forced a reappraisal so that both the President and Congress are proposing both increased research and development support and organizational changes to facilitate the emergence of a new energy policy.

Such changes are to be welcomed and encouraged. Unfortunately, many energy issues are complex, multifaceted, and have long term implications. Politicians generally think in rather short time scales. Let us hope that concern for solving current problems does not commit us to quick and easy solutions which neglect the long term implications of such policy. The time has come to act, with courage and with foresight, to meet the challenge of both energy and environment.

Bibliography

[1] Energy 9: interview with Russel Peterson. *Intellectual Digest*, August, 1973.

APPENDIX

INDIVIDUAL ACTION FOR ENERGY CONSERVATION

PREPARED BY THE

SUBCOMMITTEE ON ENERGY

OF THE

COMMITTEE ON SCIENCE AND ASTRONAUTICS
U.S. HOUSE OF REPRESENTATIVES
NINETY-THIRD CONGRESS
FIRST SESSION

Serial C

JUNE 1973

303

Printed for the use of the Committee on Science and Astronautics

U.S. GOVERNMENT PRINTING OFFICE
WASHINGTON : 1973

96–138 O

INDIVIDUAL ACTION FOR ENERGY CONSERVATION

The use of energy for transportation and in homes accounts for 44 percent of our total energy consumption. Thus, by reducing personal energy consumption in these two areas, individuals like yourself can make an important contribution toward reducing the total U.S. energy consumption.

TABLE I

UNITED STATES ENERGY CONSUMPTION (1968 DATA)

13 percent for Commercial Uses   19 percent for Residential Uses
43 percent for Industrial Uses   25 percent for Transportation

TRANSPORTATION

As you can see from Table I, 25 percent of the nation's energy is used for transportation. Since most of this is consumed in private automobiles in the form of gasoline, it is clear that reducing the use of gasoline will have a significant impact in easing fuel shortages. Here are some actions you can take:

Walk, take public transportation, or ride a bike for short trips.

Learn the schedules and routings of public transportation. Use it whenever possible to get to work, school, or shopping. Reduce your dependence upon automobiles.

If public transportation does not meet your needs, encourage additional routing and scheduling.

Encourage development of bike trails in your community.

Consolidate small tasks requiring an automobile into one trip, and thus reduce your total automobile mileage.

Create and support car pools for transportation to work, school, or shopping.

DRIVING AN AUTOMOBILE

Keep your engine tuned at all times.

Keep your tires properly inflated; under-inflated tires decrease gas mileage.

After starting your engine, drive slowly for the first mile instead of warming the engine up while standing still.

Drive slower. Increasing the speed with which you drive greatly increases fuel consumption. Driving 70 miles per hour will increase the gasoline you use by 33 percent compared to driving 50 miles per hour, and 12 percent compared to driving 60 miles per hour.

Anticipate speed changes and, where possible, allow your car to slow down before applying the brakes. Excessive braking increases gas consumption.

Drive smoothly. Changes in speed wastes gasoline.

Do not race the engine. If the automobile idles poorly, it may indicate the need for a tune-up.

Do not idle your engine for over three minutes while waiting.

While driving at highway speeds, check to see if the air conditioner is necessary. If possible, drive with it off. (You will need your air conditioner less if you avoid driving during the hottest hours of the day.)

Set your air conditioner to the warmest level that is still comfortable.

PURCHASING AN AUTOMOBILE

When considering the purchase of an automobile, include fuel economy as a major consideration.

Purchase a car no larger or more powerful than you need. Try to eliminate unnecessary optional electrical features.

Remember that larger cars with more powerful engines consume more fuel than smaller ones, in direct proportion to their weights. (An automobile weighing 5,000 pounds uses over twice as much fuel as one weighing 2,000 pounds.)

Air conditioning units and automatic transmissions increase fuel consumption.

RESIDENTIAL

COOLING

Shade windows from direct sunlight. It is best to shade them from the outside with trees, shutters, awnings, or roof overhangs. Be sure that this exterior shading does not trap hot air. (Deciduous trees give shade in the summer, but when they lose their foilage in the winter, they provide direct sunlight to windows and aid in heating.)

If the windows cannot be protected from the outside from direct sunlight, use light colored opaque draperies inside. These should be kept closed when the window is exposed to direct sunlight. In this way, you will reduce solar heating of your house through windows by 50%.

If you cannot shade a window from the outside, and do not wish to cover it with draperies, consider installing heat absorbing or reflecting glass. (This can reduce heat entering a house through the windows by 70%.)

Leave storm windows on windows that are not going to be opened during the summer months. This will reduce the transfer of outdoor heat into the house. Even with storm windows in place, it is important to shade windows from direct sunlight.

Make sure that your house is properly sealed so that the amount of warm air that can enter the house from the outside will be minimized. This should be done by checking areas of the house that could be sources of leaks. Check seals on windows and doors. Check and seal cracks in roofs and floors. Seal all exterior cracks. Use weatherstripping.

Close the fireplace damper. (This is important. It keeps hot air out in the summer and cold air out in the winter.)

Increase the insulation between the house and the attic to six inches of insulating material.

Allow for the ventilation of air through the attic. Reduce heat build-up by opening vents or windows. Using a small fan to exhaust attic air is particularly helpful.

If you are going to repaint or reshingle the house, use a light color. (Dark surfaces can become as much as 60 degrees warmer than the surrounding air. Under the same circumstances, a light surface would only be 20 degrees warmer.)

During hot weather, try to reduce the use of electrical or gas appliances within the house. These appliances give off excess heat during operation, and add to the load of cooling the house.

If possible, construct exterior vents for major appliances such as stoves and clothes dryers. Any excess hot air that can be expelled into the outside will mean less that will have to be cooled inside.

Minimize the use of hot water in your home. Wash in warm or cool water. Do not waste hot water when showering or bathing.

Turn off the lights when not in use.

HEATING

Check your house for insulation. It has been estimated that 15 to 30% of the heat required to warm a house is lost due to poor insulation. Check the insulation of your house against the following chart:

Heating system	Ceilings (inches)	Walls (inches)
Electrical_ _ _ _ _ _ _ _ _ _ _ _ _ _ _ _ _ _ _	9	3½
Gas or oil_ _ _ _ _ _ _ _ _ _ _ _ _ _ _ _ _ _ _	6	3½

If your insulation does not measure up to these standards, your energy output for heating will be greater than is necessary.

Install storm doors and windows.

Check for leakage to the attic and outside.

If possible, replace large glass areas with insulating or double pane glass. Close draperies in the evening or during exceptionally cold periods to reduce the heat loss through the glass.

Close the damper of the fireplace when not in use. If the fireplace is no longer in operation, provide an airtight seal in the chimney.

Have the furnace checked once a year and change the filters frequently during use.

Lower the daytime setting of the thermostat. Lowering the thermostat setting by one degree results in a 3 to 4% drop in fuel consumption; by 5 degrees, 15 to 20% less fuel.

Lower the thermostat at night.

Close or reduce ventilation to rooms that are not in use or are used for limited periods.

All appliances should be evaluated for their usefulness when compared to the energy they consume.

When purchasing new appliances, decide how much you will use optional extras—they require extra energy.

Air Conditioners

Check your requirements before you purchase. An air conditioner with too large or too small a capacity requires more energy and will often not work as well as an air conditioner matched to your needs.

Determine the efficiency of an air conditioner before purchase. To obtain the efficiency, divide the rating of the machine in BTU's per hour by the number of watts required to operate the machine. Models on sale today have efficiencies (defined above) ranging from 5 to 12. The higher the number, the more efficient the machine; the more efficient the machine, the less energy required for a given amount of cooling power.

Keep your air conditioning system clean and in good working order. Clean filters are required for the machine to work at its maximum efficiency. Check all filters every thirty days during use and if necessary replace them. Before use, check and lubricate the bearings as recommended in the manufacturer's manual. Check for proper tension and wear on all pulley belts.

Inspect the ducts in a central air conditioning system for blockage or leakage. The ducts should have a minimum of 1½ inches of insulation.

Gas Appliances

Since approximately 10% of all natural gas used in homes is consumed by pilot lights, consider switch operated electric starters instead of continuous burning pilot lights when purchasing new equipment.

Extinguish all pilot lights on appliances that will not be used for long periods of time. Make sure no gas is flowing.

Television Sets

Turn off television sets when not in use. (If yours has the "Instant-On" feature, unplug the set when not in use.)

Refrigerators and Freezers

Frost-free refrigerators require 50% more energy to operate than a standard model. Side-by-side refrigerator/freezer models use up to 45% more energy than conventional models.

Decide whether you need a full size freezer before purchase: it can add up to $4 per month to your fuel cost. If you do use a freezer, keep in mind that a full freezer is more efficient than an empty one.

Washers and Dryers

When possible, wash dishes and clothes in warm or cold water. The water heater accounts for 15% of a home's utility bill.

If weather conditions are suitable, use outside clotheslines for drying clothes.

Check for dripping hot water faucets and fix if necessary. Such a leak wastes money, water and energy.

Set water heater to a lower temperature.

VACATIONS

In the months ahead, the energy crisis may reach many of us while we vacation. Even while on vacation, we should consider measures that conserve energy.

BEFORE YOU LEAVE

Make sure that all gas outlets in your home are closed before leaving. If there are any that you want working when you return, have a neighbor turn them on the day before you reach home.

Use a timer (or neighbor) to turn the lights on and off in the evening rather than leaving them on while you are gone.

If you vacation in the winter, set the thermostat at the lowest setting. (Turn your heating system off if there is no danger of freezing your water pipes.)

Turn off your water heater.

ON THE ROAD

While driving, remember to slow down to save gas.

Try to minimize the use of your automobile air conditioner. Make sure that it is cleaned and checked before leaving.

IF YOU HAVE A TRAILER OR CAMPER

Slow down. The speed at which you travel affects gas mileage even more than if you were in a passenger car.

Check propane or butane lines for leaks. Turn off all outlets during travel.

In the summer, choose sites for the trailer or camper that have natural shade. Open windows at night.

ENERGY RESEARCH AND DEVELOPMENT

REPORT

OF THE

TASK FORCE ON ENERGY

OF THE

SUBCOMMITTEE ON SCIENCE, RESEARCH, AND DEVELOPMENT

OF THE

COMMITTEE ON SCIENCE AND ASTRONAUTICS
U.S. HOUSE OF REPRESENTATIVES

NINETY-SECOND CONGRESS

SECOND SESSION

Serial EE

DECEMBER, 1972

309

Printed for the use of the Committee on Science and Astronautics

---

U.S. GOVERNMENT PRINTING OFFICE

89–612   WASHINGTON : 1973

Chapter IV

CONCLUSIONS AND RECOMMENDATIONS

During its year and one-half of intensive investigation on Energy Research and Development, the Task Force has become aware of the many complexities and interrelationships affecting present and future energy uses. Although recognizing the need for further careful study, the Task Force makes the following recommendations:

1. Now is the time to implement a greatly increased national energy research and development effort. Studies alone are not enough. Adequate funds and technical manpower must also be committed.

It is clear that a short-term energy crisis is upon us. But there is a long-term energy crisis which is just as real, and now is the time for making those decisions for action necessary for the long-term. Report-writing, discussion, and debate have gone far enough to identify where additional emphasis is needed. Research and development will have a great effect in solving these long-range problems, and adequate R & D programs must get underway now.

An appropriate agenda for research was developed in 1964 by the Interdepartmental Energy Study commissioned by President Kennedy. Most of the excellent recommendations from that report relative to such topics as nuclear power, substitutes for crude oil and natural gas, and environmental pollution abatement are still valid today—valid because so little action has been taken to implement them.

The total government and private funding for Energy R & D has remained at 0.15% of the GNP (about $1.5 billion now) during the nine years since the Interdepartmental report was written. This is inadequate to meet future energy needs and should be significantly increased. An additional one billion dollars annually for Energy Research and Development is needed now.

Historical Trends in Energy Utilization

Before the industrial revolution, man's utilization of energy was limited mainly to his own strength and that of his domestic animals. This was supplemented by crude harnessing of wind, falling water and burning wood. These sources depended ultimately on the sun, and were for all intents and purposes inexhaustible.

The history of the United States coincides with the period of great increase in the use of energy which produced the industrial revolution. By the mid 1800's, the U.S. use of energy per capita was about 25 times the energy content of food consumed per capita. This ratio changed little until the early 1900's, when it began its steady and rapid increase to the present value of about 80.

310

A seemingly insatiable demand for energy, especially in the form of electricity, characterizes the United States as it approaches the end of the twentieth century. However, we know that this consumption, which has grown exponentially for almost a century, must eventually level off. The present "energy crisis" may indicate that the era of cheap and ample energy is coming to an end.

Future Demand for Energy

The historical increase in U.S. energy consumption becomes alarming when past trends are simply projected into the future. Total U.S. energy use has been doubling about every 20 years, with the demand for electricity doubling every decade. The implications of such short doubling times are formidable, both for energy resources and for the environment.

Anything that doubles in a fixed period of time has the characteristic that it increases tenfold in slightly more than 3 doubling times and one hundredfold in less than seven doubling periods. This kind of growth (exponential) also has other important properties. For example, since U.S. electricity demand is expoential, the amount of electricity consumed in the decade of the 60's equaled the total consumed in all of history up to 1960. Projected to the decade beginning in 2030 U.S. electricity demand would be more than 100 times the total electrical energy consumed until 1960.

The economic and environmental implications of a ten year doubling time are enormous. If future demand follows projection of past trends, great amounts of capital will have to be raised to finance new construction in the electricity industry, as well as in the supporting fuel and transportation industries. Severe insults to the natural environment will come from sulphur dioxide, nitrogen oxides, particulates, carbon monoxide, and waste heat from energy conversion equipment such as central power stations and automobiles. Increasing amounts of our land area will have to be dedicated to powerplants, refineries, electrical transmission lines and highways—all energy-related activities.

Some studies indicate future growth in demand for energy will be greatly depressed due to increased prices. Studies of the elasticity of demand for electricity even predict negative growth rates under certain price assumptions.

Recent energy shortages and the direct impact of those shortages upon the lives and work of many people are a hint of what may lie ahead if future imbalances between demand and supply occur. A rigorous examination of the forecasting process as it is related to energy supply and demand is needed. Policymakers must have at their disposal sophisticated economic models that factor in microeconomic data on our resources base and other parameters affecting energy demand. Simple projections of historical trends are not accurate enough.

Dwindling Resource Base

The implications of projecting historical energy trends for the future of our natural resources are no less dramatic. The earth's resources of oil, gas, coal and uranium are finite. Resource experts project that U.S. resources of gas and oil will be largely depleted within the next few decades. Foreign fossil fuel resources may provide a temporary respite for the United States, but as other nations strive for our standard of living we cannot expect to indefinitely command a disproportionate share of these foreign reserves. U.S. coal reserves, although large, face difficult environment problems that inhibit their exploitation. Reserves of our fissionable material are only slightly larger than our fossil reserves, unless we can assume the timely success of the nuclear breeder reactor program.

As late as World War II the United States was able to export large quantities of fuel to its allies, and there was at that time little anticipation that within a few years the Nation would become a net importer. The balance shifted in 1950 when fuel imports first exceeded exports. The overall energy deficit has increased since then, reaching 10 per cent of our total energy needs in 1971.

Our deficit of oil has increased sharply since 1950. Then our exports approximated 5 per cent of domestic production; in 1971 our net imports were 24 per cent, despite restrictions on oil imports. Natural gas, too, has been imported since 1950. In 1971 these imports amounted to about 4 per cent of domestic consumption. The Department of the Interior forecasts a 25 per cent dependency upon foreign gas and a 40 per cent dependency on imported oil by 1985. Other analysts agree substantially with these projections, and there is widespread concern within Congress and among many citizens over the international implications of this situation. The effect on our international balance of payments alone is expected to be $30 billion by 1985.

Uranium, coal, and oil shale are energy resources with which the United States is richly endowed. Environmental concerns are limiting the burning of coal in traditional ways, and inhibit mining operations for both coal and oil shale. Environmental concerns have also slowed the deployment of nuclear power reactors, and have resulted in slowing down the nuclear breeder reactor development program. Research and development may lead to the technology that will permit full utilization of these indigenous resources.

Energy and Environmental Quality

It has been stated that, with a given technology, the environment is damaged in direct proportion to the amount of energy consumed. Some ways in which this occurs are through the destruction of land through extraction of energy resources such as coal and uranium; and pollution of the air and water with exhaust products and waste heat.

In fact, the environmental damage need not be in direct proportion to the energy used. Technology has made automobiles and central power stations more efficient, resulting in less rejected heat and less noxious fumes. Research and careful planning can reduce the probability of accidents and health hazards to workers in energy industries to extremely low levels.

Many of the environmental goals require the consumption of more energy. Examples are automobile pollution standards which reduce engine efficiencies and require about 25% more fuel, and sulfur dioxide removal from fuels at high energy and economic penalties.

Attaining future environmental quality goals will require more energy and substantially increased research and development.

312

Energy and Economic Prosperity

There is a direct correlation between energy consumption and economic prosperity. The wealthy, industrialized nations use much more energy per capita than the poor, underdeveloped ones. The wealth of the U.S. has grown with its consumption of energy. In fact, the factor by which one multiplies per capita energy consumption to obtain per capita gross national product (GNP) is approximately constant over time and between nations. To a first approximation this relationship is easy to understand. Energy powers machines which do work for people; they multiply the ability of people to do work, to produce goods and provide services. Almost by definition this increases the per capita GNP.

However, a causal relationship between per capita energy consumption and per capita GNP has not been firmly established. This is an area worthy of more study and research. However, it does seem clear that public policies to decrease energy consumption will have rough sledding in the political arena if they also result in a decline in economic prosperity.

Prior Studies on Energy R & D

Abundant studies have been done on the status of and needs for energy research and development. The initial chapter of this report describes 30 of these studies that have been conducted since 1960.

"Energy R&D and National Progress", published in 1964, is probably one of the most comprehensive reports written on this subject. It was produced by an interdepartmental study group from Federal agencies which was established by President Kennedy in 1963. It recommended specific national opportunities in energy R & D related to energy resources, conversion, transmission, and utilization, as well as health and environmental problems associated with energy. These included oil drilling technology, coal gasification and thermonuclear fusion. The recommendations of this report are almost all relevant today.

The National Petroleum Council, in response to a request of the Secretary of the Interior, has carried out a massive study of the U.S. energy problem. Its "Summary Report" has just been published (December 1972) and makes a number of recommendations regarding policies designed to achieve increased U.S. energy supplies. One recommendation is:

> *Energy Research and Technology Must Be Permitted to Make the Advances Necessary for the Nation's Longer Term Development of Energy Resources.*

Research into a broad range of energy related technology could provide the means to increase future energy supplies.

If research is to make its maximum contribution, energy policies must recognize that strengthened incentives for research spending are needed. Reduced profitability in the energy industries has retarded the expansion of funds available for research and development. Improved revenues are essential to a healthy and growing research effort. In addition, commitment of large amounts of capital dollars for research requires an expectation that future government policies will continue to recognize the importance of expanding research and development programs.

Historically, research expenditures by the oil and gas industry have primarily been privately funded. Other fuel suppliers, however, particularly coal and nuclear, have historically relied largely on government funding. The National Petroleum Council endorses continued reliance on private industry as the principal source of funds for oil and gas research and takes no position on the optimal way to fund research in other fuel areas.

Areas for augmenting energy supplies that require particular attention are: perfection of a stack gas control device which would permit the use of high-sulfur coal consistent with environmental standards; research on conversion of oil shale and coal into synthetic fuels; and development of advanced nuclear reactor technology.

The Task Force itself has published an *Inventory of Research* in March, 1972. This effort attempted to answer the fundamental question "where are we now—what is the magnitude and emphasis of our present R&D effort?" The Inventory identified 4,400 energy R&D projects. Because funding levels of many projects were proprietary and because annual support levels were missing from many others, only a lower limit for the total investment in these 4,400 research projects is known ($441 million). It is estimated, if funding were known for all projects, that the entire inventory represents public and private R&D totaling over one billion dollars.

These studies, as well as others not reviewed here, have been useful in one way or another. But none has accomplished the most important objective of all: launching the massive R&D effort needed to cope with the energy crisis, both in the next decade and in the next century. Time is running out, and this effort must get underway without further delay.

Current Status of Energy R&D

The Task Force estimates the total government and private funding for energy research and development to be about $1.5 billion annually. This compares with $944 million in 1964, and has remained at 0.15 per cent of the gross national product during the nine years since the interdepartmental report was published. This is too modest an investment in the future, and is inadequate to cope with the needs of the country.

The figure of $1.5 billion for total energy R&D expenditures is consistent with the Task Force "Inventory" noted above. It is also consistent with the National Science Foundation estimates of private energy R&D expenditures. Using NSF and Electrical Research Council figures, the Task Force projects 1971 expenditures of about $600 million by the petroleum industry and $300 million by electrical utilities and manufacturers. Other energy R&D funded by industry should bring the total to about $1 billion. The Office of Science and Technology estimates Federal outlays for energy research and development to be $405 million in fiscal year 1971, $525 million in 1972 and $622 million in 1973. The ratio of industrial to governmental support has remained about the same since 1964, 2:1.

The nation as a whole spends about 2.5 per cent of its more than $1 trillion gross national product for research and development. Of the approximately $26 billion so expended in 1970, for example, about $16 billion came from Federal appropriations. With about 10 per cent of the GNP directly related to energy, and with the technologically intensive nature of the energy industries, it is not unreasonable to expect that 10 per cent of the national research and development effort be assigned to energy. This would mean an annual expenditure of $2.5 to $3 billion, almost twice our current energy R&D funding. It will take at least an additional billion dollars a year to bring the total effort into line with needs. This increased level of effort is consistent with funding levels in other areas of national importance.

The Electric Research Council recommended $30 billion be spent for research and development related to electricity alone over the next three decades. This averages out to $1 billion a year. Similar efforts are needed by the coal, oil, gas and nuclear industries if an adequate national level of effort for energy research and development is to be reached. Only by making such R&D expenditures and evaluating them carefully over the coming years and decades will the new energy technologies be available when needed.

Unbalanced R&D Priorities

The total Federal funding of about one-half billion dollars for energy R&D looks impressive, until it is realized that most of it is identified with nuclear power. Funding for R&D on non-nuclear sources of energy, energy transmission and conservation of energy are inadequate to provide timely, practicable solutions to the worsening balance between energy demand and supply.

Research and development for nuclear power have long dominated the Federal energy R & D budget. Many more Federal scientists and engineers are at work on nuclear power than are involved with coal, oil and gas. The 1964 Interdepartmental Energy Study also noted this imbalance in Federal priorities. It has not been corrected, in part because energy R & D expenditures have barely kept up with the growth of the economy since 1964.

A better balance in energy R & D priorities must be established. This should be done by increasing significantly expenditures for non-nuclear energy R & D.

Priorities for Future R & D

There is no lack of worthwhile opportunities for energy R & D. Hard choices must be made between competing areas of research, and between individual programs in a given area.

The amount of money available for energy R & D will determine the upper limit for progress in developing new energy technologies. Other important factors include strict judgments to attain the highest scientific quality in the R & D programs, and effective incentives to get new knowledge to commercial use as soon as possible, compatible with concerns for health, safety, and the quality of the environment.

More funds will not necessarily assure a research and development program of highest quality. They are, however, a necessary condition to such a program, and will increase the probability of producing new energy technologies in the shortest possible time.

2. Organizational reforms are needed in the executive branch of government in order to effectively coordinate and direct a greatly increased national energy R & D effort within the context of an overall national energy policy.

(a) A focal point for energy policy must exist in the White House.

This policy group should constantly review the energy situation— both short- and long-range problems—taking account of both international and domestic developments. It must take the responsibility for making policy recommendations to the President, and then overseeing the implementation of those policies (including research and development) which are promulgated. In addition to its responsibility for setting Energy R & D policy within the executive branch, if it is to be effective it must also be responsive to the Congress.

Energy Policy and the White House

The Nation needs vigorous leadership in creating and applying new energy technologies. The focal point for that effort must be the White House. Only the President has the requisite influence and resources to develop and implement a national energy policy. Congress should participate in the development of that policy, and ensure its implementation.

The present energy policy framework is the historical outcome of a laissez-faire attitude of government towards energy. This attitude grew up in an era of abundant energy resources. Now we face an energy deficit, and this fact must be taken into account.

These changed circumstances make the need for a national energy policy urgent. This is especially true for energy research and development, because of the long lead times required and the need for stable funding to assure the building up of competent scientific and technical groups to pursue the R & D objectives.

The details of such a national energy policy cannot be given in a report such as this. Such a policy can result only from careful decisions based on the complex set of foreign policy, economic, environmental and technological issues.

A focal point for energy in the White House is especially important for research and development because there are so many interagency and interdisciplinary factors involved. Energy, including energy R & D, is not a separable entity, and cannot fit into a neat organizational chart. Energy policy will inevitably cut across agency lines in the Federal government; it will also affect diverse segments of the private sector of our economy.

Because of the complex structure of the Executive Office of the President, and its constantly changing organizational details, the Task Force refrains from prescribing any specific organizational solution. Instead, it puts a mandate upon the President to formulate national policy for energy and the related research and development, and to establish a focal point for energy policy in the White House itself.

Alternative Policy Organizations

Presently two organizations formulate and coordinate Energy R & D policy at the White House level: the Domestic Council and the Office of Science and Technology (OST). The former has a Subcommittee on Energy, chaired by the Secretary of Interior, and has wide responsibilities related to energy. OST has conducted analyses of energy R & D alternatives, and has had limited responsibilities for coordinating the R & D programs of Federal agencies.

An Energy Policy Council in the Executive Office of the President has been proposed in bills introduced in both the House and the Senate. The Council would serve as a focal point for energy policy close to the President, and provide coordination and advisory functions. It would also have long-range planning responsibilities.

Other bills have been introduced which would establish Advisory Boards or Commissions with energy policy responsibilities. The basic objective of legislation such as this is the same as that of the Task Force. The difference lies in the mode of implementation: the Task Force believes that the structural details of such a focal point for energy policy in the White House should originate with the President, at the same time, the needs for Congressional advice and approval must be recognized.

Information for Policy Making

Effective planning, management and coordination of energy research and development must be based on accurate and up-to-date information. Although efficient and innovative management is a leading strength of the United States, it is surprising to discover that there now exists no comprehensive central clearing house for information on energy related research and development.

Several useful sources of information exist, including the Interagency Advanced Power Group, the Science Information Exchange of the Smithsonian Institution, and the Defense Documentation Center. Data on energy research and development also have been developed from time to time by ad hoc studies such as the Interdepartmental Energy Study of 1964. A major assessment of energy research and development has just been completed for the Federal Council for Science and Technology, but has not been released even though it was financed in large part by research funds appropriated to the National Science Foundation.

Some industrial groups have collected and published information on selected aspects of energy research and development. An example is the 1971 survey of research issued by the Electric Research Council that reported on some 2,270 projects. A major study of energy policy issues funded by the Ford Foundation also can be expected to yield important information and insights into energy research and development.

Probably the most comprehensive survey to date of energy research and development activities was published by the Task Force itself in February 1972. This inventory has information on more than 4,400 projects and is exhaustively indexed to make its contents a helpful reference in examining the status of energy research and development. The survey is nevertheless incomplete and has not been adequately analyzed for serious policy formation.

None of the above efforts has been organized to provide the kind of information needed for planning and policy making. They deal more with what has happened than with what is happening and what is planned.

A continuing Energy Research and Development Information capability is needed to collect and analyze data and information on energy research and development. It should not only support the needs of the Federal government, including Congress, but those of private industry as well. It must include industrial R & D data yet at the same time protect proprietary information. It would also be appropriate to have a comprehensive annual status report on energy research, development and technology prepared for the President and the Congress, identifying and updating past evaluations of scientific and technological opportunities, and projecting future directions and funding for energy R & D.

The Regulatory Process

The regulatory process is an increasingly important factor in our nations de facto energy policy. Originally begun for economic reasons, regulation of energy-related industries now extends to environmental effects and to public health and safety. Much of what can be accomplished by regulation depends upon the technologies available. Regulations can require clean air, for example, but until adequate air cleaning equipment is on the market, the regulation has limited effect.

The regulatory process has not been fully responsive to the problem of adequately balancing supply and demand for energy with environmental safety and public health issues. This situation will not improve until we learn to do the regulatory job more flexibly, reasonably, without so much delay, and yet with improved opportunity for public participation and understanding. This will be difficult; however, we must continue to work towards more responsive methods of regulation.

As the number of mines, oil depots, LNG terminals, pipelines, drilling platforms, power plants, transmission lines and waste disposal sites continues to grow, innovations in regulation will be needed. But increased efficiency of regulation should not be at the expense of those who should be heard. The current trend towards litigation as a way to regulate the supply and use of energy—now so evident for nuclear power and in setting rates for electricity—is a principal issue for national energy policy. A better understanding of the nature and effects of the regulatory process upon energy activities is needed.

Resource Data Base

Future policy decisions about energy must be based on the best information available. Yet there remain many gaps in information about the nature and extent of basic energy resources both in the United States and elsewhere in the world. At present many policy decisions have to rely upon resource information from special interest groups, information rarely verified independently.

It is difficult to discuss the relative merits of various energy technologies without an adequate knowledge of the size of their respective resource bases; it is also impossible to evaluate the proper urgency for developing each new energy source if the resource base of old sources are in doubt. Money and effort can be wasted if unneeded crash programs are initiated; but far more money and effort will be wasted if needed technologies are not developed as they are required.

The energy resource bases include fossil, nuclear, geothermal and solar energy. There are important other natural resources whose importance to future energy supplies are not quite so obvious, such as helium likely to be needed for future superconducting technologies. In the past, the AEC has encouraged industry and prospectors in their search for uranium. It may be appropriate for the government to explore adequate incentives for other resource base explorations as well.

There should be established within the Federal government a capability for generating and continually updating data on primary energy resources. This data base will be invaluable to policy making organizations, such as that proposed herein.

Other Policy Issues

There are a multitude of other policy issues which are appropriate for consideration at both congressional and White House levels. These include ways for adequately financing energy research and development, such as an energy tax or a tax credit for privately funded R & D. Decisions must be made on who will ultimately pay for environmental measures related to energy production and use.

> **(b) An operating agency with responsibility for managing Government supported energy R & D should be established as soon as practicable.**

This will require centralizing within a single organization the management of many energy R & D programs which now reside in various departments, commissions, and independent agencies. This operating agency would carry out, along with other executive agencies, the policies enumerated by the President acting upon the advice of the policy organization recommended above. The agency would answer to the Congress and its various legislative and appropriations committees in developing its specific responsibilities and in budgetary matters.

Need for Energy R & D Agency

No matter how ably the national energy policy is thought out, the organizational forms which underlie the performance of energy R & D can be as important as the total expenditures. At the present time there is a lack of coordination within the Federal Government in its own support of R & D. Some areas, such as nuclear research, are strongly supported. Other equally important R & D activities, such as coal gasification, are grossly under-funded and lack the expert management and high quality technical oversight which are required for success.

The policy organization recommended above can correct this situation to some extent. It cannot, however, provide detailed oversight and coordination of Federal energy R & D programs. This function must be the responsibility of an operating agency. Such an agency with wider responsibilities than any existing agency is urgently needed.

Current Reorganization Proposals

President Nixon proposed creation of a Department of Natural Resources (DNR) in 1971. This new department would consolidate operations for energy research and development in an Energy and Mineral Resources Administration (EMRA). The primary reasons given for this reorganization proposal were the fragmentation of Federal responsibility for energy, and the need to organize the Federal government by national goals.

Most of the constituent agencies of EMRA, except for the AEC, are presently located in the Interior Department. The major shift would involve transfer of the civilian power programs from the AEC. The reorganization would consolidate AEC's major civilian energy activities in an agency charged with the mission of insuring that the total energy resources of the Nation are effectively used.

This proposed reorganization is designed to assure a more rational energy policy, and give broader scope and greater balance to the national effort in energy research and development.

There is substantial support for converting the Atomic Energy Commission into a National Energy Commission and transferring the AEC military and regulatory functions elsewhere.

The AEC has some of the best laboratories in the country with scientists and engineers who are leaders in many fields of energy R & D. It also has experience and existing organizations for managing large development and demonstration projects, and in working closely with industry to get new technologies out of laboratories and into commercial use.

There are, however, objections that an energy superagency built around the AEC would have a bias in favor of nuclear energy. The Commission structure is also criticized as an ineffective management format by those who prefer a departmental structure with centralized authority.

Drastic reorganization will not provide magical solutions to organizational problems which exist in the energy area. Some recently established agencies still show signs of internal discord as the different groups that were combined to form them continue to struggle for bureaucratic power. Limited and incremental steps in reorganization may be better than trying to reorganize everything at once. Building upon an existing agency is such an incremental alternative. If the energy problem is to have a timely resolution, pragmatism in reorganization should take priority over ideology and dogmatism.

Role of National Laboratories

The national (or Federal) Laboratories of the AEC, NASA, and the Departments of Defense, Interior and Commerce represent a great public asset bought and paid for by public funds. They should be quickly brought into the mainstream of energy research and development. The Committee on Science and Astronautics has long held to the principle that the human and physical resources established in these laboratories should be used on whatever pertinent national problems need solution. National laboratories should not be viewed as the private property of the agencies, to be jealously guarded and hoarded. They are a national scientific and technical resource, and should be used in seeking solutions of energy problems.

The energy R & D Agency proposed by the Task Force should utilize the talents in our existing National laboratories to the maximum extent compatible with timely and economical execution of R & D programs.

Demonstration of New Energy Technologies

Research and development is an essential but insufficient step toward solution of the energy problem. Demonstrations of new technologies are needed so that industry will have enough engineering, operating and economic information to decide whether, how and when to move ahead with large scale deployment.

The costs of such large scale demonstrations, however, appear to be more than private investors are willing or able to risk. For example, the demonstration of a commercial coal gasification process will be enormously more expensive and complicated than was the demonstration of the seagoing use of the steam engine in the S.S. *Savannah* in 1819. Thus, the Federal government has become more heavily involved through direct funding or joint ventures. Federal funds underwrite or limit possible private losses from such demonstrations.

No single organizational mold can be specified for demonstrating nor or improved energy technologies. Because of continuing pressures on the Federal budget, it is desirable that government funds exert as much leverage as possible.

Combined efforts of several companies may be needed for such projects as development of new methods for energy conversion, improved processing equipment for extractive industries, or new devices for abatement of pollution. Changes may be needed in patent and antitrust policies to provide the proper environment for these ventures.

Management of demonstration projects for new energy technologies will be an appropriate function of a new or enlarged operating agency for energy R & D.

Industry Participation

There is a need to insure that industry have a voice in the planning and performance of research, development and demonstration for energy. It is industry that ultimately will have to produce and market the new systems, equipment, machinery and services. So the influence of the marketplace should be introduced into the R & D cycle at an early stage.

It is not only desirable to increase cooperation between the Federal government and industry in R & D activities, but to minimize the adversary and defendant aspects that have so often characterized relations between industry and government in the United States. Our foremost competitors from industrial nations abroad often have a cooperative rather than an adversary relationship with their governments, thus gaining significant advantage when in meeting us in the world markets. The U.S. should be willing to adopt this attitude when it is in the national interest to do so.

International Cooperation in Energy Research and Development

As discoveries and innovations move out of the laboratories into the real world of the marketplace, practical considerations of trade secrecy and protecting private investments decrease the prospects for international cooperation in energy research and development. The unhappy experience of Euratom in developing nuclear power technology in Europe is a case in point.

There are, however, prospects for useful international cooperation in the research stage where the embryonic technologies are not close enough to commercial use to induce secrecy and inhibit cooperation. Energy research in such fields as solar, fusion, and superconductivity are at the stage where international cooperation has been feasible and should continue. The United States, as a matter of policy, should encourage international exchange of scientific and technical information related to energy research and development. It should also encourage joint ventures in energy R & D when appropriate. Large scale scientific experiments for energy are increasing in cost, and the prospects of international cooperation offer ways to reduce the costs and manpower demands for the participating nations while providing new ideas and insights from the various national scientific and technical communities.

Large scale experiments for fusion and for satellite solar power appear ideal for international cooperation. The widespread international cooperation in fusion research since 1958 has been so successful that its arrangements merit study and use as a model for other international cooperation in energy research.

3. The issues of environmental protection and energy conservation must be paramount in any national energy policy and should receive greatly increased research and development support.

Energy consumption cannot continue to increase indefinitely into the future at its present rate, since our planet cannot cope with the vast amounts of thermal and material pollution which this would produce. Research programs directed toward more rational and efficient utilization of energy, health and safety of our people, and protection of the natural environment should have the highest priority.

Concomitant with the need for conserving energy and protecting the environment is the necessity for more careful utilization of our limited natural resources. Research and development offer great opportunities in accomplishing these goals through more effective resource recovery, and more efficient energy conversion, transmission, and utilization. Recycling of materials and the use of solid wastes as sources deserve substantial R &D support.

Energy and Environmental Quality

National policy for energy research and development must look beyond the single task of meeting future demands for energy. It must also take into account the effects upon the environment of extracting fuels from the earth and using the energy provided from those fuels. There must be R & D programs directly related to the extraction of fuels and to the conversion and use of energy.

A simply stated goal of energy conservation is complicated in practice by the divergence of interests and goals in our society. An example is to be found in the case of air pollution control. Policy that leads to the abatement of air pollution from existing motor vehicles with internal combustion engines runs counter to a policy of increasing efficiency in motor transportation. The Department of Transportation indicated to the Task Force that the fuel penalty for air pollution control could be as much as 25 per cent if a suitable catalyst is not found for devices to control the emission of nitrogen oxides from gasoline engines. Had such devices been applied to all motor vehicles in 1970, the amount of fuel consumed for the same vehicle use would have increased by as much as 23 billion gallons.

This interdependence of energy and the environment requires that issues of environmental protection and energy conservation be paramount in any national policy for energy R & D.

The experience of the 1960's demonstrates that the large scale supply and use of energy can adversely affect our environment. Some of these effects threaten to become so objectionable that they can no longer be tolerated. Basic policy for energy research and development must give priority to technologies that, if successful, would keep environmental effects of energy activities within acceptable limits.

Appropriate objectives for research and development related to environmental effects of energy should include:

—Establish the characteristics of the unpolluted environment as a base line.

—Determine the nature and extent of present energy related pollution.

—Determine quantitatively the effects of this pollution upon health and the natural environment.

—Develop new sources of clean fuels.

—Develop technology to control environmental effects of energy related activities.

Need For Base-Line Information

If society is to rationally regulate the supply and use of energy in order to keep environmental effects within acceptable bounds, systematic collection of base-line information on the environment must be undertaken. It is difficult if not impossible to analyze the effects of pollution unless the characteristics of the unpolluted environment are known. This knowledge can be obtained only by high quality basic and applied research programs utilizing improvements in technology for collection, analysis and interpretation of relevant data. The International Biological Program of the National Science Foundation is an example of such a program for acquiring and refining such information.

Effects of Energy Utilization on the Environment

Our current understanding of the environmental effects of supplying and using energy is insufficient for effective regulation, but current decisions can only be made on the basis of present information. These decisions can thus be only tentative; future refinement and possible modifications of these decisions will need detailed, reliable information about the nature and extent of environmental effects.

The waste heat problem has attracted much attention in recent years, especially with the advent of 1000 megawatt steam electric power plants. Discharge of heated cooling waters from such plants has an effect on the water life. Yet there remains a need to gather and assess information in order to set water temperature standards. Research in the life sciences as well as work in engineering are clearly indicated.

Effects of Energy Utilization on Health

Present information on the effects of supplying and using energy on public health and occupational health and safety is spotty. On the one hand, the effects of radiation from nuclear wastes have probably been researched more thoroughly than any other potential danger. But for a common pollutant like sulfur dioxide, the Environmental Protection Administration advised this year that ". . . we cannot say with certainty what the effects we have observed are directly traceable to sulfur oxides and/or particulates . . ."

Federal and state agencies are now setting standards for emission of sulfur and nitrogen oxides from motor vehicles. Their decisions just as those for other pollutants associated with energy should be based upon substantial scientific information on the effects of these pollutants. But much of this needed information is not now available. Research policy should aim to identify and fill such gaps. Lacking such information, regulators may be too severe, with consequent excessive economic costs and a lowered standard of living, or they may err on the side of insufficient rigor and we may find technological surprises in the form of unexpected adverse effects upon people or the environment. Standards and regulations for regulation of energy activities should be based on reliable evidence that such regulations will, in fact, achieve the desired goals.

Clean Fuel From Coal

One way to reduce air pollution is to burn clean fuels. At a time when clean natural gas is in short supply and when much of our abundant coal supply is barred from use because of high sulfur content, it becomes more important to synthesize clean fuels from available coal. The current pace of research, development and demonstration for manufacture of synthetic gas from coal is too slow and should be greatly increased. Likewise, the growing demand for gasoline at a time when our overseas sources of oil are becoming less reliable underscores the urgent need to expand present research and development to make clean liquid fuels from coal.

Control Technologies

Basically there are two ways to reduce undesirable environmental effects of supplying and using energy. One is to increase the efficiency of the various steps in utilizing energy so that the same amount of useful energy can be supplied with less fuel, and consequently less pollution and environmental damage. The other way is to improve the technologies for controlling the pollutants that are produced.

As indicated in chapter two of this report, there are many technological avenues to be opened or improved if energy is to be supplied without unacceptable damage to the environment or detrimental effects on public and occupational health and safety. These opportunities range from measures to protect the health and safety of miners of coal and uranium to the control of gases and ash from burning fuels. They include improved ways to dissipate waste heat, means for using waste heat, improving efficiencies of engines for motor vehicles, reducing radioactive emissions from nuclear power plants, controlling oil pollution from tankers and pipeline accidents, and reclaiming mined lands.

324

The ultimate outcome for all of these opportunities depends on an adequate effective national policy for energy research and development.

Energy Conservation

Reducing the growth in demand for energy through conservation measures is a policy option that promises short-term payoff. First, less oil and gas would have to be imported from abroad with consequent benefit for our international trade balance and national security. The Office of Emergency Preparedness estimates that energy conservation could reduce U. S. energy demand in 1980 by the equivalant of 7.3 million barrels of oil daily, representing an annual value of $10.7 billion, this equivalent to two-thirds of the oil imports forecast for that time.

Second, conserving energy by reducing its use can reduce environmental problems. For example, for every kilowatt hour of electricity saved, waste heat equivalent to almost two additional kilowatt hours is not dissipated into the water and air. Every kilowatt hour saved means a saving of about one pound of coal at the powerplant.

Conservation of our energy fuel supply can be attained by using renewable energy sources, such as solar energy and wind. These technologies are unfortunately still largely in the talking stage, and only slow progress is being made toward commercial use.

Conservation in Mining and Processing

Not all the coal, oil and natural gas in presently known deposits will be recovered, or even most of it. For example, only about 32 per cent of the oil in place in a field is actually recovered at the present time. There is room for considerable improvements in the technologies of recovery so that more of these energy resources can be utilized. Improvements in deep mining technology, in secondary and tertiary recovery of oil, in ways to free natural gas trapped in tight rock formations will all depend upon the outcome of research, development and demonstration activities.

Conservation in Conversion

Another way to conserve primary energy resources is to increase the efficiency of converting heat energy into electricity or some other desirable energy form. Thermodynamic efficiencies of steam turbines in the electricity industry seem to have reached a plateau of about 40 percent for new installation, and are considerably less for older plants.

Two opportunities for increasing conversion efficiency for generating plants are magnetohydrodynamics (MHD) and gas turbines, either in a combined cycle or as separate prime movers for generation of electricity. In principle either approach could offer efficiencies of as much as 55 or 60 percent. Increased R&D funding can generate reliable information as to the technical and economic feasibility of these and other advanced conversion cycles.

There are also prospects of improving the efficiency of combustion for fossil fuels, particularly in the lower grades of coal. Only more R&D can determine whether these ideas will proceed to the demonstration stage and be introduced into the market with a consequent saving in fuels.

Conservation Through Nuclear Breeding

A special case of conservation for fuel materials is the breeder reactor. Its success could multiply the energy recoverable from uranium deposits perhaps fifty or one hundred fold and also make thorium a useful nuclear fuel. But planning the demonstration of breeding technology has raised some thorny issues of R&D policy. One issue is the wisdom of focusing the scientific and financial resources upon demonstration of a single approach, which the AEC is doing with the Liquid Metal Fast Breeder Reactor (LMFBR). The alternative is to develop and demonstrate alternative approaches such as the gas-cooled fast breeder or the molten salt breeder. The AEC is funding the gas cooled fast breeder concept and the molten salt breeder at levels which are insufficient to produce an alternative in the same time frame as the LMFBR. Such concentration of resources on the LMFBR incurs some risk of failure for nuclear breeding. Increased funding for other approaches is a form of technological insurance.

One innovative proposal put to the Task Force for breeding was to use the laser-fusion process as a plentiful, cheap supply of neutrons to convert uranium-238 or thorium-232 into nuclear fuels for use in conventional nuclear power plants. This approach would do away with the critical assembly of fissionable materials and the chain reaction of the breeder and thus substantially reduce problems of nuclear accidents and nuclear safety. The idea of using a neutron source to convert uranium-238 is not new, for it has been discussed since the 1950s. What is new is the improving possibilities of using the laser fusion process to supply the neutrons. Perfecting a fusion neutron source appears to be much less demanding of science and technology, especially materials technology, than the usual fusion reactor schemes. This idea deserves close scrutiny and adequate R&D funding.

Conservation in Building Design and Construction

Conserving energy by improved insulation of homes and by increased efficiency of furnaces and air conditioners is not a new idea. Lack of progress is due to problems that are more economic, sociological and governmental than technological. There is also a real possibility of using solar energy in many parts of the country for heating and air conditioning. But once again innovations in manufacturing, marketing, financing, taxation and regulation of building design and construction are as much needed as technological improvements. Experiments and demonstrations are needed to prove technical and economic feasibility to the builder and owner.

Conservation in Industrial Use

Until recently management could resort to more and more mechanization and automation to improve productivity, confident that ample supplies of inexpensive energy were at hand to substitute kilowatt hours for man hours. Now as industry moves toward tight and uncertain fuel supplies, there is fresh need for research and development to increase efficiency of energy use. A good example of what can be accomplished is the recent announcement by Alcoa of a new process for making aluminum that can cut electrical requirements by almost a third. More R&D is needed to improve industrial efficiency in utilization of energy.

Conservation in Transmission

The trend toward larger power plants is aggravating the problem of energy loss in transmission of electricity. Proposals to establish a national electric grid, and to put nuclear power plants in remote places may further increase transmission distances for large amounts of power, with attendant increases in energy loss. While several technological options are receiving some attention, the total R&D effort to reduce transmission losses is small and fragmented. R&D efforts in industry are bringing some improvements, but progress is too slow and does not reflect the national need to conserve energy.

Conservation in Transportation

Transportation directly accounts for about 25 percent of the total energy consumed in the United States (and perhaps as much as 40% if all indirect energy costs are included, such as those associated with the manufacture of automobiles or the construction of highways.) It shows an annual growth rate of 4 percent. Of some 15.1 trillion Btu of energy used in transportation in 1968, 14.5 came from petroleum products. Jet fuels accounted for 13 percent, gasoline for 68 percent and distillate fuels for 8 percent.

One way to conserve motor fuel is to increase the efficiency of engines. Current air pollution requirements are working at cross purposes, and the difficulties are great for developing an engine that is both efficient and acceptably non-polluting.

Another option is to change the pattern of use for motor vehicles, particularly the automobile. It is now conventional wisdom to prescribe a changeover from automobiles to public mass transportation. Before this change can be made by other than compulsion, much more needs to be known about the qualities of mass transportation that would attract automobile users. Careful systems analysis approaches are needed in studying the entire transportation system, taking into account preferences of our citizens.

Another alternative for reducing energy requirements for transportation are land use policies that get people to live closer to their work. Another approach is to reduce the need for business travel by improving communications technology enough for salesmen and other business travelers to communicate electronically rather than face-to-face.

Increasing efficiency and conservation of energy in transportation is a goal that would result in saving large amounts of fuel and is worthy of greatly increased R&D expenditures.

Conservation and Storage of Energy

If it were possible to store large amounts of electricity, generating stations could be run at full output for long periods of time. That would result in the highest thermal efficiency and economy. But electricity cannot be stored in large quantities.

An indirect approach has been pumped storage for hydro plants. Here, however, the process is limited by availability of acceptable sites and public objections to their environmental effects. Compressed air is a similar storage medium with some advantages over water. Interruptible supplies of electricity such as that from solar energy or wind turbines could be used if technical and economic feasibility were shown.

Another alternative is to use thermal, chemical or electrical energy to dissociate water into hydrogen and oxygen. The hydrogen could be stored indefinitely and later used as a fuel for transportation or in fuel cells to generate electricity. The idea of the hydrogen economy is attractive, but much remains to be done to show that it is indeed feasible. The scientific community supports the idea. On the other hand, there are safety and economic problems that can be solved only by research and development.

4. The Nation must set priorities among technological opportunities for investment in research and development. We cannot support all energy research and development alternatives at the levels which are suggested by their proponents. Evaluation of current data indicates the following areas of activity should have the highest priority.

(a) Basic Research

Since basic research is inherently cheap compared to applied research and development, and the basic knowledge obtained from it undergirds all advances in energy technology, the progress of basic research should be limited by scientific and technical barriers rather than financial ones. Scientifically sound research in unconventional as well as conventional fields of Energy R&D must be pursued at a vigorous pace.

A necessary first step in developing the scientific basis for new energy technology is basic research. It is not enough to say that unconventional sources of energy exist or that better ways of transporting energy must be found. Hard scientific facts must be gathered and demonstrations of scientific feasibility must be made in order to make possible technological solutions to the energy crisis.

Applied research which builds on basic scientific data is the logical next step in the chain which produces new energy technology. Added emphasis is needed for a broad range of applied research programs that will attack in parallel those opportunities revealed by basic science.

In supporting basic and applied research, it must be realized that many projects will not lead to new energy technology. This investment, however, should not be considered as wasted, because a negative answer is often as important as a positive one. Since basic and applied research are relatively inexpensive, these negative answers can be useful in avoiding large needless expenditures in the development or demonstration plant stages. In addition, those basic and applied research projects that do lead to new technologies give such a high return on the research investment that they more than repay the cost of unsuccessful research.

We must, therefore, assure adequate support of basic and applied research in those scientific areas relating to energy. The NSF has a special responsibility in this regard. Through its RANN program, the NSF cannot only support specific applied energy research programs, but can also take steps to assure a rapid exploitation of new basic research knowledge through its applied programs.

(b) Materials Research

Materials Research and Development, including materials testing, should receive special emphasis since almost all technological progress related to energy is limited by the properties of available materials.

Materials sciences underlie virtually every phase of present and projected energy technologies. Accordingly, they merit special research and development emphasis.

The long term future of nuclear breeders and fusion reactors will depend upon materials that can function satisfactorily in extremely hostile environments for long periods of time. The economic viability of the direct conversion of solar energy to electricity requires development of much cheaper solar cells and optical coatings. Likewise, successful development of MHD and large gas turbines appears to be largely dependent upon materials that can withstand higher temperatures while retaining their structural integrity. Furthermore, if such materials were available, the operating efficiencies of conventional steam electric power plants might be significantly increased.

Materials research and development can also increase the efficiency of electric energy transmission if the problems associated with superconducting materials can be solved. The efficiency of energy utilization can be increased if better insulating materials are developed.

For these reasons, high priority should be given to materials research throughout programs of the Federal agencies. Coordination should be established to assure that materials R&D programs need the needs of energy technologies.

Better methods are needed for transferring and utilizing this new knowledge in the energy industries. Government organizations which fund and perform energy research and development should make special effort to couple scientific and engineering knowledge in materials sciences to practical applications.

(c) Solar Energy

Because of its continuous and virtually inexhaustible nature Solar Energy R&D should receive greatly increased funding. Near term applications of solar power for household uses seem likely, and central station terrestrial solar power, and satellite solar power are attractive long-term possibilities.

The fossil fuels we depend on today were formed by solar energy of the past. Food, wind, wood, and hydropower are all derived from solar energy which fell on the earth more recently. Solar energy is available everywhere and is almost limitless. If we can learn to use solar energy economically, it is a nearly ideal source of energy.

Three distinct uses of solar energy, each with its own problems and time scale, are worthy of increased attention: dispersed, small-scale use for heating and cooling buildings and water; large-scale terrestrial solar energy collection and conversion; and large-scale space satellite electric power plants.

It appears that, with minor engineering development and relatively simple architectural modifications, solar energy can now be used for space heating of residential and industrial buildings, and the heating of water. In a few years solar energy might be practical for cooling as well. Such use would lead to a significant decrease in consumption of depletable resources.

There are many R&D approaches to large-scale terrestrial solar energy use, all of them underfunded. Though the National Science Foundation supports some solar energy research, there is no national program to assess these approaches and develop the most promising ones. It is essential that we make a national commitment to bring one or more techniques for large-scale terrestrial solar energy collection to commercial demonstration.

Though it is much further into the future, the eventual development of economic power from satellites cannot be dismissed. Such a scheme has several advantages over terrestrial collection of solar energy: less land is needed, energy storage is only a small problem, and power can be beamed to locations on earth that have inadequate sunshine for useful terrestrial collection.

Because of its present economic disadvantage, and the need to develop both a space shuttle and a space tug, satellite solar energy R & D should have a lower priority than terrestrial solar technology.

(d) Geothermal Energy

Because of the vast reservoirs of thermal energy located in the earth's underground water and rocks and its widespread distribution, geothermal energy should have greatly increased R&D emphasis.

Basic and applied research in the field of geothermal energy should be increased many times over the present level. Because little attention has been given to this area in the past, it is potentially highly leveraged. The investment of a few tens of millions of dollars now has the possibility of opening for development a vast new source of energy.

There are two specific questions about geothermal energy that need answers: how large is the geothermal energy resource? Can we economically obtain energy from dry geothermal reservoirs? The first question can be resolved by a combination of terrestrial exploration and satellite studies of earth resources. The second question can only be answered by direct experimentation on a fractured, hot, dry, geothermal heat reservoir. This work on geothermal energy should receive highest priority.

(e) Nuclear Breeders

The present effort to develop a safe, dependable Liquid Metal Fast Breeder Reactor (LMFBR) must be continued with its high priority. Breeder concepts alternative to the LMFBR must be pursued in parallel and have the same priority. Methods for safe, secure handling of nuclear fuels and safe, long-term disposal of radioactive wastes must be developed and implemented.

It is essential to develop and demonstrate several safe and reliable technologies for breeding nuclear fuel in order to fully exploit the advantages of nuclear power from our fissionable resources (uranium and thorium). Without a workable breeder, the potential supply of nuclear fuels is measured in decades; with an integrated reactor system using both nuclear breeders and the nuclear "burners" of today, we would eventually generate approximately 100 times as much useable energy from our resource base. We must maintain the present high priority and schedule for developing and demonstrating a Liquid Metal Fast Breeder Reactor (LMFBR).

Considering the complicated technology involved in any type of nuclear reactor, and the need to develop at least one safe and economical breeder, work on alternate breeder concepts and fuel cycles must be pursued in parallel with the LMFBR. This alternate breeder R & D should have the same priority, in order to assure bringing at least one other approach to breeding to the demonstration stage by the late 1980's.

Procedures and technologies to reduce the hazards associated with mining, transporting, and processing nuclear fuels must be developed and implemented. We must also assure that the radioactive wastes produced from all reactors can be disposed of safely for as long as necessary.

(f) Coal

Technologies to obtain clean energy from coal must be brought to commercial demonstration as rapidly as possible. Development of clean, economic coal gasification, liquefaction and solid coal combustion techniques would greatly reduce our dependence on oil and natural gas. Such R & D should be financed by both the public and private sectors at greatly increased levels.

Natural gas services 61% of all homes and our transportation system depends almost exclusively on liquid petroleum products. We must recognize that changing this existing energy infrastructure without seriously damaging our economy will take decades. It is therefore imperative to maintain a supply of liquid and gaseous fuels compatible with existing capital equipment.

In order to supplement those natural reserves of gas and oil that do exist, and to allow proper use of our coal reserves, the development of commercially feasible combustible gas from coal must be given a priority equal in every way to the breeder program. It must be noted that, because of the much less sophisticated technology involved and the relative lack of safety problems, such a program would almost certainly cost considerably less than the development of breeder reactors, and would be even more certain of prompt success. To be most useful, coal gasification should be available on a commercial scale by the mid-1980's, implying that commercially feasible demonstration plants must be on line by the early 1980's. Thus, priority should be given to accelerated design and testing of processes on a commercial demonstration scale.

Almost as important, and directly related to coal gasification, is the production of liquid fuel from coal. It is likely that developments in the technology of coal gasification would, almost as a fringe benefit, also advance the prospects for coal liquefaction.

(g) Fusion

Controlled thermonuclear fusion presents an exciting challenge to mankind. The enormous payoff from taming this virtually inexhaustible energy resource makes it mandatory to make the investment needed to overcome huge scientific and materials problems.

331

A controlled thermonuclear fusion reactor power plant is one of the most ideal energy sources yet suggested. Such a reactor would provide essentially limitless power. In addition, if fusion energy could be directly converted into electricity with a high efficiency fusion reactors could have much less environmental impact than today's electric powerplants. Indeed, following the successful development of fusion power, the only limits on energy use would come from the effects of waste heat upon the environment or from non-technological issues. Success with fusion would mean that coal and oil could be reserved for petrochemical feed materials, for which today there are no economic substitutes.

Scientists and engineers working on fusion research and development have yet to attain simultaneously the difficult technical conditions necessary to show the scientific feasibility of fusion power. Even if that milestone is reached, which could come in the late 1970's or early 1980's, much more work will be necessary to show economic and engineering feasibility. It seems most unlikely that fusion power will be a factor in energy supply before the late 1990's at the very earliest, unless an unexpected breakthrough occurs. Some fusion proponents think that laser ignition of a fusion reaction may be such a breakthrough.

On the whole, the importance of fusion to our future energy supply requires that we vigorously pursue the present program in fusion research, never allowing it to become budget limited. It should be recognized that once a laboratory demonstration of a useful fusion process has been achieved, the costs of developing the subsequent pilot plants and commercial demonstrations will be high, and may have to be borne largely by the Federal Government.

INDEX

333

H

Half-life, 15
Hardin, G., 264
Heat, 39
Heat balance of earth, 6, 211–15
Heat engine, 45
Heat pipe, 164
Heat pump, 247
Heat reservoir, 45n
Helium, 99
Heronemus, Prof., 185
Hindenburg syndrome, 200
Home energy consumption, 249–53, 307
Horsepower (hp), 30t
Hydro storage, 69, 192, 297, 327
Hydroelectric power, 177
Hydrogen
  heat content of, 196
  production from seawater, 169
  storage of, 198–99
Hydrogen atom, 12
Hydrogen economy, 196–201, 298
Hydrogen isotopes, 136t

I

Infrared radiation, 52
Insulation, 248–49
Isobutane, 175
Isotopes, 15–16, 110
  of hydrogen, 136t
  of uranium, 112

J

Joule, 25t
Joule, J., 41

K

Kantrowitz, Dr., 180
Kelvin, Lord, 6
Kelvin temperature scale, 39
Kerala Coast, 123

Kilocalorie, 30t
Kilogram, 25
Kilowatt-hour, 30t
Kinetic energy, 28, 34
!Kung Bushmen, 275–76

L

Laser, 142
Lawson criterion, 137, 141t
Leukemia, 123
Light water reactor (LWR), 113, 295
Lighting, 245, 251
Limits to growth, 270
Liquid metal fast breeder reactor (LMFBR), 130–31
Liquid petroleum gas (LPG), 201
Liquified natural gas (LNG), 201
Lithium, 145
Load factor, 234t
Logarithm, 74
Low level emissions, 125–27
Ludington pump storage facility, 193

M

Magnetic field, 19
Magnetic mirror, 139
Magnetohydrodynamics (MHD), 179–81, 243, 325
Market, 260
Mass, 14, 24
Mass transit, 238, 327
Maximum permissable dose (MPD), 124
Meinel, A., 162
Meinel, M., 162
Methane, 104
Microwaves, 17, 165
Middle East oil, 288–89
Mks units, 25
Models
  economic, 259
  scientific, 11–12
Moderator, 113–14
Molecules, 12